The Way Back

INSIDE THE MIND OF A MULTIPLE PERSONALITY DISORDER

Donna Mae Rose

Outskirts Press, Inc.
Denver, Colorado

The opinions expressed in this manuscript are solely the opinions of the author and do not represent the opinions or thoughts of the publisher.

The Way Back
Inside the mind of a multiple personality
All Rights Reserved
Copyright © 2007 Donna Mae Rose
V2.0R1.1

Cover Image © 2007 JupiterImages Corporation
All Rights Reserved. Used With Permission.

This book may not be reproduced, transmitted, or stored in whole or in part by any means, including graphic, electronic, or mechanical without the express written consent of the publisher except in the case of brief quotations embodied in critical articles and reviews.

Author:
Donna Hunt
3600 Ave. G SP.19
White City, OR 97503
(541) 826-6456 E-mail: wilna1@embarqmail.com

Outskirts Press
http://www.outskirtspress.com

ISBN-10: 1-4327-0605-5
ISBN-13: 978-1-4327-0605-0

Outskirts Press and the "OP" logo are trademarks belonging to Outskirts Press, Inc.

Printed in the United States of America

This book is dedicated to Dr. Boyd. As a child cannot be born without a father, so this book could not be written without his knowledge and brilliant insight.

Acknowledgement

I look back over the years with a grateful heart and give thanks to each and everyone who helped me along the way to wellness. In every situation and circumstance I found myself, there were those special people who came into my life. First and foremost was my adopted son Russell. He was not born of my flesh, he was born of my soul and dwelled within my heart until perfect timing presented itself and Russell became my very own. Being his mother gave me the motivation to be someone he could always be proud of. Then there's my present day husband, who through his example taught me the patience needed to go though the healing process at my own pace. I love him very much, not because he's perfect but because he keeps loving me when I'm not being perfect. My first counselor, Dr. Weber, showed me the compassion that I believed was a gift only women had. It was refreshing and pleasing to me to see I was wrong. Pat Carter became my close friend the first day I came to Oregon. For the first time in my life I had left my family and friends behind, I was definitely out of my comfort zone. She introduced herself to me, gave me a big hug and said, "welcome to Oregon." The warmth in which she said this to me was as if she had found a long lost relative. I felt a great comfort come over me and I love her to this day. Dezra was an English major I met while going to Rogue Community College in Medford, Oregon. She took a genuine interest in my desire to learn. I gained a great deal from her. She enhanced my self-esteem and gave me a sense of knowing I could achieve any goal if I put the necessary effort into it. My first Unity minister, Rev. Colleen Graham through the Unity teachings and her guidance I was given a deeper understanding of life and an awareness of the spiritual nature unfolding within myself. These are just a few of the ones that came at just the right time to give me their help, their guidance and the courage to move through whatever place I was in, until I could see beyond the cleansing that had taken place through the years. Looking beyond the appearance of my life that had kept me frozen in fear, I found the "me" that God had created. Again, I say, I am exceedingly grateful.

To My Readers:

This is a true story of tremendous tragedy and triumph, a story of extreme sorrow and great joy. Sorrow because of the human dilemma we all experience, joy because of the healing power that lives within each and every one of us.

With strong desire, much courage, and my eye on the goal, I healed the lifetime of deep trauma that shattered the core of my being. If you take just one thing from this book let it be that you, too, can overcome.

Desire is the seed that eventually grows into the accomplished intent. In my case, perfect healing was the motivation behind the desire. It was a longing to know my

Wholeness, to know I was scattered from within and that it didn't have to be this way. Our Creator never intended for me to live this way. With a yearning that would not let me go and a hunger so strong that my passion to overcome would lead me to the healthy person I wanted to be. There always seemed to be a constant undertow of persuasion, sometimes gentle, sometimes not so gentle, a command to put the pieces of my soul back together again.

There was much work to be done, and so with all the zeal I could muster, I reached out to the task set before me. Many times courage seemed to be nowhere in sight. At times, I felt desperate beyond all belief; hopelessness and misery appeared to be everywhere. There was no place where gloom was not. It was as if my very being was buried under all this rubble of anguish, preventing the truth of who I am from seeing the light of day. And then strength would come, a strength called courage, that innate gift we all have, a tool given to each one of us. Sometimes this gift is buried so deep within us it is impossible to see. Courage surfaces when we accept the fear of what lies ahead. Take the time to find it; look within; it's waiting for you. Embrace your fear and courage will carry you one step closer to your destination.

Keeping your eye on the goal can be tough but not impossible. It takes the best of your ability, honesty, and the truth as you know it. When the pain comes, and trust me there will be pain, make every effort to see the victory as you want it. Believe in that victory! In time your faith will bring you through the fear. Oh, yes! The fear will surely come, and when it does, trust in the completed task and the fear will subside. The healer within will guide and direct you to a place of rest. This course of action will happen throughout the healing process; your inner guide will help you meet any situation. When you fall, you will rise again, and in time, you will solve your difficulties. Even you who have experienced great trauma, yes, you too can be healed.

Plant your desire within your soul's memory and it will evolve. With unwavering determination you will know yourself as you are intended to be. As you persevere, you will realize your completeness.

Subtle Resistance

"Well, we meet again. Why am I here, in your office?"

"Hello, Mrs. Hunt. Why do *you* think you're here?"

"Maybe it might have something to do with the marriage counseling my husband and I do with Dr. Williams. That's where I met you, over at his office. Am I close?"

"Your counseling with me could most certainly help with the problems you and your husband are working through. And, you and Bill should continue with Dr. Williams. But I didn't have you come here to discuss issues about your husband."

"Then why, Dr. Boyd? Why am I here?"

He looked directly at me. "Would you, for right now,

let me ask the questions?"

"Sure, why not? I know about counseling. I've done a lot of it."

"Tell me about your counseling. What went on in your sessions?"

"I just needed to talk with someone, a professional, to help me clear my head. I didn't have the greatest childhood in the world."

"Can you tell me about your parents?

"Yes. I loved my mom dearly. And feared my dad with a fear that was indescribable."

"You said 'was' indescribable. Talk to me about that a little more, Mrs. Hunt."

"I said 'was' because he's dead. He had a violent temper. It scared the hell out of all of us. I feel the anxiety right now, just talking and thinking about it. The memories are too painful."

"Okay, then let's not go there right now. Can you tell me about your family? You mentioned that he 'scared the hell out of all of you.' Who did he scare?"

"My mom, my sisters and my brothers. The oldest is my brother Ray. Actually he's my half-brother, my dad's son from a previous marriage. My mom raised him as if he was her very own. Then comes my oldest sister, Dorothy, then Louise, then my brother Bill, next is Marge. Billy was killed when he was seventeen, on his motorcycle. Last is my youngest sister, Happy, and that's my family."

"How are you doing right now, Mrs. Hunt?"

"I'd do a lot better if you'd call me Donna."

"If you prefer being called Donna, I can do that," said Dr. Boyd.

"I do like it better. Mrs. Hunt sounds too stuffy."

"We do have a little time left today to talk. Would you be willing to see me on a continuous basis?"

"I suppose, but being able to handle my life without counseling is a goal of mine. I don't want to get into any serious painful stuff. What do you want me to talk about with the time we have left?"

"How about your family, can you elaborate a little on each member?"

"Yeah, I think so. But not my brother, Bill. Okay?"

"We got a deal, Donna."

"Dorothy was the oldest born to my parents. I remember her babysitting, when my folks were gone, which was seldom, THANK GOD! She was strict. I think she thought I was a brat. In fact, I know she thought that about me. Maybe she thought she could straighten out the "little brat" in a few hours while she had me to herself."

"Dorothy and I were never close to each other. The differences in our ages counted for some of it; sibling rivalry, I believe, played a big part of it. Our lives just drifted apart when we didn't live in the same house anymore."

"Louise was the next born. My memories of her and Dorothy are the fists fights they got into with each other. They outgrew fighting as they grew up and became friends, going out together and having fun. Louise and I never really had much in common either — other than being born into the same family. Louise and I were just two people growing up under the same roof and living the same terror inflicted by the man we called dad. I have always liked her and love her as my sister. She is, in my opinion, a courageous woman with a great deal of strength. She's had her own demons to deal with."

"Marge is next. We were typical sisters. It was nothing like the relationship with my two older sisters. Marge and I didn't have a relationship based on some hidden agenda that caused hostility and resentment. It was more in the natural order of things. We talked, we played, we fought, and then we made up again. We soon forgot our disagreements, and that was the end of it. We are close sisters to this day. We always laugh a lot when we're together; we can also get into some serious conversations when we need to. We simply enjoy each other's company."

"So Dorothy had you pegged as a brat. Tell me about that."

"For one thing, I would stand at the screen door and scream almost the whole time mom was gone. Maybe I was a brat, maybe I just didn't like being away from my mom. Mom used to fix me a bowl of cocoa and sugar; I loved it. One time, I talked Dorothy into fixing it for me. I had to promise her I would eat every bit of it and not waste it. I promised, but didn't keep up my end of the bargain. I got full and hid it in the closet. When my brother Ray came home, I told him what I did, and he went and got it and dumped it for me. Yep, I was a brat."

"That's wonderful. Nothing wrong with being a brat," he said with a big grin on his face. We've got a little more time left. What about your half-brother?"

"My oldest brother. That's the way I think of him. He's a happy-go-lucky guy, loves to laugh. He has a great sense of humor and a kindness about him that makes people want to be around him. And he knew how to make my mother laugh, in spite of the sadness in her life. Ray loves mom very much and felt compassion toward her for the life she lived with dad. Ray was always nice to me and I loved the attention he gave me. I knew he liked me because he would find the time to play games with me, and he talked to me much more than my two older sisters did. But he wasn't always home. He went to school and started liking girls at an early age. He would hang out with them for as long as he could. Coming home to our house was difficult for all of us."

"My father was both physically and verbally abusive to him. Ray was almost always in trouble with dad. He would stay out late, sometimes all night. He wouldn't get a job, like my dad wanted him to. Sometimes he got money from my mom, that is, when she had some to give him. It could never have been too much, mom didn't have much money. We lived during the Depression and were poor, but mom managed to squeeze out a little cash for Ray now and then. He gave a lot in return; he helped make my mother's life somewhat bearable in an otherwise unbearable existence."

"Ray was loved by all in the family. It was a sad day when he moved out. He'd come over once in awhile to see my mom. He'd let me sit on his lap and would always give me a great big hug right before he'd leave. Are we almost done here? I'm feeling tired."

"You look tired. We can stop now."

"I am very tired. I've got a couple of days off. Boy! Am I glad."

"You work at the State Hospital, don't you?"

"Yes, I do. Lanterman State Hospital. I work with the mentally retarded. I'm a Psychiatric Technician."

"Okay, Donna. Let the receptionist make an appointment for you in three weeks.

Thanks for coming in."

* * * * *

"Good morning, Donna. I'm glad you're here, I thought maybe you'd back off."

"I wanted to. I'm not sure why I even bothered to show up."

"How are you feeling?" he asked.

"Okay, not so okay. I'm feeling upset and a little on edge for some reason," I answered honestly.

5

"What's been going on with you these last three weeks?"

"I don't know. I really don't. I just know I really feel cranky. I'm angry and very resistive to being here."

"Why is that, Donna? Why are you feeling this way?"

"Because I've already been in therapy. I got my life straightened out. I went to college and got an education, I have a good paying job, and I feel good about myself."

"It sounds to me there's a 'but' in what all you just said. Is there?

"Yes, there is. The reason is why Bill and I are in marriage counseling with Dr. Williams. The 'but' is about Bill's impotence."

"Tell me about Bill."

"He's easy-going, never gets mad like my father did. I like that in him, but he's too passive. I want to help him overcome his impotence. If coming here will help do that, then I guess the least I can do is come here for awhile. Will it help us, Dr. Boyd?"

"I believe it will, in time. Let's talk about your feelings of anger. Where's that coming from? What's going on? You mentioned Bill never gets mad like your father did. Let's stay with that."

"I remember dad's anger. Just thinking about it makes my stomach churn. If it'll help, I'll tell you about it. Should I?"

"Yes, please do. It will help. In time, it will help a lot."

"Dad never stopped his rampages, his sadistic pleasure in keeping all of us frozen in fear. I remember an evening at the dinner table that made all of us jump out of our skin. When I got old enough to sit at the dinner table mom put me next to him, don't ask me why, 'cause I'll never know. But there I was every night. Dad sat at one end of the table, "the head of the table," and I was the first one to his left.

6

This was definitely one of his "I'm going to find something to get pissed off about" nights. He reached for the apricot jam, his favorite, it slipped out of his hand. I reached out to grab it and he did too, at the same time. Our hands tangled in each other's and the jam went crashing to the floor, glass shattering everywhere. Dad found his moment and exploded: "You stupid, clumsy brat! What in the hell did you do that for?"

"In spite of my fear, I tried to explain that I was trying to catch it for him. Dad was furious, ranting, raving, using every cuss word that ever was. The four letter word was his favorite in his peak of madness.

Billy, my brave brother who sat next to me, jumped up and took my arm, "Come on, Donna. Stay with me." I followed him out to the backyard. The yard was fenced and Billy said, "We're going to jump the fence. Come on, hurry!"

"You know, Dr. Boyd, Billy was always trying to get me to jump that fence. I could never do it until that night. I glided over that fence like a graceful fawn. Well, maybe not that graceful, but I flew over the fence and was on the other side in an instant. We stood in the backyard of a vacant house."

"Go over there," Billy said pointing to a hole the previous tenants' dog had dug. Once in the hole he said, "We're going to sit here and pray." And so we did. Billy prayed, "Dear God, please let mama be okay and please tell me what to do." That was it, short and to the point. It didn't even take a minute. With my hands still clasped and head bowed in prayer, Billy said, "Come on, let's go." I was expecting more prayer or at least the "amen."

We got up, Billy taking my hand. He must have received an instant answer to his prayer, because he seemed to know exactly where he was going. We went to a house about four blocks away from ours, and Billy knocked on the door. A man answered and immediately recognized my brother. I learned later that Billy did yard work for this man.

"Well, hi. Come on in, Bill," the man said in a friendly voice. We went inside. The man looked at me and then at Billy, "Is everything okay? What is it, Bill?"

"I need to leave my little sister here for awhile. Will that be okay?" Billy asked.

"I'm sure it is," he responded. "Judy's in the kitchen, I'll go ask her." He looked down at me and said, "My name is Don. What's yours?"

Because he was a stranger to me, I hung my head down and answered in a whisper, "Donna."

Leaning closer, he said, "I didn't hear you. What is your name?"

My head still hung and in a little louder voice, I repeated, "Donna."

"That's a nice name," he said while putting his hand on my shoulder.

After Don went into the kitchen, Billy said, "I want you to stay here for just a little while. I need to go see if mom is okay. You'll be alright here; they're really nice people." I nodded, giving Billy the okay sign.

In a short time Don and a woman walked out of the kitchen. "Donna, this is my wife, Judy. Looking at Billy, he said, "Donna can stay with us, go take care of your business."

Billy thanked them emphatically and told them he wouldn't be long. Billy turned toward me and, with assurance in his voice, said, "I'll be right back. I promise. These are nice people. You'll be okay." He turned to Don and asked, "Will you walk me to the door?" They stood at the door and talked about something before Billy left.

I was uncomfortable being with strangers and especially being without my mama.

"Would you like some cookies and milk," Judy asked me. I nodded, still not looking up. "Don, will you go get some milk and cookies for this pretty girl?"

"I sure will." And he left to go get the cookies.

"Are you okay, dear?" asked Judy. I nodded, this time raising my head a little. Actually I was terrified, my stomach was churning. That's what my dad did to me.

Don brought milk and cookies from the kitchen. "I didn't think to ask if you like milk," he said.

"Yes, I do. Mama always has milk for us. I like it cold."

"Good, that's fine because it is very cold. What kind of games do you like to play?" he asked with genuine interest.

In between bites of cookies and drinks of milk, I said, "I like hopscotch and playing jacks. Marge and I play together. That's my sister." He kept talking to me in such a kind way. He gave me the recognition and the respect that I so much wanted from my father. He did most of the talking, while I either nodded my head in response to questions or answered with a quick "yes" or "no." Judy returned to the kitchen, taking time to explain to me that she had some dishes to do.

"We have checkers. Do you know how to play checkers?"

"Yes, we play checkers at home, and sometimes I play with Billy or my sister Marge." I started to relax enough to begin talking to this friendly stranger.

"Do you want to play a game with me?" He was giving me the freedom to make up my own mind. What a great feeling! No telling me I had to do it, just letting me make the choice. I said yes. We played a couple of rounds, and I won both times. Did he let me win? I don't know for sure, but I do know I was having a good time."

Don smiled at me and said, "You're really a good player," and we both laughed. I was having such a good time. Judy came out of the kitchen and sat down with us to watch us finish our game. Then the three of us talked together. They came down to my level and encouraged me to talk about my interests. I became so comfortable, that even the churning in my stomach disappeared."

"Do you like school?" asked Don.

"Sometimes I do, sometimes I don't. The work at school is easy but mostly I like to stay home with my mom. I feel funny when I can't see her."

Dr. Boyd interrupted me, "Do you know why you felt funny when you weren't with your mom?"

"I don't know, I think I felt something was missing. I felt vulnerable without her. You know, fragile."

"Okay. What else did you talk about with Don and Judy that day?"

"I told them how I helped Billy with the chickens and rabbits my dad raised for eating purposes. They asked how old I was, and I told them I was almost eight. I felt so wonderful with them, a wonderful happiness in my stomach. I don't ever remember feeling so good as a child, other than being with my mother."

"Billy finally returned. He came over to me and said, "We can go home now. Dad's in bed; Dorothy and Louise say everything is calm." I didn't want to go home, but Billy said we had to. He thanked the couple and we left. When I saw my mom, I reached out to her, and was so glad to be in her arms again. Yet, I felt a kind of sadness I had never felt before."

"I never saw Don and Judy again. They gave me so much that day, something to carry within my soul, the gift of hope and the knowing that someday I would again feel the way I did with them. I spent only a short time with them, but the joy I experienced was a treasure beyond description. They probably never knew just what they had done for me. But, I knew and my spirit knew."

"Other than looking tired, worried, and scared, mom seemed all right. The tired-worried-and-scared look was something I had seen many times before and many times after the night I didn't catch the jam. Billy and I found out that dad kept raging long after we left. Mom kept trying to calm him down, but he was out of control and beyond the point of listening to anyone. He started breaking dishes. Mom slipped, fell, and cut her leg, a deep cut that the girls said needed stitches. But, dad wouldn't let her go to the emergency room. He told the girls to take care of her. My sisters tried to stop the bleeding by wrapping her leg in a sheet. Marge told us mom was bleeding a lot. Dorothy and Louise had her lie on the couch and kept putting towels on the cut. Eventually the bleeding stopped, and in time, mom's leg healed without the care of a doctor, but the ache in her heart remained. Marge said my older sisters begged him to take mom to the doctor but he wouldn't let them."

"Why do you think that was, Donna?" asked Dr. Boyd.

"He was scared the police would come. He was deathly afraid of the police. Dorothy kept asking him to get help for her. Her love for mom gave her the courage to persist. 'She needs to go to the doctor, dad, she needs stitches. Daddy, it's really deep.'"

"Marge told me Dorothy tried so hard for mama's sake, but he wouldn't give in. 'She was brave to approach dad that way. I bet you her love for mom overtook her fear of dad.'"

"Marge said dad shouted, 'I'm not taking her to the doctor and that's that,' before going out the front door and sitting in the car. He came back into the house later and asked if our mom was okay. Mama heard him asking about

11

her and in her comforting way said 'I'm okay, honey; everything's okay. You go on to bed and don't worry.' Good grief, Dr. Boyd, what makes a woman like my mom *be* like my mom?"

"This isn't the time to go into that. It's not a one sentence answer," he wisely replied.

"I don't have the answer to my mom. I just know I love her." I said.

"Maybe that is your answer. We seem to be able to love in spite of the behavior."

"Maybe, who knows? Anyway, dad went to bed that night, and mom told Dorothy and Louise to go find us, Billy and me. Marge stayed home with mom. Billy and our sisters found each other as the girls searched for us and Billy headed home to see if dad had calmed down. That's when Billy returned for me.

There was no phone in our home at the time this all happened. If there had been, I know my sisters would have used it to call the police, because dad was crazed that night.

The next day while dad was at work, mom packed up everything and we all left him behind. But like every other time she left him, she also returned; he would cry and beg her to come back, promising to never lose his temper again. Mom always gave in to him, and we went back to living the same old way. For awhile, after we returned dad always made an effort to be different. It never lasted. He was stuck in his own past, bringing along his fears, his anger, and his pain into the present. The result was a living hell. The painful emotions that lived within my dad fueled a destructive urge that he seemed to have no control over. To not be in control was his deepest fear. He would never have consented to confront such scary thoughts and feelings."

"Donna that is a very insightful thing you just said. Did you learn these things from your other counselor?"

12

"I know what it's like to be out of control. And yes, I did learn an awful lot from Dr. Weber."

"Will you elaborate on some of your visits with Dr. Weber?"

"I will not!" I immediately returned to the incident of my father's temper. "You know something else about that night, Marge told me that after it was over, Dorothy and Louise talked about killing dad. They never did, though. He died of cancer."

"How old was he when he died?"

"Seventy-three or seventy-four."

"It would have been much more of a tragedy to deal with if your sisters had killed him."

"I know, instead they left home as soon as they were old enough to take care of themselves. Ray was already gone the night that happened. My brother Billy left this Earth completely when he died on his motorcycle. He was only seventeen. It makes me feel very sad to think about it. And no, I don't want to talk about it. Okay?"

"You know it's okay, maybe later, when you're ready."

I nodded my head in agreement. "I was the one that lived with mom the longest. Some of the family said it was because I was a mama's baby. The truth is, living on my own was very scary. I needed to be with my mom to feel safe and secure." I felt weary, and thought it must be close to the end of our session,

"That was a wonderful experience you had with Don and Judy, wasn't it?"

"Oh, yes. It was. The most important thing I learned from them was that not every family was like mine. Until that experience, I could only see my world as all there was.

Don and Judy opened my eyes to see and feel another way of living. I hung on to the joy of that time with them for as long as I could, but in time, I forgot, consciously that is. I kept the memory of it deep in my subconscious. I saw things could be better, that someday I would break the chains that temporarily kept me a puppet on a string. After that delightful time with Don and Judy, I grew up knowing that my life was a distorted sense of reality. I couldn't put it exactly in these words, but here I am, ready to be free. When Bill and I can have a healthy sex life, I know I will be healed. I feel confident that it will happen."

"Yes, that's right. You're on your way to freedom. Your father put you in a most difficult situation and now you're here undoing what he did. Great job, Donna!"

"I feel as if it's time to end the session. Will that be alright? I'll come back if you think it's going to help my situation with Bill."

"Yes, please come back. Let's make it for three weeks again. And get some rest."

"I'll see you in three weeks then doctor."

* * * * *

I did get some rest. The three weeks went by and I was back in his office.

"Come on in, Donna. How have you been?"

"I'm fine because I made up my mind. I'm not going to talk about anything that's going to upset me. And that's that!"

"From the sound of your voice, you must have made up your mind. That's good, Donna. Do you think I tell you what to say? I don't feel like I do."

"No, you don't. You just have a way of bringing me in to subjects I don't want to discuss. I'm not going to let you do that anymore."

"I believe we're seeing this from different points of

14

view. Haven't I always told you to only talk about the things you need to talk about?"

"I guess. Maybe. Yes, you do tell me that. I just don't want to be manipulated. I hate that."

"I would never do that. What do you want to talk about?"

"I haven't told you about my sister, Happy. I could tell you about her, if you're interested and it's something easy for me to talk about.

"I'm very interested. Tell me about Happy, please."

"Hazel is her real name. She got her nickname when she was six-weeks old. Dad said he gave her the nickname because she was always smiling. Mom said it was gas pains. Whatever it was, the name stuck. She was a sweet baby. Louise adored her and cared for her a lot. Mom wasn't well after the birth of Happy and was more than glad to let Louise take care of her. We found out later, mom had a tumor growing inside of her and had to return to the hospital to have it removed about two months after she gave birth to our baby sister. Huh, my dad, oh! Oh! Oh! My dad, my dad, my dad."

"What's the matter, Donna? Donna, do you hear me?"

"Yeah, I hear you. My head is dizzy. It's hard for me to speak."

"What's happening right now? Donna, tell me, please can you hear me? Can you talk to me?"

"Give me a minute...I'll be alright...What was I saying? Oh yeah, I remember. My dad gave Happy a lot of attention, having promised mom he would be a good father this time. From all outward appearances, it would seem he idolized her. Yet, if you talk to Happy, she would tell you she was as scared of him as the rest of us. I loved my little sister, yet I watched with bewilderment how much attention he gave her. In my confusion I believed that I was so bad a

15

person that I was not worthy of any of his 'good attention.' In an effort to gain his approval, I, too, showered her with much attention, accepting as truth the myth that I was not worth his love. Now I know that's not true at all."

"You're right, that's not true at all and I'm glad you know it. What was happening to you, back there, Donna? You didn't seem to be connecting with me. Can you tell me?"

"I really don't know. I guess I lost my train of thought. It happens to me once in awhile. I just fade out of the present moment. I remember now what we were talking about. I know I'm not a bad person. Bewildered but not bad."

"You are so worthwhile, Donna. I hope you truly believe it."

"I do, I'd have to believe it, to focus so much on my desire to become a totally healthy person. I think I can tell you about my brother, Billy. And then we can forget my boring family."

"Okay, that would be great! And, I don't find you boring at all. I see a bright and very intelligent person. Tell me about your brother."

"I'll tell you as much as I can. He took care of me the best he could. I think he did a good job. Billy went out of his way to be good to me. When he was around, he tried to protect me by keeping me away from dad. He was about three and a half years older than me, and he was my friend. We loved each other. I felt good when I was in his presence, he cared about me and I sensed it. Being loved by him was a special thing to me. He left this Earth at seventeen. It pains me to think about it. He was so young."

"How did he die, Donna?"

"On his motorcycle with his buddy on the back. He was

taking his friend to work and going very fast because he had to get to his job, which was in the opposite direction. There was an accident with other cars and he died instantly. His friend died the next day. My beloved brother was gone from me, from us."

"I'm so sorry for your loss."

"I don't want to talk about it anymore, right now. Maybe later."

"You don't have to talk about it ever again if you don't want to."

"Tell me, doctor, what is the point of all this talking about my past. It seems to me, I should be getting on with my life."

"In a very real sense that's exactly what you are doing, getting on with your life."

"But how can talking about the past bring me to the place I want to be? There's so much turmoil in me. I don't want that."

"Of course you don't. You're coming out of the past, so you can leave it behind and begin to live in the Now, without the burden of the past."

"That makes sense, a lot of sense. I feel much more relaxed about all this therapy stuff, now that I understand it better."

"Good, Donna, I'm glad. Some of your childhood experiences have been ingrained in you since birth. It'll take persistence on your part to overcome it."

"I can do that. My family tells me I'm persistent to a fault. More like stubborn."

"Call it what you will. But if you use that persistence, that stubbornness, in the right direction, you can reach whatever you desire."

"My desire is to be whole, a complete woman. From now on, I'm going to focus on being healed. How does that sound?"

"It sounds wonderful and you sound excited!"

"I am, Dr. Boyd. And encouraged."

"Did you find what you were looking for with your other therapist? What I mean is, did it help you in anyway?"

"Yes, it did." I was remembering why I decided to seek counseling.

"Donna, you're not saying anything. Talk to me. Was it a positive experience for you?"

"Just a minute and I'll tell you." The reason was troubling to me. "When I started going to my other therapist, I was running around on my then husband. I wanted to stay married to him and thought maybe therapy would save my marriage. It helped me, but not my marriage. After fourteen years, my marriage to Dick was over."

"Let's talk about how it helped you."

"I don't know. It's going to be hard. I'm not proud of how I used to live, I'm very much ashamed."

"Okay, Donna, just take it slow. Remember your persistence, your desire."

"I'll try, I'll try. I, I, I…there's no other way to say this, except, I was a whore. Before I met Dick, I slept with different men all the time. It was more than being a whore, more like a female cat in heat. And there were male cats; we would find each other and satisfy our animal instinct. I was driven, the need to keep repeating this behavior continued, that is until I met Dick. We cared about each other and the sex was about wanting to touch each other, to satisfy and be satisfied. We only wanted each other. She was gone. We went together for fourteen months."

"Wait a minute, Donna, wait a minute. What did you mean 'she was gone?' Who was gone?"

"What did I mean? Huh, I Guess I meant the urges left me. You know, that part of me that was driven was for some reason gone."

"Can you talk about that part of you, your urges, as you called it?"

"There's nothing to say, really. I was in love. To me, that's all that mattered. The urges were gone. We were married after fourteen months of dating. And for the first five years, things seemed just fine, then the urge to be with a stranger slowly returned. I denied the feelings at first, but after awhile, the urge grew stronger and stronger until I gave into it. I started finding ways to get out, to get this thing started, this, whatever it was, all over again. I sent myself baby shower cards, girls' night out, anything. I was out of control. I could only think of being with someone beside my husband again. The female cat called the shots for several years, until I decided to stop it through therapy. The talking it out with a professional helped a lot. Plus discovering, huh, I found out. Wow!"

"What is it, Donna? Trust me, it will be alright. I'm here for you. Get it out."

"It was, was, my very own father. He…you know."

"You can tell me Donna. Please tell me."

"He raped me, Dr. Boyd. My very own father raped me!" I cried softly into my hands.

"You don't need to be ashamed, my dear. It's your father that should have carried the shame. This should be his burden, not yours."

"I can't talk about it anymore. I can tell you remembering this ugly thing freed me to the point that I stopped the behavior, but it destroyed my marriage."

"Embrace yourself, Donna, for the courageous, insightful person you are. Your courage gave you a more noble way to see yourself, as you really are. What you value in your life won the victory and gave you a different way of thinking."

"Life still seems so difficult for me. Will the struggle ever be over?"

"I believe it will. It will take sometime, but it's on its way. Our time is up Donna. Will you be okay when you leave here?"

"Yes, I will. I feel more peaceful. I guess it does help to talk things out. I know it won't be tomorrow or the next day but it will be someday. It's on its way."

"Yes it is. Go do something good for yourself."

Relinquishing

"I have had a hard time these last three weeks, a very hard time."

"Can you elaborate? Tell me what's been going on."

"Frustration for one thing, sadness for another. It's been difficult time for me, as well as deeply disturbing trying to deal with it."

"Are you saying you've been looking closely at yourself, your emotions, maybe recalling some distressing memories?"

"Yes, that's it exactly. It's overwhelming."

"I should think so. I know these emotions are hard to deal with. Can I give you a little bit of advice?" He waited for me to answer.

I nodded.

"It might be better if you didn't try to solve your problems between appointments. Donna, this may take a long time to get through. Don't suffer unnecessarily in an effort to get this over quickly. This is not a quick fix. I know I keep telling you this. Try to focus on your living now, and find some enjoyment. If you remember something in the past that is painful and confusing, write it down and try not to let it take you away from finding some joy now. Don't let this thing absorb your every thought."

"That's easier said than done. My feelings and thoughts keep coming into my consciousness and it spaces me out. I don't like the feeling at all. "

"Perhaps we can talk about those feelings today. Remember this Donna, that although I want to encourage you to find some answers to your dilemma, you did not choose this battle, this struggle you're going through, your father gave it to you to bear. You are strong, you are intelligent, and you are courageous. And with these tools you may gain a deeper sense of yourself. Would it all be worth it if you could achieve this goal?"

"Oh, yes! Very much so. This is my purpose, to become more of who I am and to know who I am."

"Okay then. We've got some work ahead of us. You will have to look deep and understand that you can make great strides by going through this challenge. Are you ready to work, work, work?"

"I am, am, am." I smiled after I said this, so did he.

"It's very important that you trust me, Donna. Do you?"

"I think I do. Trusting people is not easy for me."

"I'm not saying to turn over control to me. I'm asking if you trust that I want to help you to live and to be happy in this world."

"The way you put it, I can truthfully say I do trust that you have my best interest at heart. Not having to turn over control makes me feel less anxious. But, I still have a great deal of conflict going on in me."

"That is perfectly understandable. We'll work this out together. What matters is for you to see that you matter and are not alone in this. I can see your desperation. Be as patient with yourself as you can be, as willing as you can, and as you go deep within yourself, you will help me see the obstacles standing in the way. Together, we will slowly remove the stuff blocking you from seeing what it means to be human."

"You know me pretty well. I don't know what it feels like to be a healthy human being. I would really like that."

"I know, Donna, I know. You have been dehumanized. I know you want to experience a life without fear. And, I will help guide you into this new place. But, I need to know you trust me."

"I do trust you. I don't trust that my future will be as good as you say it can be, not right at this moment anyway. But, I like your vision so I'll do my best."

"That's good enough for me."

"I can tell you about the time the goat ate my bottle."

"Okay, let's hear it."

"I was just a few months from being three years old. Mom was
    always —"

"Wait a minute, Donna. Are you telling me you can remember back that far?"

"Well, yes. I actually can, but in this case, it isn't just me remembering the incident. This story was told periodically throughout our growing years. I heard about it many times, about when 'the goat ate Donna's bottle.'"

"Is it a funny story?"

"Not at all. It's about my dad's rotten temper. My mom told me a lot about the situation. And since I've started coming here, I've deliberately asked her questions about my childhood. We drink coffee together everyday, and it's a good time to get into things I need to know."

"Okay, let's hear it."

"Mama said everyone in the family was always nagging her to take my bottle away. I loved that bottle and would scream if I didn't know where it was. My family hated it when I screamed.

"Mama, make Donna quit screaming. She's a brat. Make her stop," said my sister Marge.

Mom answered her gently, "She's lost her bottle again. You know how upset she gets when her bottle's not with her." Loud screams came out of my mouth, and mom tried to soothe me, to no avail. "Will you help mama find it for her?" Mom looked at me and said, "Thank God, your father's not home."

"Will you give me some pennies if I find it?" Marge asked.

"Yes, I will, but you have to wait 'til daddy gets paid." Mama echoed an extra request, "Find it as soon as you can, daddy will be home in just a few minutes."

Marge ran out to the yard, followed by mom with me in her arms. Dorothy, my oldest sister was walking towards the house. Before Marge could say anything, Dorothy said, "What are you doing, looking for the big baby's bottle again?" Dorothy kept walking, and in the same sarcastic tone said, "How many pennies did mom promise you this time?"

"I don't know, I have to wait 'til daddy gets paid. You better be quiet, mom's on the other side of the house and can hear everything you say."

Dorothy paid no attention. "If you find it before daddy gets home you'll probably get a bonus," Dorothy said even louder, in her this-is-so-disgusting voice as she walked right to where mom and I were. Mom had me on her hip, looking for my bottle in the high grass.

"Mom," Dorothy said, "when are you going to take the bottle away from her?

She's almost three. Are you going to let her be a baby all her life?"

"No, she's not going to be a baby all her life. Your dad's going to be home any minute now and I don't want her screaming."

"If you keep her glued to your hip, she'll be okay." Dorothy answered.

"I know you're right dear. It is time to break her from the bottle, but not right now." My sweet mama always tried to keep everyone happy.

Marge came running around the house, waving the bottle and saying, "I found it, I found it. Look, here it is!"

"Thank you, thank you, I love you, you're such a good girl. Will you do one more thing for me?"

"I know what you want," Marge said. "I'll go fill it up with milk. She'll keep quiet now, huh mama? Shall I put her in the crib?"

"Better let me do that, she's really crabby and she'll keep crying if you try to put her down. Hurry up, Marge. I need to start dinner as soon as I put her down."

Marge hurried into the kitchen to fill the bottle. "Dorothy, I'm going to take the bottle away from her for good in a few days, I promise." Dorothy didn't say a word. Marge came out of the house and handed the milk-filled bottle to mom. I reached for it right away and mom laid me down, kissing me and telling me I was a good girl.

Dorothy went to her room, a room she shared with Louise and Marge. Marge stayed outside. Everything was quiet again. Mom started dinner. Dad would be home soon and the family, each and every one of us, would be puppets on a string.

The situation with my bottle and me had been a bone of contention for almost a year, mama told me. She had tried to break me from the bottle, but my screaming spells always won out. The bottle was more than something with milk in it. Second to mom, it was my everything. I laughed and played with it when I was happy. I drank from it when I was hungry, threw it when I was angry, and held it close when I was afraid. All my feelings were put into my bottle. Mom had long since changed my bottle from a regular wide-mouth glass one used in those days to a baking soda can which the wide nipple fit perfectly. She did this because in my fits of anger I would throw it out of my crib. Glass would shatter everywhere in tiny bits and pieces. The baking soda can was the perfect solution. Mom didn't give in just because I screamed, but because it also gave her some much needed time to get things done around the house. It was her way of finding some quiet time for herself and of keeping dad from blowing his top. I learned that all I had to do to get my way was to scream, but that was about to stop.

A delicious smell from the kitchen told us we were having spaghetti for dinner. Mom went to the girls' bedroom, as she always did around this time. "Louise, come help with dinner. You can set the table." It was more of a request than a demand.

"Okay, in just a minute. I want to finish this chapter."

And before mom had a chance to speak, a voice all too familiar said, "Did you hear your mother? Do it now. Do you hear me?" This was a demand on no uncertain terms, a loud gruff demand.

"Yes, dad, I hear you." Louise said in a voice just above a whisper. She was up and gone without a word."

"We all got like this, Dr. Boyd, when dad used his gruff voice. My mom told me that dad's tone of voice was gruffer than usual this particular night. Something had happened at work and we were going to pay for it. Sitting at the dinner was going to be extremely uncomfortable. Everyone would try to say the right thing or not say anything at all, but he always found something to get mad about. Our family would hurry up and eat in order to leave the table, except mom that is. Like puppets each one would dance to the one who controlled the strings.

Dinner was always a scary time, even if he was in a fairly good mood, which tonight he wasn't. He would need to show us in some unpleasant way that he was king and master of his family. This very night, we would most definitely have the privilege of listening to him rant and rave. And the topic would be the bottle and me.

And so it was. "You fixed Donna another bottle, didn't you? I checked her crib and saw the bottle hanging out of her mouth. What is wrong with you, mother?" Dad said in his totally angry voice, "What in the goddamn hell is wrong with you?"

"Now honey, don't get mad. Please don't get mad," said mom, giving dad the power he wanted. No! Giving him the power he *demanded*. "I'm going to take the bottle away from her tomorrow," said mom in a low, quivery voice. Unable to hide the fear, she went on, "Honest dear, tomorrow Donna will not have the bottle anymore! Now, please calm down, please!"

"I don't know why in the hell it's taking you so long, she's almost three for God's sake. "You're as stupid as my supervisor. You two would make a good pair." Dad's voice was getting loud as usual, and everyone stiffened with fear. He pounded his fist on the table and said, "Jesus Christ, do I have to come home to the same shit I have to put up with at work?"

Mom said all the kids jumped from the noise of his fists

on the table, and that I woke up crying. Mom hurriedly got me from my crib and put me in my high chair. She said, "You be a good girl now." I was terrified of this big man I called daddy and clammed up.

Like so many nights before, we were not going to be able to stay out of harm's way tonight. We felt helpless, like an animal caught in a trap, and did what we always did when in this kind of predicament. Unable to resolve the situation, we looked to mom to pull us out of another stressful, anxious encounter with the man we couldn't control.

"Please, please, don't get mad at us," mom pleaded with dad.

Ignoring her, he raved on, "I should be able to come home to my family and get some goddamn peace. That son-of-a-bitch at work is bad enough. I'm going to break his fuckin' neck if he doesn't get off my back!"

"Okay dear, okay, we'll try to do better." said mom, allowing him to believe his rotten temper was our fault. She told my two older sisters to finish their dinner and start the dishes.

"I'm through, mom," said Dorothy, anxious to get away from dad.

"So am I," repeated Louise with a tremble in her voice.

"What about your dessert, girls? Don't you want dessert?" said dad, knowing full well their dessert tonight would be to get out of his sight.

"No dessert for me, thanks. Do you want any Louise?" asked Dorothy.

"No, I'm too full. May we please be excused?"

Dad gave a nod, "You girls start cleaning up the dishes now."

Mom was doing her best to get us away from dad's temper. She looked to Billy, my youngest brother who hadn't said a word up to this point. "Billy, you and Margie take the baby and keep an eye on her while daddy and I finish our dinner."

"Sure, mom." said Billy. They both popped up, more than glad to have a reason to leave the table. Billy picked me up out of the high chair, I started to cry and mama said, "If you can't quiet her down, fix her a bottle and put her to bed." That last remark put fuel to the fire. In his loudest voice, one notch below a scream, dad replied, "Son-of-a-bitch, fuckin' hell! You better quit calling her the baby, and you sure as hell better take that bottle away from her tomorrow or there's going to be hell to pay."

At this point, Marge left with Billy as he carried me out of the dining room and out of sight.

Mom had got us out of the dining room, knowing full well dad would focus on her. She said to him, "I am absolutely going to take the bottle from her tomorrow. I just wanted to finish our meal without the children. I promise you; tonight is the last time she will get her bottle." This calmed him down somewhat but mom had to listen to his rage over his boss, as if it was her fault. She got her cubs out of immediate danger posed by a very angry, almost insane man. And dad, well he accomplished his goal, too. He needed to be in control at all times, but work made him feel trapped. He had to exert his control at home to feel the power again. Yes, he was able to make himself feel all powerful again with small children and a little woman, an insecure, frightened woman who used what courage she had to protect her children. She was not able, however, to stop the damage that fear creates in the mind. The anticipation of the "next time" was a source of constant stress. I felt in danger and lived in fear on a daily basis. The terror I experienced most definitely caused psychological damage within my psyche. Understanding the dynamics of it all, taught me to believe this is the way life is. That is until I met Don and Judy."

"That is so true. You were smart to see it then and you're insightful to realize it now." Dr. Boyd responded. "But where is the part where the goat eats the bottle?"

"I'm getting there, I'm getting there. Don't rush me. Thank you for that very nice remark you just said about me. I appreciate it." He nodded his head up and down in a you're welcome gesture." I want to tell you something about my mom before I go on. I was raised during the depression and not having enough money was an everyday occurrence in our family. Sometimes the utilities would get shut off and yet I was given a loving mother. A gentle, sweet, loving mother. She was my savior in an otherwise difficult world. And although she gave me the kind of love that made me feel like a well loved only child, she was unable to give the kind of life that children need to grow in to become a healthy, happy, productive adult. It looks as if that is now my responsibility. That caring positive love she gave me and still gives me is the tool I need to carry me through to the place where I desire to be. I guess what you've been saying is the choice is mine to make."

"Now you're thinking straight, a very wise way of looking at it. The choice is yours and yours alone."

"Mom unknowingly continues to help me. When I start to remember something that's not completely clear in my mind, she helps me put the pieces together. She doesn't know what my father did to me. I'll never tell her."

"There's no need to. It could hurt instead of help."

"I know, Dr. Boyd. I just know that it would break her heart, and she's had it broken enough already. Okay, I think I'm ready to tell you the rest of the story now.

Mom and dad remained at the table for quite awhile. Sitting there talking to dad gave mom the time she needed to let dad cool off. It didn't always work. Sometimes, he reached a point of anger that was much, much worse than this particular evening. Sometimes, the rage took over and nothing would bring him out of it. It was even out of his control. He would eventually exhaust himself and go to bed to sleep off the rest of his anger. In fact, dad always went to bed early, soon after dinner. He would go into his bedroom, and we wouldn't see him until close to dinner time the next day. We learned to be very quiet when he went to bed. There was no way we wanted to wake him.

Ray came in that evening quite late. "Where have you been?" asked mom.

"Nowhere, mom. What's to eat? I'm starving," he said, walking toward the kitchen.

"I'll warm you up some spaghetti," said mom and headed in the same direction as Ray.

"Did dad ask where I was?"

"No. Lucky for you, he had other things on his mind. I have to take the bottle away from Donna. What can I do Ray? You know how many times that bottle kept her quiet and out of dad's way. Giving her that bottle has been a God send.

Without hesitation, he said, "Tell her the goat ate it." Mom told us he laughed right after he said it. I could just hear him, that wonderful laugh of his that always put a smile on her face.

But mom didn't laugh. Instead she said, "You know, Ray, that just might work." By this time, Ray was eating his warmed up spaghetti. She continued, "Maybe that's the answer. I'm going to take her to see the goat tomorrow. She loves that goat. I've got to do something."

"I hope it does the trick, mom," remarked Ray. "You know, mom, it is time to take it away from her. She's too old to be sucking on that bottle all the time." He got up

31

from his empty plate and gave mom a big kiss on the cheek. "I'm going to bed. The spaghetti was delicious, I love you."

"I love you, too. You be home by dinnertime tomorrow." There was no answer.

Our house was in the low-rent district of Los Angeles. Next to our house was a vacant field where a goat lived. The owner kept him there to keep the grass and weeds from getting too high. One of the highlights of my childhood was to see the goat.

The town we lived in was called Belvedere, now called East L.A. We didn't have the gangs then, and crime in the area was minimal back then. Our fear did not come from what happened outside of our house; our fear was of a different kind. We were prisoners of an authority that came from within our home, a power that wielded complete control over us. Our crime was being innocent, helpless victims, powerless to get ourselves out of the mess we were in. And, our mom feared the unknown more than the familiar fear she had grown accustomed to. She had brought her own fears and insecurities into the relationship with my dad and put the energy of her constant anxiety upon us. Without realizing it, of course, she gave this spirit of dread to her children, and it was reinforced by our father. We each learned to cope with our dilemma in our own way.

Dad was a hard worker, he went whenever and wherever he could to make money. He dealt with his own stress, wondering where his next dollar was coming from. The Depression was hard on us psychologically as well as financially. Dad's sense of responsibility never allowed him the option of walking out on us. He saw the obligation of taking care of us financially as a duty not to be abandoned."

"Why are you sticking up for him?" asked Dr. Boyd to my surprise.

"I'm not, I'm just telling you about my dad. You said you wanted to know things about my family." I answered somewhat annoyed.

"What about a sense of decency, his lack of caring? He should have been helping you to feel safe. To protect you, like fathers are supposed to do," he said with the tone of a man who not only knew how to be decent and caring, but who also didn't make excuses for someone like my dad.

"I don't know, Dr. Boyd. I don't have the answer to those things. Or, the reason why he was the way that he was."

"I know you don't. You've gone through so much. It's an awful way for children to have to live."

"I agree, one hundred percent." I paused, remembering those terribly crazy days. "Oh well, back to my bottle story. Mom knew dad meant business, so the next day after dad went to work, the others had gone to school, and Ray went to wherever he went, mama asked me, "Want to go see the goat?"

"Yeah, take me to see the goat," I answered.

"Take mama's hand," she said, and reached out for my hand. We walked out of the house to the field, where the goat was eating weeds. Mama bent down and pulled up a handful of grass and gave it to me, "Here sweetie, you can feed this to the goat." As I fed the goat she said, "Do you remember what else the goat eats? Remember what I told you?" She was trying to work her magic, hoping I wouldn't want my bottle anymore with what she was about to tell me.

"The goat eats cans and his name is Billy?" I said.

"That's right. The goat eats all the cans he can find. And you know what?" Mom got down on her knees, down to my level, and with her gentle voice said, "The goat ate your bottle. There's no more bottle, so now when you want milk to drink, we'll put it in a glass just like the other kids. Okay?" She always talked soft and slow to me. Sometimes it helped me understand what she was saying to me, sometimes not. "He's a bad goat, huh mama?"

"Yes, he is. Your bottle's all gone and that bad old goat ate it all up."

I got very quiet. I didn't cry, and I didn't have a temper tantrum as she expected I would. She kissed and hugged me, telling me I was a good girl. She thought I was being a good girl, but the truth was I didn't totally understand what she was telling me. I had no clue. I did not make the connection between the goat eating my bottle and my not being able to have the bottle anymore. The quietness was not coming from a "good girl," rather from a blank, unknowing mind. Mama told the whole family how well I took the news that my bottle was gone for good.

The security my bottle provided was gone, and it had a most devastating effect on me. Mom tried to put me in bed without it, but it didn't work. I would rock back and forth, flipping my hand in front of my eyes while making a loud "aaaah" sound. The noise would get louder and my rocking faster. The noise nearly became a scream. In the daytime, mom would give me a glass of milk and then rock me until I fell asleep. In the evening, mom would pick me up, take me to the older children, and make them keep me quiet until dad went to bed. Then she would rock me until I fell asleep. Once I fell asleep, I generally didn't wake up until the early part of the morning. Dad would be at work by then, so mom would put me in bed with her and I would get the comfort that I needed, wanted, and loved."

"Do you remember what would happen if your dad was home in the daytime?"

"My crib was in a corner of Billy and Ray's room, the room next to mom and dad's bedroom. If I woke before dad went to work, the boys were to entertain me until dad was gone. Mom had a "'round the clock program" to keep me from having a temper tantrum so that the man of the house, called father, would not have his own fit. There was always someone home on the weekends. I know I got rocked a lot, and sometimes, mama said she would find me asleep in a corner of the house. She would pick me up and put me in bed. I remember daddy got very mad when he caught me making loud noises.

Every Sunday, the whole family, except dad and Ray, went to Sunday school and church. It was rare for mom not to go, but if dad was in a bad mood, she would send us by ourselves so she could stay home and pamper him. One Sunday morning, I woke up extremely early. Ray was gone as usual and Billy was deep in sleep. I began flipping my hand and making my weird, loud noises, bringing it up to a near scream. I was out of touch, off in my own little world. I was deep within myself and found a place of comfort. As I became stimulated, the sound I made would get louder and louder. As far as I was concerned, they were happy noises, but for my father, they were unacceptable. Gradually, I began to hear a familiar but distressing noise outside of myself. I have no idea how long this unpleasant sound had been going on, it eventually became clear as to who was making the noise.

"You better shut your goddamn mouth or I'll shut it for you!" Dad's voice, it was dad's voice! I stopped for only a few seconds; I was spaced out and my inner world had priority.

Mom came in at this point and said, "You better behave yourself. Your dad's going to get you if you don't be quiet. At the sound of her voice— even though she was trying to be stern, the gentleness was still there— I started coming out of the trance I was in. She picked me up and walked me into their bedroom. She said to my dad, "I'm going to go get her a glass of milk."

"Is she still bellyaching over that bottle?" He asked mom.

"I guess so. She's been like this since we took it away from her. I'll go get her some milk and I think she'll be okay," replied mom, hoping to God she could keep dad from blowing up. "I'll stay home with you this morning, dear. I know it's really early. Are you hungry?" She said in her timid voice, knowing he was in a bad mood.

"Yes, fix me something to eat," he demanded.

Mom went into the kitchen and started preparing breakfast for dad. She put me in the high chair and gave me a glass of milk.

Dad came into the kitchen, sat down at the table, and started in on mom. "Are you giving her a bottle when I'm not around?"

"No. The children help me when she gets cranky. Ray spent the night with one of his friends, and the rest of the kids are still sleeping. She just woke up earlier than usual.

I'm going to go wake the children now to help me with her. They need to start getting ready for Sunday school anyway."

Mom left the kitchen and I started to cry. She came right back into the kitchen, picked me up, and took me with her to wake Billy and the girls. She returned to the kitchen with me on her hip and started cooking dad's breakfast. When dad finished his breakfast of oatmeal, toast, and a tall glass of milk, he went outside, a regular habit of his. With dad outside, mom put me back in the highchair and proceeded to fix breakfast for us. When breakfast was over, the older kids went to get ready for church.

Dad came to mom and said, "You go to church, I'm okay."

"Okay, I'll get Donna ready right now."

"Donna's not going," said dad. "She's got to learn she can't have her way all the time."

"She's not getting her way, dear, honest. I'm not sneaking her the bottle!" she said nervously.

"You take the kids and go to church. I'll handle little Edith Rose." Dad said this in his you-better-jump-to-my-strings voice. Nobody else called me Edith Rose except dad, and only when he was totally upset with me.

Mom did as she was told. She knew dad had made up his mind and nobody was going to change it. She put me in the crib, saying, "You be a good girl for daddy and I'll be home real soon. Mommy loves you." I started to cry, but she had to ignore me. I cried even louder. I didn't understand what was going on, it was the tone in her voice that taught me to recognize when something bad was going to happen. When he called me Edith Rose in that hateful voice of his, I became a bundle of fear. Mom and the others left me all alone with dad. I hated it and mom told me she hated to leave me with him, because of his temper.

I don't know how long I cried. The anxiety I felt without mom was a most painful thing. Dad eventually came to the crib, picked me up, took me into his bedroom, and threw me on the bed. He put his face up close to mine and said, "You shut the fuck up. Your mama's not here to protect you, so shut your mouth right now!"

I shut up as fast as I could but couldn't stop sobbing. I would catch my breath in an effort to stop. His presence terrified me. I can't remember a time he didn't scare me. Even as an infant, mom told me he would try to hold me and I would start crying as soon as he picked me up."

I stopped talking and stared into space, until I heard Dr. Boyd's voice.

"Donna. You've been quiet for so long. Can you explain what's going on? Your feelings, talk to me about your feelings."

"How long is 'so long'?" I said slowly.

"Seven, maybe ten minutes. Your mind seems to be somewhere else. Talk to me about it."

"You want me to talk about my feelings? I'm not sure what they are, right now."

"Can you tell me what is going on with you right now?"

"I don't think I want to be in therapy anymore."

"I know this is a terrible burden for you. This is a difficult and extremely emotional thing that's going on with you. I know and I am very sorry that anything like this has happened to you. But it has, and the only way to rid yourself of it is to confront it. I know how tough it is for you right now. Accepting the truth is the only way. I know you have been hurt badly, that you have experienced great suffering. If I could wish it away for you, I would. But I can't. Your healing must begin from within. Are you listening to me, Donna?"

"I am listening. I thought I was through all this, after I counseled with Dr. Weber. I don't want to keep thinking about my unpleasant childhood. It pains me too much."

"I know it does. I have observed the tension in your body and the struggle that's going on in your mind, but I know of no other way."

"I sometimes wonder who I am, who I really am. More than sometimes, quite often to be truthful. In fact it's a hunger within me. There are spaces in me and I have no idea why. Do you know why?"

"We can find out together. Only you can choose how

you want to spend your time based on what you believe is valuable and worthy of your time."

The sound of his voice and what he said was hard to ignore. As agitated as my mind was at this time, I could say to myself, "How else can I come to the place I want to be, other than by remembering my past childhood memories?"

"I'll try to go on," I said before continuing. "He punished me for making those loud noises. I didn't understand it at all."

"Are you making a free choice to go on, or are you doing it to please me?"

"A little of both, I think. That's okay, isn't it?'

"Yes, that's okay. Stop whenever you need."

"Okay, I will.

My dad told me, "You do as your told, little girl!" His voice was so harsh, "Take off your clothes, right now!" I hurriedly took off my clothes off. Then he said, "Get on your knees and sit up straight." I did and he pulled me to the edge of the bed and turned me around, facing away from him. He then put his right hand between my legs, and with the weight of his hand between my legs, lifted me up to my feet. I was frantic! I was dazed and totally puzzled as to what was going on. He then took my left arm with his free hand and reaching it as high as it would go, put my fingers in his mouth and bit down as hard as he could. It took awhile, slowly I began to feel the pain and let out a blood-curdling scream.

As the pain became unbearable, breathing became difficult. A choking sensation kept coming up in my throat. I felt as if I was fading into nothingness, and the blackness of fear mixed with a chilling gray pain overwhelmed me. The intense emotions gave way to a sense of floating, of actually being in a safe place. The next thing I remember was my dad telling me to put my clothes on and to get back to bed. I did just what he told me. As I walked out of the bedroom, he said, "Don't ever scream for your bottle again, and don't ever tell your mother what I did to you. Now get to bed."

"Did you ever tell your mom?" Dr. Boyd asked

"No. I couldn't. I didn't remember anything to tell her. I think that's all I can handle for today. I'm going home."

"You did great. I'll see you next time."

"How long is this going to take?"

"I have no idea, probably a very long time. I wish I could give you better news, Donna, but I can't."

"Is there something we can do to make it go faster?"

"You just need to keep remembering things from your past. I *can* tell you, you will need to talk to me about the morning your father raped you, among others things but especially about that morning. I believe there's a key there that will unlock the hidden agenda within your mind. I truly believe that Donna. If you decide not to talk about it for awhile, nothing bad will happen to you. Do you understand? There's no urgency, it's your choice."

"I understand. I'll think about it."

Absolute Fear

"Donna, I know this is an extremely difficult decision you've made. Talking about the morning your father raped you is not only brave and courageous on your part, it's also necessary. Take your time stop if you need to, whenever you need to. Remember, Donna, I am right here. Okay?"

I nodded my head and in my mind went back to the worse morning of my life.

"Daddy, will you help me with my dress? I can't button the back of it." I was wringing my hands together the whole time I asked him. My anxiety was intense. There was no one else in the house for me to ask. He was in the living room, reading the paper. He put it down as I spoke to him and looked directly at me.

Sure, honey. Come here. Don't be afraid." His voice was friendly enough and I relaxed a little. "Don't stand in the doorway. Come sit on daddy's lap, and we'll see about the snaps on that pretty dress of yours."

His voice sounded nice. Actually, it was the tone of manipulation but what did I know? I was six-years old; to me, it was a friendly voice. Still standing in the hallway I asked, "You're not too tired are you? Mama said to leave you alone if you're too tired to do things for me. I don't want to get in trouble." "I'm not too tired. You're not going to get in trouble. Come on over, let daddy help you."

When I was close enough, he picked me up and put me on his lap. He put his arms around me and gave me a gentle hug. I loved it! In the past, he had either ignored me or ridiculed me. This time he seemed to act loving toward me, and I responded by kissing him on the cheek. I should have remembered that there was no one around for him to humiliate me in front of. He didn't have an audience. But the joy of a six-year old, six years and three months to be exact, getting attention from my daddy in a loving way took over. All the scary feelings I had felt toward him simply disappeared. I needed him. My loving, gentle, understanding mother was in the hospital, and I missed her with all my heart. And now, here was my father being nice to me. I was thrilled!

He began to rub his hands up and down my legs, lifting my dress from under my buttocks, he continued putting his hands all over my body. I suddenly realized I was not fully dressed. "Daddy, I forgot to put on my underpants. Let me down so I can finish getting dressed."

I made an effort to slide off his lap. He pulled me back. "No! You're okay just the way you are!" He rubbed his hands between my legs and asked, "Does that feel good? Do you like what daddy's doing to you?"

His voice sounded strange. I felt uneasy. I wished I hadn't ask him to help me get dressed. My stomach was churning.

Something was happening to him. Feeling extremely uncomfortable but with insight enough to tell him what he wanted to hear, my throat full of fear and quivering, I said, "Yes, daddy. It feels good."

He picked me up at this point, his hands still rubbing me up and down my back and butt. He walked us toward his bedroom. Dread filled every part of my body. He said, "Daddy's going to make you feel even better." That strange voice again, it sounded so odd. The dread turned into terror; my stomach was in knots. I felt so helpless, and mama was nowhere around. He set me on their plain iron bed. I looked around the barren space with no curtain covering the one window in the room. Slowly moving my eyes I saw that old dresser with rollers on it but no mama; she was nowhere to be found. With great fear, I remembered it was not safe for me. I was in danger! I was confused, totally bewildered and ambivalent as to what was going on. I wanted his attention, yet I knew something was not right. I felt eerie.

"Take off your dress so we won't get it wrinkled." He said in a demanding tone.

I was tossing my head back and forth, trying to figure a way out of this horrible situation. I did not want to take my dress off, it made me feel like a "bad girl." But out of fear I always did what he wanted me to do. My needs and wants meant nothing to him. "I said take off the damn dress, now!"

Panic welled up in me; there was absolutely no place to go. I froze in submission. I took the dress off and lay back down. I was naked and felt ashamed. He started kissing me all over. I spotted a tiny black spider in the corner of the ceiling and fixed my eyes on it. He started raping me with his finger, putting it partly in and then stopping to make me touch his penis. I tried to pull away and he said, "Stop that right now! Do you hear me?"

"Okay, daddy, okay!" The anxiety ran through my whole body. I wanted him to stop. I didn't want him to do the things to me that he was doing, or to do the things that he made me do to him. There was no way out. I had to obey him. I knew he'd get really mad if I asked him to stop. After awhile, he rolled onto his back and finished the job of masturbating himself. When he was done, he laid there; I could hear him breathing. I kept my eye on the black spider that helped me maintain some sense of myself. I managed to muster up the courage to say, "Daddy, I'll go get ready for school now, okay?"

"You stay right where you are and do as your told, young lady!" His voice was so angry, so demanding. I was scared out of my wits. He sat up onto the edge of the bed then stood up. I took my eyes off the spider to see what he was going to do. I watched as he took off his pants, sat back down, and said in that weird voice again, "Now watch what I'm going to do." He leaned down and kissed me on my private parts. I made every effort to hold back the tears.

"Now don't cry, be a good girl. I want you to get on your knees and kiss daddy right here." He pointed to his private parts. With panic crawling all over me, I began to get light headed, my stomach aching from the terror. I tried again to talk him out of it.

My voice broke into a cry as I pleaded, "Please, daddy, let me go! I can't do that. Please stop!"

"Don't fight me, little girl!" He paid no attention to my plea. I prayed to God to help me. But nothing seemed to prevent my dad from doing what he wanted. He was pulling my hair and shouting. "Stop that crying or I'll give you something to cry about! Do you hear me?"

In a yielding voice I answered, "Yes, daddy, I hear you." And so I did as he told me. He pushed my head down and made me perform oral sex on him. I was choking and gagging. It appalled me. It was a bad thing and I knew it. He released his hand on my head, and in that moment, I lifted my head away and cried out, "I can't, I can't, I can't!" My desperation overwhelmed me.

He moved his body away from me and lay there, breathing loudly. We both lay there. I wanted to die; it was horrible. And I thought it was over. But, oh my God! It wasn't over. He brought me to the edge of the bed, with my legs dangling. He got on his knees on the floor. He was right in front of me, towering over me, overwhelming me with unbelievable fear. I could no longer hold back the tears rolling down my cheeks. I sobbed, my body jerking in an effort to stop the tears. The lump in my throat made it difficult for me to breath. I scooted back onto the bed and sat up to catch my breath. I was choking and coughing and crying and begging.

Instead of an angry voice, he said softly, "Now don't be a baby. You want me to like you, don't you? Just relax, calm yourself, I'll go easy." As he said this, he once again brought me to the edge of the bed and laid my body down. "I'm only going to put the tip of it inside of you….Do you feel it?"

"Yes, I feel it," I said in a small voice. My eyes fixated on the little spider in the corner of the ceiling. It moved from the corner and headed my direction. He put more and more inside of me. The pain was fierce; absolute fear possessed me. My arms floundered in an attempt to push him away. I did everything I could to get away. I did not want to be me any longer. He pinned me down by putting his knees on my hands. I was screaming, screaming, *screaming*! He put one of his hands over my mouth; I was helpless. The burden being put upon me was too much to bear. 'What can I do? Help me somebody, help me please!' The pain in my stomach tore me up physically and emotionally. My heart broke and my body hurt all over. It was impossible to get away from him.

I looked straight into the heavens, and the spider was directly overhead getting bigger and bigger, weaving itself down toward me. My hands were numb from the pressure of his knees against them. The spider had grown huge and was directly over my face. My head exploded. I felt like a helpless creature, lost in a maze of confusion. I entered a world of nothingness. Darkness covered me completely. The big, black spider landed on me, its eight legs clinging tightly to my skin. Out of control and grunting loudly, my father raped me. *The spider wasn't over me! My father was!*

My six-year-old imagination had seen the spider coming down over me. In reality, the spider never moved from the corner on the ceiling. It was an illusion from the long laborious trauma that had been forced onto me. My eyes had closed soon after I first saw that little spider, and I entered into a trance. Fear separated me from fact. Torture contributed to my dissociation. Multiple layers of protection were exchanged for the suffering I could no longer endure. I felt as if I was being torn into pieces. Many expressions of Self came to my aid that morning. The eight spider legs grasping on so tightly became eight separate personalities. I split completely. I was protecting myself, saving myself. In a way, I answered my own prayer. I was losing consciousness, and as I faded into darkness, I saw the eight legs protruding from the big black spider, overpowering me.

Everything got quiet except for my dad's heavy breathing. The black belly of the spider opened up, and the eight personalities were swallowed up. Everything turned black. Then, there was nothingness."

"Oh my God! Oh my God! Oh my God!" I shook my head, my hands coverings my face.

"It's okay, it's okay. Donna, it's okay! You're safe. You're here in my office. This is Dr. Boyd talking to you. Do you hear me? Donna, do you hear me?"

The sound of his voice slowly brought me back to the present. I started to calm down. "I hear you," I said, taking my hands from my face and looking all around. The feeling of security returned. "I feel drained."

"I'm sure you do," he replied. "You've had a real breakthrough."

"I've never told anyone about that morning so explicitly. I feel as if I'm waking up from a deep sleep." I looked at Dr. Boyd and tried to say something else, but no words came.

"Sit back and relax, Donna, you're in shock." His words gave me the reassurance I needed. "You're going to be okay, trust me. You are going to be okay."

"Those people, all those people, they were scattered throughout my mind. They were running everywhere. It seemed like an explosion. I don't know why that happened to me." I said in a shaky voice, feeling the panic inside of me.

"You're extremely upset right now. It must have been terrible for you. It's over now. He can't hurt you anymore. Take some more time to calm down. We don't have to talk anymore today."

"I'm okay, honest. I want to talk; I need to talk. I just never remembered all those details before. You know? Now that I think of it "the people" weren't in a panic at all; I was the one going crazy. They seemed to know exactly what to do. They were organized, they took their places.

They took me to a cocoon-like place, where I would be safe and protected from fatal disaster. Yes, I was the one in a panic." I thought I was going to collapse from what I had just discovered. "This is too bizarre, too unbelievable. I can't deal with all of this Dr. Boyd. Tell me it's not true."

He walked over to me from behind his desk, knelt down beside me, and with a voice full of compassion said, "We can lick this thing. You can get better; it's your decision. I'm right here for you. You must draw on that wonderful courage of yours and face the truth as it is. And together we'll change your life into what you want it to be. You do have a multiple personality disorder. That's where you are right now. Shall we work on getting you well? Only you can do what needs to be done. I'll be here for you, but no one can do it for you."

I was devastated. I knew it was not going to be easy and I knew it was going to be painful, but I dreaded the thought of what was to come. "It's sort of like a rebirth."

"It's not *a* rebirth, Donna, it's *your* rebirth."

"Okay, let's do it. I'll probably be a basket case most of the time."

"I'm going to give you a prescription for Valium. That'll help you a lot."

"I need to ask you a question and it's going to sound really crazy."

"Crazier than today's session?" he said, testing my sense of humor.

I laughed and said, "I guess not," before asking him my question: "How long have I been coming to you?"

"For about six months. You never missed an appointment. You've kept every one. Well, anyway, someone has kept them." He said, with a little grin on his face.

"What have I been talking about? Or, what has *someone*

48

been talking about?" I asked, grinning back at him.

"You talked about your parents and how afraid you were of your dad, about your sisters and brothers. You told me about some of your scary times with your dad, and, let's see, you talked a little about your husband Bill. That's just a few of the things that were discussed. Our time is up, Donna."

"One more question Dr. Boyd. Why is the last six months so blurry to me? Why can't I remember?"

"We'll start working on that question next time. Your memory lapse of the last six months may clear over the next three weeks. Our time is up, my dear."

I spent the next three weeks one day at a time. I worked the swing shift, 3:00 PM to 11:00 PM, at a state hospital for the mentally retarded. I visited my mom almost every day before going to work. Bill and I didn't have too much time together. He went to school in the day and worked part-time in the evening. On my days off, I had time to think, to try to remember what happened the last six months during the sessions with Dr. Boyd.

My mind went back to when Bill and I had married in October of 1974. He was impotent and I did not like our dysfunctional sex life at all. My goal was to live a healthy life which in my opinion consisted of a healthy sex life. After struggling with it for a year and a half we decided to get into marriage counseling. I had been in therapy many years before and it had helped a lot. Three years passed since I'd counseled with anyone, and I felt as if I was doing quite well. I hated getting back into therapy, but if it could help solve our problem, I was willing to try.

Dr. Williams was a psychologist, and he explained that he had a head psychiatrist who came in once a week to evaluate new clients. There was also a test we needed to take in order to provide this psychiatrist with a little background on both Bill and me. The results of the psychiatrist's evaluation would help determine the best approach to our problem.

"The psychiatrist's name is Dr. Boyd," Dr. Williams informed us. Bill and I took the test and each made our appointment with Dr. Boyd, as he wanted to see us separately. The session was only for fifteen minutes. The doctor went over the test I had taken, which consisted of a lot of multiple-choice questions. I n about a week, Dr. Williams called to tell me Dr. Boyd would like to have another session with me if I was willing. I was puzzled and somewhat nervous, but I agreed. "He wants to see you for thirty minutes this time. Will that be alright, Mrs. Hunt?"

"Yes, I guess so." I wondered why he wanted to talk to me and not to Bill.

After all, it was Bill's impotence that was the problem.

"Tell me about yourself, Donna."

"What do you want me to tell you?"

"Whatever comes into your mind."

So, I told him about my nervous breakdown eighteen years ago. I told him that I had been in and out of mental hospitals, that I had shock treatments once and had spent a lot of time in therapy as an outpatient. That it had been many years since I've had to be in a mental hospital, and that I haven't had to be in therapy for three years until now because of Bill's problem.

"It seems you've had some serious mental problems, Mrs. Hunt. Can you go into a little more detail?"

"No! I've worked through all that and I want to get on with my life. I've been doing just fine. I completed a three-semester program in a neighboring community college and passed the state board exam and am now employed at the State Hospital for the Mentally Retarded as a psychiatric technician."

"You've most certainly done well. Did you find out what was causing all the problems?"

"I was diagnosed as a schizophrenic."

"Do you take medication?'

"No, none at all," I said proudly.

"Mrs. Hunt, will you make another appointment to see me, a full session this time?"

"Well, I, I guess so." I said, feeling awkward and nervous. I wondered why but didn't question him. There was something about him that made me feel comfortable while at the same time a bit uneasy.

Bill and I continued to see Dr. Williams. There was a big block between us when it came to sex. I was also seeing Dr. Boyd once a month, which seemed very strange to me. On the fourth visit Dr. Boyd ask me, "Donna, what do you think of me as a doctor?"

"I like you or else I wouldn't keep coming to you; I don't know why I keep seeing you. You're an up-front, no-nonsense doctor and I like that in you."

"Good," he said, "Very good. Would you be willing to counsel with me at my main office?"

"Why would I need to, do you think I need therapy?"

"Yes, I do," he said in that direct way of his.

"I *could* do that," I said bewildered. "Is there something wrong with me?"

"Why don't you make an appointment to see me and we'll talk about it then. The secretary will give you my office address and phone number."

"Okay," I replied, still confused as to why he thought I needed one-on-one counseling. I had been feeling pretty good with what I believed was progress. I just thought Bill and I needed to work on our sex problem.

Memories of the last six months with Dr. Boyd were still blurry. The first two visits at his office were a complete blank. But, I remembered a question he asked during the third visit, "Donna, do you know what respite care means?" He leaned forward in his chair, focused intently on my answer.

"Yes, I do, it means to provide a period of temporary relief."

"That's right, and I believe that's what you do for yourself when you become overwhelmed." He continued speaking and maintaining direct eye contact. It was difficult for me to look back at his eyes. And then he simply said, "I believe you have multiple personalities."

I didn't know what he was talking about, at least, I pretended not to know what he was talking about. My heart raced; I could hear it pounding. My stomach started to churn with anxiety, causing it to ache. My head was fuzzy, my eyes blurred, and I was dizzy. I lowered my head to avoid his eyes. He asked a question that shocked me, "Do you have your personalities named?"

I couldn't speak. I was fading away; my subconscious made every effort to reach consciousness. It took time to process what he asked me. The silence between us seemed to last forever. Then my face slowly turned to his and made eye contact. Somewhere deep within my secret place, the strength came. 'I can trust him. This doctor can help me. Let him know.'

"Yes, they're named." I felt relieved that I had finally found someone with whom I could share my burdened secret.

"Will you tell me their names?"

"No!" I said, in a loud emphatic voice. He didn't persist.

He knew I needed to make this choice on my own, without pressure. He went on to explain about multiple personality disorder, also known as dissociate hysteria. I could not hear all he said; his voice faded in and out. I could see his mouth moving but I didn't hear all the words. I didn't want to hear what he was saying. I went inside myself to calm down from the shock of my reality, a reality to difficult to deal with. The silence was with me again, deafening me from the raw emotion I felt. After a very long while, I slowly returned to the here-and-now, and knowing I could trust him, I said their names: "Wanda, Edith Rose and Susie."

With a smile of satisfaction, he said, "We don't have to talk about this anymore today. Please make another appointment, Donna, and we'll take this one step at a time. Sit for awhile if you need to. Take some deep breaths."

I was devastated yet overjoyed that at long last someone had seen the truth that lived in me. He was the only one, including myself, who could see the depth of my need for healing. His words ran through my mind: 'You have multiple personalities, you have multiple personalities, you have multiple personalities! Are they named? Are they named? Are they named! Oh God! I don't want to deal with this, I can't. I won't.' I sat there as he said I could, in silence. Finally, I got up and left his office. I didn't go to work that day.

My visits with Dr. Boyd were beginning to come back to me. 'How weird is this, that I can't remember things? Why is that?' I thought to myself. In one of the sessions Dr. Boyd asked me to talk about my childhood.

"My father was a mean man with a very bad temper. What else can I say?"

"A lot more Donna, a lot more. Now listen to me, I am not your enemy. How can I help you if you won't help yourself?"

With this comment, I softened a bit. "There are so many holes in my childhood. It makes it difficult for me to talk about. But I'll try. Where shall I start?"

"Whatever comes to your mind and remember, you can stop whenever you feel the need to."

"Well, for one thing, I never liked being without my mother. I do remember that after my mom gave birth to my youngest sister she had to go back to the hospital. She was in a great deal of pain and still looked as if she was pregnant. The doctors removed an eight pound benign tumor from my mother's stomach. She had to stay in the hospital for six weeks." I stopped talking, drew in a deep breath, and let it out slowly. I felt like I had been running hard and fast.

"Take another deep breath," Dr. Boyd said. "Do you want to stop?"

I took another deep breath and waited for a few minutes.

"It's just that I was so scared of my dad and more so when my mom wasn't with me. It was such a long time for me to be without her. I was scared the whole time."

He spoke to me in his compassionate voice, "There's no good or bad way to tell it, Donna, no right or wrong way. Say it in your own words and in your own way. I'm right here. Your father is no longer here to bother you, remember?" These were reassuring words and I needed to hear them.

"I was left alone with my father in the mornings, until it was time for me to leave for school."

"Where were the other children?" Dr. Boyd asked me.

"They all left for school before me." Something happened to me at this point, the panic in me escalated. I gasped. My body tensed. I brought my hands to my face in utter fear.

"Donna, take deep breaths. Donna, breathe and relax, breathe and relax." I did what he told me to do. I felt better. He kept talking to me. "Do you want to stop? Don't forget to breathe and relax." Finally he said, "Let's stop the session. Lean back in the chair and stay there for as long as you need."

"I'm alright, really. I feel dumb and clumsy, I always felt this way when he was mad at me. I guess all this happened, huh…well…because I was so frightened of my father, and being alone with him, without my mom for six-weeks, just brought it all back, brought back how awful I felt when I was without her. I'm feeling really tired. I agree with you; let's call it a day."

"You're doing a good job, Donna. You can call me anytime. Don't hesitate to call if you need to, okay?"

"Okay. I'll just sit here for awhile." When I left his office, I left bewildered.

On one of my days off, while Bill was gone, I was sitting quietly and staring off into space when absolute clarity came into view. The vision of the black spider getting bigger and bigger, closer and closer came into my consciousness. I was frantic. Fear gripped me just like it always did in my childhood. The eight legs turned into eight personalities swirling within the belly of the spider. I was hysterical inside, yet silent. While I hallucinated this nightmare, the phone rang, bringing me out of my stupor. I didn't answer it. I remembered Dr. Boyd telling me I could call him anytime and I did just that. It was nine o'clock in the morning and I prayed he was in his office. He was. The receptionist put me through right away. In a quivering voice, I said, "Dr. Boyd, I remember, I remember, I remember. I'm so afraid! Please, can you help me!?"

"Okay, Donna, okay. Tell me what's going on right now."

"I remember the last six months! I hate it. I don't want to remember anymore. I remember more stuff and I don't want to! Help me!"

"Donna, Donna, listen to me. What has happened to you is a good thing. Can you tell me some more?"

I told him about the personalities coming out of the big black spider. "All this is too emotional; what's the point anyway." I asked in a calmer way. The sound of his voice quieted me down. I was able to reason somewhat. "I don't want to be a freak."

"You're not a freak. Your personalities are seeking expression and the point is for you to uncover your truth if you want to be free. You can be free, Donna, you can do it. This is not going to be a snap of the fingers and you're going to need to look back in order to move forward. Do you understand what I'm saying to you?"

"Yes, yes, I understand. So 'we, the people' want to voice our opinions, is that it?" I said, letting him know my sense of humor had returned.

"That's it, Donna. It's also the beginning of making your life the way you want it. Isn't that worth whatever struggle is ahead of you?"

"I want more than anything to change my life. If this is the only way to do it, I guess I better accept it, no matter how difficult it's going to be."

"That's the way to look at it. When is your next appointment with me?'

"In a couple of days. Before I hang up I need to tell you that I was hallucinating about that black spider. It scared me, it really scared me.

"Donna, I think we need to go into some more detail about that black spider. What are your thoughts on it?"

I smiled inside because he was asking my opinion. I liked that. "Maybe we'll find some hidden answers there." I said, "I think maybe you're right. I'll see you in a few days."

"Thanks." We hung up. In this very moment, I was so very glad I had found him.

Bizarre Revelation

"Good morning, Donna. Come in, come in. It's good to see you. What's been happening since I talked to you on the phone?" asked Dr. Boyd.

"I've had better days," I answered, meaning every word of it. "It's not easy being me. Nothing much has happened since we talked on the phone. Bill and I are still trying to make our problem go away." I said, not wanting to get into anything deep.

"What's going on with you and Bill? Is the therapy helping?"

"Not really, I feel discouraged with our relationship. We were happy when we first got married and excited about getting somewhere in life. Getting an education is stimulating for both of us, but that's about all that's stimulating in our relationship. Oh well, I'll discuss that with Dr. Williams. What's on the agenda for us today? I'm guessing it's going to be all about 'the people'."

"Are you willing to answer some questions?" He asked me.

"If they don't scare the hell out of me, I am. The Valium is helping, but I'm still in a daze about everything. It's so difficult for me to believe; I feel as if I'm in a bad dream and I'm going to wake up soon."

"I know it's difficult for you, but it's not a dream. You mentioned hallucinating when we were on the phone. Can you tell me more about that?"

"It was more like imagination than hallucinating. I think, you know, in my mind. It was inside of me."

"Can you try to see it now? Maybe, it will be easier to deal with here in my office, where you feel safe. You do feel safe with me, don't you, Donna?"

"Yes, I do. Okay, I'll close my eyes and bring the spider into view." I leaned back in the chair, closed my eyes and within a few seconds it was there. "There it is! It's coming closer."

"What do you feel, Donna. How are you feeling right now?"

"This is scary. Fear, I'm feeling fear. It's big and black. His eight legs are coming out from underneath him. "Oh, sweet Jesus, I think it's going to explode! His belly is opening." Emotions rose up in me. My voice anxious and my body tense with fear, I said, "I...I...I didn't know I was separated. I, oh dear, I didn't know, I didn't know about all those people! I can't believe it, *I can't believe it!*" My voice rose louder, much louder than normal, as I told him about this unbelievable thing happening to me. Then the spider lowered. "It's not true, all the people, all the people. Where did they come from? Wanda, Mary, Laura, Edgar, John,

Mildred, Edith Rose, Donna Mae. Where did they all come from? Dr. Boyd, Dr. Boyd, Dr. Boyd, where did they all come from? Where are you Dr. Boyd?" I asked with my eyes still closed.

"I'm right here, Donna. Open your eyes. It's all right to be upset. You're letting 'the people' come into consciousness. It's a giant step. Take some deep breaths. Do you realize what you just did? You named them one by one. This is great progress. Deep breaths, Donna, take deep breaths."

I took many deep breaths and sat quietly for a few minutes. "I feel better. I get so frustrated with everything. This mental disorder thing drives me nuts. I want it to be over. 'The people,' how many more are there?"

"If there are more, they'll find their way into your consciousness. It's going to be quite awhile before it's all over. I'm sure you know that by now. Take it one day at a time and live the best you can." Dr. Boyd said, giving me wonderful advice.

"I know, I know. I do feel better."

"Good enough to answer those questions?"

"Depends on what they are."

"Can you tell me anything about the morning you were raped, after you came to?"

"I remember my stomach hurt something awful and so did my hands. I felt limp and exhausted, but most of all I felt ashamed."

"The shame belongs to your dad, not you. Understand?"

"I think so. I'm trying." I remember him washing my face with a cold cloth. He was saying, "Are you all right? Are you all right, honey?" The whole thing puzzled me. I didn't know why he was asking me if I was alright. I didn't know why he was wiping my face. He told me, "Lie there for awhile, 'til you feel better." He headed towards the door and said, "I'll be right back; I'm going to cool your cloth with cold water. I put your dress back on and snapped it for you." I was in a fog, I had no idea why I was in mom and dad's bedroom. I laid there as my father had told me to do. I didn't forget to do exactly as he told me. When he returned he said, "You won't be going to school today, but you can still wear your pretty dress if you want." I nodded. I wanted to wear the dress that was so special to me. Then he said a crazy thing to me; I had no idea what he meant by it. "I was just trying to love you." The way he said it made me feel ashamed as if I had done something wrong. He had a way of making me feel guilty and humiliated. I couldn't recall what had happened that morning.

"You've gone through an incredible trauma, Donna, incredible. Take some deep breaths, if you need to. How are you feeling?"

"Like a big boulder has hit me square in the face."

"You're a courageous woman and you were a brave little girl."

"I was only six, only six. I don't feel brave at all. I feel angry, angry that my dad destroyed my life. And you keep telling me, in so many words, that it's my responsibility to work through the damage."

"That's exactly what I'm saying. I'm also saying that it will take a long time to confront this thing squarely in the face, if I may make use of your exact words."

"I don't want to hear what you're saying. I, ah, I think, ah… I faded away, staring into space. My head dropped and I could see only a clear black slate.

"Hello, Dr. Boyd. It's me, Joyce."

"Hello, Joyce, where is Donna?"

"She's not able to cope right now, but I'm willing to help in anyway I can."

"Thank you. Why don't you tell me what you know

about Donna." He suggested.

"I know about the rape, if that's what you mean. I know about the black spider, and I know about 'the people'." Joyce said in a matter of fact tone.

"Let's talk about the morning of the rape."

"I can only tell you what she told me. I wasn't there, you know." Joyce answered with the confidence of a well experienced private secretary.

"What did she tell you about that morning?" Dr. Boyd asked with genuine interest.

"Well, I won't repeat anything she's already told you. That would be a waste of time, wouldn't it?" Not waiting for an answer, she continued. "There was no blood when she came to. The bed was stripped of any sheets, whereas before 'it' happened, there had been sheets on the bed. It seemed to me she should have died that morning. And, I bet he turned the mattress over, too. It's just my opinion, and Donna has always valued my opinion. Giving you the names of 'the people' was a smart thing to do. This will help her go forward." Her voice was devoid of any emotion, just someone relating a story that had happened to someone else.

"You seem to think a lot of her," said Dr. Boyd to Joyce.

"Donna and I are very close. You might say, we're the best of friends." And, that was it. As fast as Joyce came, Joyce was gone.

"I remember something. It's horrible, really horrible!" I said.

"Donna?" asked Dr. Boyd, making sure I had returned, returned as Donna that is.

"Yes. What?"

"Are you ready to tell me now?"

I want to tell you now. I know by now that it helps to

tell. I don't want to see that big black spider again. Maybe it'll go away if I tell you."

"The big black spider is not real, Donna. It's a childhood monster you made up when you were a kid. It's your fear in the guise of a spider, you know, like the boogie man." He deliberately took my mind off of what I just remembered. This helped reduce the overwhelming feelings I was experiencing.

"You're right; I'm afraid all the time, more sometimes than others. I hate the feeling."

"You're also right about exposing your fears. Talking about them will reduce your anxiety. Talking about all your feelings will help you to heal. What is it you remember?"

"It's about the morning he raped me. No, no, it was very early the next morning. It was still dark. My dad got up early every morning. He came into my bedroom, and when I opened my eyes, his face was right in front of mine. His nose almost touched mine. I think he shook me to wake me up. When he saw that my eyes were open, he backed up a little and put his finger to his mouth. He made me get out of bed and take off my pajamas before having me squat down in a position where my knees touched my chest. I felt dread come over me and I started to shake. Once again, terror gripped me. I knew I was in danger. My body trembled all over. I prayed, 'Oh God, oh God! Please don't let him hurt me. *Please!*'"

I had to pause at this point of telling Dr. Boyd about the terrible experience. Dr. Boyd never said a word. We waited together until I could go on. With emotions running high, I continued, "My father told me, 'I'm not going to do what I did to you yesterday. Don't worry; you're too young for that. I'll be back to you for sex when you're older.' My mind was a blank. I just didn't understand what he was saying to me." Again, I had to stop talking about this horrendous thing that had happened to me so long ago, this horror that still ripped at me as if it had just happened.

"Are you okay, Donna?" There was Dr. Boyd's voice again, the voice full of compassion, the voice that had a way of calming me.

"I just need a minute." I said. Eyes closed, I tried to gain the courage to go on. It took time to get past the emotion. After what seemed like a long, long time, I began again, "He brought his, I can't say it. Give me a minute…" More time passed before, "We had oral sex and he went all the way. You know what I mean, Dr. Boyd, he… he…did it, did it in my mouth. And he made me, huh, he had me, oh, oh, oh! He wouldn't let me spit it out." I flinched at these words I had just said. "Wait a minute, wait a minute, wait a minute." I squirmed in my seat, hands over my face. "Oh my God! Dr. Boyd. What in the hell did he do to me?"

"Deep breaths, Donna, take deep breaths. You're not there, Donna. You're here, in my office. He can't hurt you. Do you realize? He can't hurt you anymore?"

"A robot. I was like a robot. I had to detach my feelings from my body. I was totally passive to his demands. It was the only way I could endure what was happening to me. I turned myself into a thing without feelings. That's what I was to him, he depersonalized me. I was less than human, his slave, to do with as he wanted."

"Didn't you feel any anger?" Dr. Boyd asked.

"She didn't, but I did."

"Who is she and who are you?" Dr. Boyd asked.

"Oh yeah, I forgot. I'm supposed to tell you who I am. I'm Wanda and 'she' is Donna. You damn well betcha I was mad. More like a rage. My mind was on fire, sparks of red shot from my brain. Yeah, it was rage alright. He had no right to hurt me like that. He injured Donna, too. But she couldn't feel the anger. Oh no! She was doing daddy's bidding; she had no right to be angry. Anyway, that's the way she looked at it." And as with Joyce, as fast as Wanda came, she was gone.

"No, I didn't feel any anger. When he was through with me, he said, 'Never tell anyone what I did to you or you will regret it. Do you understand?"

"I nodded and asked without any emotion, 'Can I go back to bed now?'"

"'Yes, go on to bed.' He answered."

I was quiet. Dr. Boyd spoke.

"Oh, Donna, I don't know what to say except I'm so sorry all this had happened to you."

I tried to be brave, but when he said that to me, I completely broke down. I couldn't stop sobbing. I cried and cried until I had no more tears left. The release the crying provided helped untie the knot in my stomach. "I feel so ashamed," I said, bringing my hands up to my face. "I can't look at you."

"Why can't you look at me? This is not your fault. Do you hear me? This is not your fault. Your life is valuable. He diminished you, but you're not under his power anymore. Take your valuable life back."

"I can hear you. My heart is so sad; I feel like it's broken in half."

"I know it is. Your father was a self-centered son-of-a-bitch. I'll say it again; he put a great burden on you. Can you bring your hands away and look at me?"

I took my hands from my face and looked at this savior of mine and smiled.

"Donna, we've run over our time. Why don't you go wash your face, and when you get home, take a long nap. You'll feel better when you wake up."

"Okay," I said.

* * * * *

He didn't mention the visits from Joyce or Wanda and I never noticed the time lapse. Life was indeed a struggle for me. My relationship with Bill was going nowhere, and I blamed him for our problems. But, I most certainly had my own agenda. We were growing farther and farther apart. My therapy with Dr. Boyd kept me emotionally drained, yet I kept trying to make it all come together.

While I was adjusting to the facts about myself, I was startled by my father's voice. It was perfectly clear, "I'm going to kill Carol." The fear of hearing his voice caused me to become irrational. I was petrified! My body began to tremble. I had been lying on the couch and sat straight up, opening my eyes and looking around the room for my dad. No one was in sight; I was the only one in the house. Bill was at school. I lay back down, dug my face into the corner of the sofa, and the words came again: "I'm going to kill Carol." The words kept repeating. Over and over, the words started out loud, "I'm going to kill Carol. I'm going to kill Carol!" Then the sound grew quieter and quieter, "I'm going to kill Carol, I'm going to kill Carol, I'm going to kill Carol, I'm going to kill Carol, I'm going to kill Carol, I'm going to kill Carol..." Eventually the voice faded into silence, total silence. And I remembered Carol.

After all these years I remembered Carol, my little friend who came to me after my bottle had been taken away from me at the age of almost three. I hadn't told Dr. Boyd about Carol during my story of "the goat that ate my bottle." For a few minutes, I remembered her with joy. I remembered what happened to her. She died that terrible morning when the pain was too much for either of us to bear. And I said out loud, "Carol, how can he kill you? You're already dead." Reason returned to me, "besides, my father can't kill you, he's been dead for years." Saying this aloud gave me the reassurance that this was another illusion; Fear left me; logic had returned and I realized "the people" were not going to devour me. I decided to call Dr. Boyd. I needed to hear his voice. I had learned to trust him completely. "Dr. Boyd, I remember another one. There's more, there's more of those people. I remember Carol."

"Yes, there are more, you haven't remembered them all yet. Let's slow down, Donna, way down. Going fast is not going to help you. I know you want to be free from them all, but we need to be completely thorough. Do you understand?"

"Yes, I think so," I said, not knowing for sure if I really did understand. I knew I wanted to go fast, wanted it to be over with. "I wanted to tell you about Carol. Something happened and I remembered her."

"Can it wait until you come in?"

"Yes, it can. But I want it to be over with, right now."

"I know you do, Donna, and I don't blame you. Relax if you can. Spend time with your girlfriend. What did you say her name is?'

"Georgie. I'll see if she can go to lunch or something."

I walked right in Dr. Boyd's office, sat down in the chair I always sat in and started right in, "Do you remember, huh, about the bottle and that awful way my dad, huh, huh —"

"Slow down Donna. Take some deep breaths, okay. Now, relax and be still for awhile. Let your head clear."

I didn't want to slow down, relax, or be still for awhile. But I knew he had my best interest at heart, so I did as he said. After about five minutes, I said, "I think I'm okay now. I'll go slower."

"I remember when you told me about your bottle being taken away and how your dad punished you. What else do you want to tell me?"

"When the pain got so bad that I started to float, I totally relaxed, and it seemed as if I could see the soft pink courage of innocence enfold me. It seemed as if someone was with me, sharing the burden. It was Carol; she was my first friend. I stopped screaming. My dad stopped biting and let go of me completely. My body fell to the bed. I was quiet as mouse. When I woke from my nap that day, I could hear my mother's voice in the other room. I called out to her, 'mama, mama!' She came to me and I clung to her. I felt safe again with her in my sight and forgot Carol. The panic of what had happened deepened in me, and little by little, I realized that it was not okay to be alone. It was not okay to acknowledge my feelings. I did not comprehend why my dad punished me in such a cruel manner. But that night, in the quiet of the moment, the incident was forgotten. Without any effort at all, little Carol returned; she had come to save me. She replaced the security of my bottle, and I once again had somewhere to put my feelings.

Dad had associated the loud noises I made, (he called it "screaming") with the taking away of the bottle. In my forgetting of the abuse, I again started flipping my hand in front of my eyes and making the noises that he hated. Again, he punished me in the same way. When the emotional response to his abuse would take over, that beautiful pale pink color would come into my mind. My friend Carol would come and help me through it all. I didn't bear this alone; Carol shared it with me. It took three times of my father's finger-biting abuse before I connected it to the loud noises. When I stopped making the noises, dad quit his sick way of punishing me. Although, he kept berating me, deliberately making me feel miserable. In time, he took away my sense of honor. But I found a way to escape the painful events he caused. And from all the turmoil within and the confusion without came my sweet Carol. With her, we had the strength to survive. I always felt a sense of innocence when she came to me."

I took a silent pause, closed my eyes, and thought for a moment. Then, I opened my eyes and looked at Dr. Boyd. I needed the reassurance and encouragement he always gave me.

Very softly, he said, "I'm right here Donna. Go ahead; say what you need to say."

"Is this really happening to me, or am I having a serious nightmare?"

"It's not happening to you now, it *did* happen to you. It is a nightmare of sorts, but you're not asleep, in fact, you're waking up." Dr. Boyd responded. "The courage of innocence can be mighty strong, Donna. You took your own courage and personified it in Carol. It's the way you coped with your ordeal. Being stripped of your identity, you live through the personalities."

"Well, that courage of innocence only lasted until my father raped me. She must have died that morning, because she wasn't there after that."

"Her death was the result of your father taking your innocence from you."

"Oh! That makes sense. What about her coming alive again? What about that? She came back to me. What is that all about?"

"I'm not sure. I suppose that by recognizing and accepting the truth of what had happened, the memory of her existence brought back that innocence."

"How do you mean?"

"In reality your father never did take it away from you. No, Donna, you kept it from your father; you protected your innocence."

"Wow! What a concept!" I said. Then tears started to

roll down my cheeks. "I feel so sorry for the innocent child that went through all that abuse."

"That innocent child is you, Donna. You are that child, and the compassion you're feeling is for yourself. I think maybe you're beginning to realize yourself. That is great!"

"If that is so, why does my mind get so befuddled, if that's a word? You know what I mean?

"I believe you mean there remains a conflict inside of you."

"Yes exactly. And it makes me curious as to what is going on, 'cause I'm not consciously keeping any secrets from you. The secrets are secrets to me, too. I'm honestly not trying to be resistant."

"I know you're not. Actually you've come a long way. I need to make it clear; you still have a long way to go. It is going to take patience. Your willingness to expose 'them' puts time on our side. Their power lies in your not remembering on a conscious level."

"I know what you're saying is true. What can I do?"

"Patience is a must. Don't be afraid that your healing is not going to happen. Your consciousness will take in only that which it knows you can handle. It will be revealed to you in due time. Those trance-like episodes you experience are moments of self-hypnosis; this is extremely helpful. Just let it flow as it happens. I can't say enough about slowing down, calming down. You will be free from all your turmoil."

Dr. Boyd talked to me in a serious manner. I needed him to lecture me once in awhile. "I am impatient. I know I need to slow down. And, I know I have made great strides. I have noticed progress, tremendous progress. But sometimes my mind becomes so disturbed with all the commotion going on inside of me. It baffles me and I don't know what to do."

"You're already doing what you can. Donna, our time is up. I want you to believe in yourself and know that this thing you're going through will end up just as you want. Okay? Will you believe that?"

"I don't know if I can, but for you, I'll try. See you next time."

* * * * *

"I don't want to go into anything too strenuous today. I'm not up to it. Nothing bad happened in the last three weeks. It's just that I don't want to get upset about anything."

"I understand, Donna. I know your anxiety level gets high. What do you want to talk about?"

"Nothing in particular. I almost cancelled today."

Why don't you tell me about your mom and dad."

"What do you want to know?'

"Where they were born, when they were born, how they met? What ever you know about them. What do you know about their childhood? Talk to me about them. It'll help me know where you're coming from, and it'll help me to help you."

"You've already described my dad very well, I must say. You know, when you called him a son-of-a-bitch? That says it all about him." I smiled.

He smiled back. "I want to hear it from your point of view, from what you know."

"I'll start with my dad. He was born in 1893, in Hamilton, Illinois. His father and mother had two daughters born to them. Both girls died at an early age. One passed away at seven months and the other died at approximately two-years old. Dad was their third and last child. His parents owned a small bakery and a restaurant. His mother managed the bakery and his dad ran the restaurant. They were religious people and never missed a service in the little Methodist church they so faithfully attended.

When my father was two they moved to Lawton, Oklahoma, and continued to live there until dad was fourteen. They moved onto a ranch in Montana. Dad never liked living on the ranch and disliked his religious upbringing even more. He hated the way his mother dressed him; he described it as "little Lord Fauntleroy clothes." He grew at a rapid pace and was 6'6'' at the age of sixteen. His mother once commented to my mother that he was always a handful and became even more difficult when they moved to the ranch. He would run away and be gone for weeks. Dad would hop freight trains to get to where he wanted to go and worked wherever he could earn money. Eventually he would come home exhausted, his clothes so dirty and worn that his mother would throw them away.

As a teenager still living with his parents, he fell in love with a girl named Edith. In time they became engaged, but Edith was scared of his frequent outbursts and broke off the engagement. This saddened my dad because he was very fond of Edith. He also loved his Aunt Rose (his mother's sister), and Rose loved him. She was a gentle person and gave him lots of attention. She seemed to understand him better than his parents did. His mother was stern and outspoken, a nice person, my mother said, but someone who showed little tenderness. She had tried to raise my dad with strict control, but my father rebelled. She didn't understand my father's need to be his own person. He was not able to live up to what she thought he should be. And, she was never able to control his excessive fits of rage. They were in constant conflict which only increased as he got older. She just didn't know how to handle his independent behavior. In her frustration toward him, she would lash out with hurtful words, she would say things like, "why couldn't it have been one of my girls that lived instead of you?" Ouch! That must have hurt my dad. His mom was German born and just didn't seem to understand anyone going against parental authority.

My dad's relationship with his father was not good either. His father always thought he should be obedient at all times, and when my dad disobeyed, he was labeled a "bad boy." His dad always protected and stood up for dad's mother. It seemed his only love growing up was his Aunt Rose. She not only gave him love, she let him love her in return. Written on the back of one of his childhood pictures were the words, "To the sweetest boy who ever walked." No one had signed it, but my mom said she believed Aunt Rose was the one who wrote it. He actually had two loves in his life as he was growing up: Edith, who eventually rejected him, and Aunt Rose, who was always there for him, that is, until death took her away. Mama told me once that Aunt Rose told her that dad's parents were sorely disappointed in having a son instead of a daughter. My dad was a sensitive man and must have felt their disappointment. Perhaps, his attempts to express his true self were seen as rebellion, not a boy just trying to be himself. It was not an easy thing for my dad to conform to anything he thought would take away his identity. Being held back from being your true self can be a most miserable thing."

"You would most certainly know how that felt," remarked Dr. Boyd.

I continued, "When dad was eighteen, he ran away to join the navy, and he never again lived with his parents. While he was in the service, he married a woman named Martha. Mama said they lived the wild life, partying, drinking and fighting with each other. They must have made up once in awhile, because they had a son, my half-brother, Ray. Dad got custody when the marriage ended.

At the time all this was going on with my dad, my mom ran a boarding home for children with her mom, my grandma (we called her nanny). When little Ray was around two-years old or so, dad would leave him at the boarding home during the week. Mama said he sometimes would visit Ray during the week. Sometimes, mom and my dad would take Ray to the park. My mom was single and loved children; the rest is history. Mom and dad fell in love. My mom is a really decent person, sweet and gentle, and as my dad said, 'completely opposite from Martha.' Mama is always soft spoken and has an honest spirit. She's an extremely caring person. My dad saw that goodness in her."

"You know a lot about your dad. How much do you know about your mom?"

"I make it a point to know all about my family. Mom and I drink coffee together everyday before I go to work and I ask her a bunch of questions." I paused at this point. I was fading, only able to see a clear black slate. My head lowered and then nothing.

"Hello, Dr. Boyd. I'm Carol."

"Hello Carol. I'm glad you came to see me."

"You are? I'm three years old and I'm Donna's first friend."

"That's nice. Are you still her friend?"

"Yes, I am, again. She remembered me and I'm her friend again. She forgot me for a long time."

"What made her forget you?"

"That morning, you know when Donna was being hurt. It was so awful. I couldn't help her like I did before. It was too much so I went away."

In a flash, Carol was gone, her visit over. I continued, unaware of any lapse in time. "Wow! I feel light-headed."

"What's happening, Donna?" asked Dr. Boyd.

"I don't know. I'm very light-headed and my eyes are blurry, like they want to cross and close. If I take some deep breaths, I think I'll be alright."

"Take your time, Donna."

I sat quietly for a couple of minutes before speaking: "I'm starting to feel better. I'll tell you about my mom. She was born in Boston, Massachusetts, December 4, 1900. She was an illegitimate child and put up for adoption. You know, being pregnant and not married in those days was almost unheard of. Another reason Nanny gave her up was because she had tuberculosis and her doctor told her she had only six months to live. But guess what? That doctor was wrong. Nanny lived to see all her grandchildren except my little sister, Happy. Mama was put in a foster home right after she was born, with plans for adoption. But, she was so shy that her foster parents adopted her. Mama told me about her shyness. She said it was painful for her throughout her whole life. Change of any kind disturbed her immensely. I was shy too, just like her, as a child. My mom comforted me, knowing full well what I was going through. Am I boring you?"

"No not at all. I'm learning more about you, through the descriptions of your parents."

"Okay then, I'll finish. When mom was seventeen, her adopted mother became ill with cancer. She had my mom investigate the possibility that her biological mother might still be alive, or at least someone within the biological family that mom could go to. Mom's adoptive dad had passed away several years earlier, and her adoptive mom knew she was not going to live much longer. The search paid off. Her real mom was still alive and living in Boston.

She had married and had a fifteen-year-old son. Her husband knew about my mom's existence, so he wasn't surprised when my mom came into their life.

My mom never returned to her adopted mother, who died shortly after Mama reunited with her real mom. Mom and my uncle Bob, her half-brother, are very close. Within six months, the whole family moved from Boston to Southern California. This is where they started a boarding home for children. Mom stayed with them until she went to live with my father. My mom and dad lived together for two and a half years before they married. They had my two older sisters before they married. Well, that's about it. Family time is over."

"And so is our time. I'll see you in three weeks, Donna. Take care of yourself and get lots of rest."

"Boy! What happened to the time? It really went fast." He looked at me, as if to say I think you know. We gave each other direct eye contact, staying that way for a few seconds. Somewhere deep within I knew the answer but wasn't ready to deal with it just yet. With a toss of my head, I said, "As the saying goes, time flies when you're having a good time." And then I laughed.

"You did a good job today, Donna," said Dr. Boyd as he walked me out his office door. "Your decision to stay away from the high anxiety stuff was a good one. And, you gave me some information I didn't have before."

"You think so? Good. I have one more question: why don't you have me come more often than once every three weeks?"

"Because my dear," he said putting his arm around me, "you're vulnerable right now. You need that time to process and accept the reality of your situation."

"Okay, I can appreciate that. Bye." I felt good that day. And it felt good to feel good.

Remembering

It was my day off. I was lying on my bed and went into the trance that was so easy for me to go into. In a brief moment the reality of all "the people" and the struggle that lay ahead came into view with such full impact that I started moaning out loud and tossing back and forth. "Oh, oh, oh, *oh*!" The internal conflict bore down on me, a mental pain that took my breath away. It lasted a short time before the pain began to subside.

Then quietness came, and the thought, 'I'm too stupid to even be called a human being.' A voice said, 'Are you ready to die?' Mesmerized, the stark naked truth jolted me into an upright sitting position. "The people" were running wild in my mind. It was chaotic, they were scattering everywhere. Then they would disappear to repeat the same behavior over again. This happened several times. At the end of the frenzy, everything became absolutely quiet once again. Only one of "the people" remained within sight. I could not see her face clearly but I could hear her: "Donna, you don't have to deal with your pain anymore."

"Who are you?" I asked.

"My name is Mary and I've come to help you. There are many ways to die, let's pick the least painful."

"I can't do that, Mary. It's wrong. There's got to be another way!"

"There is no other way. You can end your pain, once and for all. Take the pills Dr. Boyd gave you; you'll find your peace. You don't have to live through the suffering that lies ahead of you."

My mind drifted off, 'maybe she's right,' I thought. "I can't cope with this thing anymore." I decided to let Mary take my life. "The people were so real to me and I was panicked.

I sensed another person stirring within me, Edith Rose. "What are you doing here?" I asked.

"If you're going to let Mary do this, let me say good-bye to Dr. Boyd." Through me during my visits, Edith Rose had grown fond of this dear man. He had helped her feel good about herself.

"I'll call and say good-bye for you," I said. This seemed to satisfy her. I got a hold of the answering service and asked to talk to Dr. Boyd. The lady on the other end asked if it was an emergency.

A child-like voice said, "Donna's not going to live anymore and I want to say good-bye."

With that remark, the lady said, "Hang on, we'll get him for you." In a couple of minutes she returned, "Dr. Boyd will be calling you in a few minutes. I need your number." Edith Rose gave it to her and hung up. She went into the living room, sat down on the rug, and held her doll, waiting for Dr. Boyd to call. The wait was long. The phone didn't ring, but someone knocked on the door. My head was in a fog. With the knock on the door, Edith Rose left to roam around in my head. Dizzy, I went to the door.

There were two men dressed in white, one of whom said, "Is there a Mrs. Hunt here?" Upon hearing the name Mrs. Hunt, Edith Rose vanished completely.

"Yes, that's me. What do you want?" I now fully observed the men in white standing in my doorway with a gurney.

"We've received an emergency call from Dr. Boyd," said one of the men.

"But I'm okay, really I am." And I meant what I said. The memories of Mary and Edith Rose were gone.

"We're sorry, Mrs. Hunt. If you don't come with us willingly then it will have to be by force." He said this with determination.

"Alright, I'll go. I need to get my coat and purse." As I turned to go into my bedroom, the two men stepped into my apartment and followed me in. I could see they were not about to let me out of their sight. They allowed me to walk to the ambulance but informed me that I had to get on to the gurney and strap in while they took me to the hospital.

I felt so bewildered and absolutely devastated. I was checked into the hospital and lying in my assigned bed, when Dr. Boyd came in and directed me to follow him into his office. As soon as I went in and he closed the door, I became hysterical. "I can't stand 'the people' coming into my life." Frantic, I blurted out, "I can't face up to the ugliness that lives in me. No one deserves to be this ugly! I saw 'the people.' Mary wants me to kill myself, 'the people' disappear and then they come back again! Edith

Rose wanted to say good-bye to you. She was playing with her doll."

I kept jabbering something about Mary's existence and what she had tried to get me to do. While I went on a mile a minute, he got up, went to the door, called a nurse, and ordered an injection of some kind. He explained that the injection would calm me down. The nurse brought it in and handed it to Dr. Boyd. He gave it to me right away. Within a few minutes, I began to settle down. Some reason returned to me. "Jesus! Dr. Boyd, what in the hell is going on? I need to call Bill to let him know where I am."

"I'll tell the nurse to let you make your phone call. Donna, listen to me, we'll sort it all out tomorrow. Get a good night's sleep and I'll see you in the morning."

I called Bill as soon as Dr. Boyd left. "I'm in the hospital Bill, I hate it here. Get me out, talk Dr. Boyd into releasing me. He's coming back in the morning. I have to stay the night." I said almost in tears.

"Okay, Donna. I'll call him first thing in the morning. I'll come see you tomorrow and let you know what he said."

"Thanks, Bill. I'll see you in the morning."

I was very sleepy. I went to my room, got into the hospital's night clothes, and was asleep as soon as my head hit the pillow. It was not only a good night's sleep; it was a wonderful night's sleep, the best I had since the revelation of "the people." Early in the morning, I was awakened by a man in a lab coat wanting to draw my blood. It was required procedure. I knew it had to be done. Having been in a psychiatric hospital before, I knew there wasn't anything else to do but submit.

About an hour later, a Social Worker came in and said she had to ask me a few questions: "How are you feeling?" was her first.

"Okay."

"I understand you tried to commit suicide," she said in a monotone voice.

I quickly answered, "No, I didn't."

"Why are you here, Mrs. Hunt?"

The memory of Mary and what had happened flashed through my mind. "I guess I was going to kill myself, but now all I want to do is get out of here. I have to go to work today." She was jotting it all down.

"What made you want to kill yourself?" She asked as a matter of record.

"You know, things just got me down and I wasn't thinking straight," I answered. 'Let's hope that satisfies the old bitch.' I thought. That was the end of the questions. She left me to myself, and, of course, "the people." I dozed off and thought, 'How many are there, I wonder?' I slept until one of the nurses woke me to let me know it was breakfast time. It was a little before 7:00 AM. I got dressed and went into the dining room. I knew what was expected of me and felt comfortable in these surroundings. When I finished breakfast, I went into the lounge for a few minutes and then back to the dorm where my bed was. I'd lay there for awhile before going back to the lounge. Back and forth, back and forth, for several hours, without any conscious thought of anything. I was somewhere deep. I waited for Bill and the doctor to come and release me. Bill came about 1:00 PM. I was glad to see him. He told me Dr. Boyd said he would release me if it seemed appropriate, but that he needed to talk to me first.

It was a nice day. Bill and I went out to the patio and sat at one of the several tables. I don't remember all that we talked about during the nearly two-hour wait for Dr. Boyd. A few spoken words were said, but mostly long periods of silence pervaded. The quiet felt good. Bill was, by nature, a quiet man, "a man of few words," as the saying goes. "I called your job and told your supervisor you were sick with the flu, that it would be a couple of days before you'd be back."

"Thank you, Bill. I appreciate it." I relaxed a little after I knew he had made that phone call for me.

"There was a little doll lying on the living room floor," remarked Bill, not inquiring as to why.

"There was?" I said, in surprise. "Put it up somewhere. When I get home, I'll do something with it." I didn't know what else to say. The memory of Edith Rose was just that, a memory buried in my subconscious.

He didn't say anything more about it. "We didn't get any mail yesterday, unless you picked it up."

"No, I didn't. I'm feeling restless; I'll go get us some coffee. It'll give me a chance to move around."

"That would be nice," answered Bill. We seemed so uncomfortable with each other. The situation, I suppose.

I returned with the coffee and soon after Dr. Boyd came in. "Hello, Bill," he said, greeting Bill with a handshake. "Come with me, Donna."

"Wait for me, Bill. Will you?" He nodded.

Dr. Boyd led me into his office and asked, "How are things going for you, Donna?"

"I feel fragile, overwhelmed and scared. I feel calm right now but my life is in such a turmoil."

"We have a lot of work ahead of us as you now know, don't you?" He looked right into me to see if I had fully seen things as they truly were.

"Yes, I know it. I feel sad, Dr. Boyd, like I lost someone and I'm grieving. I haven't lost anyone. I don't understand."

"You have lost someone. You've lost yourself as a whole person."

I become a little excited when I tried to explain what happened. "All those people looked like spider legs, they were, like, floating, not standing on solid ground. They came to me through the belly of the spider. So many of them inside my head. Then Mary came and she wanted me to die. Oh God! Dr. Boyd, I am falling apart, aren't I?"

"I believe you're coming together. Donna, you said something about Edith Rose and her doll. Can you tell me something about that? Who is Edith Rose?"

"The doll? You say Edith Rose had a doll? Bill mentioned to me that there was a doll on the floor in our apartment. I'll have to think about that one for awhile. Can I go home now?"

"You're running away from me, Donna. Who is Edith Rose?"

"I am Edith Rose, Edith Rose is me. Umm, Edith Rose was with me before I was six, before that morning. I mean, she wasn't a personality inside of me, only a feeling of guilt. My father hated me right from the start because I wasn't a boy. He had an awful temper when things didn't go his way. I was one of his disappointments, and I paid a great price. He always named us kids at birth, but when mom asked him what he wanted to name me, he said, "I don't give a damn what you name her." So while mom was still in the hospital she named me Donna Mae. When we returned home from the hospital, my dad said he had decided to name me Edith Rose. I had two names right from the start. The tone of voice dad used when he called me Edith Rose became a thing of dread. It always happened when he was mad at me or when he was feeling mean. If he wasn't being hateful in some way toward me, he was totally indifferent. He was the only one in the family that called me Edith Rose, the rest of the family always called me Donna."

I paused for a few minutes, while I got up enough courage to ask him, "Are you going to release me?"

"Yes, I'm going to release you. Stay strong Donna. You can change your life."

I couldn't wait to get out of there. Bill and I were in the car, I was out of that hospital and feeling free.

* * * * *

"Hello," I said. I know you're going to ask me how I feel, so I might as well tell you and save you the trouble."

"You're no trouble, Donna. How are you feeling?" He asked anyway, a little grin on his face.

"Mary wanted me to kill myself. How do you think I'm feeling? I don't want to die. I want to be healthy. And yes, I know there's no spider in me. It's 'the people' that scared me."

"Why do you call them 'the people'?"

"Because they seem separate from me. They don't feel like a part of me. Should they?"

"It's not about 'should they,' it's about how you see them. If calling them 'the people' is comfortable for you then continue to do so."

"Okay, I'll tell Donna you said that. I'm Joyce. She's gone, too frazzled. Stressed out, you know. She wasn't able to stay."

"You're welcome here, too. Nice to see you again." Dr. Boyd said, not too surprised after all that had happened. "She's in a painful place, right now."

"I agree. It's not an easy time for her right now. She doesn't even know I'm here."

"I'm glad you're here, Joyce, to explain why you're here and not Donna. I have great respect for her courage. It's going to be a long, hard emotional road for her to travel. But if she could only know the tremendous release that will come from her going through this, she would also know how worthwhile it is for her to continue. I'm hoping she can see the value of her life and how deserving she is of the best that life has to offer. She's more than her disorder, much more."

"I know it is essential for her to become consciously aware in order for her to gain her freedom," said Joyce, pleased with Dr. Boyd's positive approach. "But sometimes, she doesn't believe in herself, in her ability to reach the healing she so desires."

"If she refuses to accept all this, it will debilitate her." Dr. Boyd went on to explain, "She may even lose sight of her own existence. The separation is keeping her a prisoner, and she'll remain locked up if she doesn't proceed. She must expose 'the people,' as she calls them, to eventually bring her to the healing she seeks. Can you explain this to her?"

"Yes, I can and I will. I know that by accepting the world within her she will change her way of thinking, and that will change her way of life."

"That's right. Her courage to overcome is her strength." Dr. Boyd kept talking to Joyce, attempting to remain reassuring and positive.

Joyce explained, "I believe she knows all this on some level, but her confusion is creating fear in her. The fear causes frustration and the frustration turns back into fear. The stress she's under is phenomenal."

"I know that's true," Dr. Boyd answered. "The integration will most certainly bring about change, and the change, in itself, will frighten her. I think, perhaps, she sometimes doesn't see this as moving toward healing, rather that she will be without 'the people.' Also, she's extremely ambivalent. On one hand, she's protecting them, and on the other hand, she wants to be free of them. It has to be a terrible time for her."

"You do understand the situation. I feel more relaxed now that we're having this conversation." said Joyce, soundly relieved.

"And you're a very smart lady," said Dr. Boyd. "You're extremely insightful."

"Thank you. I appreciate you saying so. I always try to be helpful where Donna is concerned. She truly wants to change her reality. It's just, well, you know, she gets so bogged down with all this stuff."

"I know she does and sometimes she goes too fast. She first needs to confront where she's at in her life before change can take place. It can take a long time. Donna has faced up to some of her painful past. Let's be satisfied with that for now. More will come, in time. Do you understand?" Dr. Boyd asked Joyce.

"I understand perfectly," Joyce responded. "Another thing we need to talk about is 'the people.' They, too, are in constant conflict, which I think increases her anxiety. 'The people' are very important to her, they've been her lifeline. Oh, it's just all so complicated right now!"

"It most certainly is. With patience and at Donna's pace, we can unravel this very complicated time in her life. I have observed that each personality has given her comfort through each of the seemingly impossible situations she's experienced. The real truth is that these personalities are parts of her. When she can feel the oneness they all share, Donna, will have taken a giant step."

"And she's worth it," said Joyce.

"Yes, she is." agreed Dr. Boyd.

"You know, Dr. Boyd, Susie's in denial," said Joyce, wanting him to know she was aware of some of the others.

"Susie? Tell me about Susie."

"It's like I said, she's in denial. I don't think she wants Donna to heal, because it scares Susie."

"Why would Donna's healing scare Susie?" asked Dr. Boyd with great interest.

"I don't know for sure. I do know she's unwilling to accept the fact that healing is necessary."

"Maybe her denial includes a feeling of being threatened, that she will disappear into nothingness if Donna exposes her. But I would hope she could understand that, in reality, the integration will be better for all of you. Each of you will live more fully when this occurs. I know the conflict in Donna is immense. Do you understand what I'm saying?" he said to Joyce, leaning forward as he always did when intent on making sure the one he was talking to comprehended what he was saying.

"Yes, yes, I do. Donna has to know what is real and what is illusion. One of her fears is that the future is going to be worse without 'the people.' How am I doing, Doc?"

"You're right on the nail," answered Dr. Boyd.

"Getting back to Susie," continued Joyce, "Her only concern is with her own preservation. Her survival is threatened and she knows it." Joyce waited to hear what Dr. Boyd had to say in response.

"Susie's survival is threatened only as she believes she is the only personality needed. As a part of Donna, there is no threat to her or any of the rest of you."

"Oh, I understand," Joyce said. "Susie's just trying to save herself from becoming extinct."

"I believe that's so. The truth is, as a part of Donna, she will continue to live."

"Thank you for helping me better understand this absolute bizarre, crazy disorder. I thought I was coming here to help you, and instead you're the one that has helped me."

"You have also helped me, Joyce. Don't think that you

haven't. I don't know everything about this disorder. Any information you give me is going to help me help Donna."

"It's been a delight talking to you. I think I'm going to leave now. Did you get the letter I sent you?"

"Yes, I did."

Joyce was gone and Susie appeared.

"Why in the hell, do I have to share my body with the others?" Were the first words from her mouth.

"Your body? Who am I speaking to?" asked Dr. Boyd knowing better than to surmise.

"It's me, Susie. I heard Joyce talking about me. She doesn't need to tell you about me, using all that wisdom she thinks she's got. I can speak for myself. It should be just my body. I'm the healthiest one of them all."

"Is that right? Will you tell me about you?" He asked.

"Let me think. I exercise, I eat healthy food. I think normal thoughts and I helped Donna get through college, which by the way, she passed the State Board to receive her Psychiatric Technician License. I will admit, Joyce did help me with the college thing, too."

"So, you interact with Joyce?" Dr. Boyd said in the form of a question.

"We know what the other one is doing, if that's what you mean."

"Do you talk with each other?"

"Yes, we do." Wanting to get back to talking about herself, she said, "I enjoy life and am one smart cookie."

"I believe you are smart." responded Dr. Boyd, meaning what he said.

"I can exist without Donna, I just know I can."

"What about the love and protection Donna gives you?"

"I don't know. What about it?" Susie was not even close to wanting to face the truth. She was gone.

"What happened? What happened?" I asked, totally

confused and anxious.

"What is happening Donna? Can you tell me?"

"My head feels woozy."

"What do you mean 'woozy'?" The doctor asked.

"You know, funny. It feels funny, like I've been on a roller coaster. My head is swirling. I'm glad I'm here. Can't think of a better place I'd rather be when I'm feeling like this."

"Donna, listen to me. Listen! Some of your people have been visiting me."

"Oh my God, do I look ugly when I change?"

"No, not at all. You close your eyes and lower your head. Donna, how are you feeling right now?" He purposely said my name, to help me clear my head, to fully come back into myself.

"I'm having a hard time focusing my eyes, and I feel a little dizzy."

"You are exposing them, by letting them come into your consciousness. Can you give me more details into your feelings at this very moment?"

"Huh? I feel like I'm falling apart; I feel like I'm coming together. I'm not sure about much of anything. It feels as if everything is being thrown at me. I remember things, awful things, hateful things, painful things! I remember 'the people' coming at me full force, swarming all around my head, filling it up and making me more confused than I already am. I don't know what to do."

"You're doing just fine. What you're going through right now is absolutely understandable. The chaos is part of the process; you're experiencing a transition. This is the way to rediscover your self."

"I'm trying to be comforted by your words, and it all sounds good, but how can I find myself if I don't know who I am. I don't know who me is without 'the people.'

The me I know always turns out to be 'the us.' I hate it. I'm telling you, I hate it!"

"Take some time to settle down and know that you're not alone. Together, we'll find the way for you to know who you are. I know you hate it, but this is all part of a series of changes you will be going through before you can be one. I know of no other way to explain it to you. What is happening Donna, is that you're undoing the past by remembering your people and it's painful. The frightening experience you're going through will, in time, lessen. It is a nightmare right now, and if I could change it for you, I would. But I know of no other way.

"I know you would Dr. Boyd. There are so many people, that sometimes I don't know where to turn. I guess I know where to turn, to you. Everything gets so distorted. I get so scared."

"Does your fear bring back the illusion of the black spider?"

"No, no. I don't have the illusion of the black spider anymore. Progress, huh? The fear comes when I can't see anything but black, like a completely erased black board. Then nothingness takes over. I think maybe that's when 'the people' start coming, but I'm not sure."

"Don't push your people away from your consciousness. This is exactly what needs to happen in order for you to gain your health back. Release them, Donna. Don't fight them from reaching *their* awareness; this will help all of you come together. You don't need to understand everything that is happening with you; leave that to me. Do you trust me enough to do that?"

"Yes, I trust you enough. But so often I think this is a dream that will go away as soon as I wake up."

"It's not a dream. For right now, it's your reality. Our goal is to eliminate your sense of separation. It's still a long way off, and the key to reaching this goal is your willingness to accept it, not as a dream but as a fact."

"I don't want to hurt 'the people' and I don't want 'the people' to hurt me." I said, feeling a lot more focused and calm.

"Neither will happen. See them as they are, parts of you, seeking to express their own personality. Let it happen, Donna. Let it happen."

"It looks like I'm not doing a good job of concealing them, so maybe I am letting it happen. I must be."

"And it's okay. Absolutely positively okay." Dr. Boyd reassured me.

"I had a dream the other night. I saw black bugs jumping on the backs of a group of people. I was standing back watching it happen. I turned around and walked away, and then I returned to see what happened. The bugs were all in a pile, and there were men spraying them with insecticide. The bugs were all dead. When I woke up, I seemed to be in a place of peace. What do you make of it all?"

"Perhaps it means you realize you don't have to leave your people behind. Only the fear and the pain will be left behind. Are you feeling better?"

"Yes, much better and much calmer. I'm ready to face it. I do realize talking about the past helps me clear my head."

"Remember, Donna, we don't have to go any faster than what you can handle. We'll sort it all out in due time, all in due time."

"I feel more positive. I hope you know I trust you with all my heart. And it is going to take a long time, isn't it?"

"I do believe that it is going to take a long while," he answered. He didn't sugar coat his answer. He was always honest with me and I loved him for that, even though I didn't always want to hear what he was saying.

"I'll tell you about Beth, another one I remember. She always looked beautiful to me. My first memory of Beth was during the scary experience my brother and I had. Billy and I were friends as well as brother and sister. He told mom I was the closest thing to having a brother. Ray had moved out and only came to see us once in awhile. I was considered the tomboy of the family because I helped Billy kill the chickens and rabbits dad raised for food.

Billy came to me once with a strange request. Maybe not so strange, for a boy his age now that I think of it. He was fifteen and a half; I was twelve and a few months.

"Donna," said Billy. I've got a favor to ask, but you have to promise to never tell anyone, ever, I mean no one, not ever." He stood in front of me with his hands on my shoulders trying to make eye contact, a difficult thing to do with me. I looked at him just a digit away from his eyes, as was the way I always looked at people without anyone seeming to ever notice.

"What do you want to ask me?" I said.

"You've got to promise first," he said to me, dead serious.

"Okay, I promise. Now tell me." I backed off from him. His arms dropped to his sides.

"I want you to let me see you, down there." He moved his head downward just a little, with his eyes looking slightly down.

"Down there?" I said, "Down where?" when I knew darn well where he meant.

He looked up at me, "I want you to pull down your pants so I can see your thing down there" he said, glancing once again in the area of my underpants. Looking up again, he said, "Mom and dad are gone grocery shopping, we can go in their bedroom and get under the bed. None of the other kids would dare go in there. Okay?"

"Are you crazy? How do you know they went shopping? What if they come back and catch us while you're looking at me?"

"They just left, Donna, you know how long they're gone. It won't take long, I promise. Please."

"Guess what, Dr. Boyd? We went under the bed and just when I had pulled my pants off, dad came into the bedroom with some people. Our house was up for sale and he was showing them around. I pulled my dress down fast! We were both startled and remained quiet as a mouse. I prayed to God that he hadn't seen us. Dad and the other people finally left the room. I hurriedly put my pants on.

"Let's get out of here, quick!" Billy said. He took my hand to help me out from underneath the bed. "Come on, let's go. Hurry!" he said, pulling me along with him. I, too, was experiencing a fear freeze. An all too familiar feeling had its grip on me. Billy saw the scared look on my face. "They're not in the house, Donna, honest. There in the yard, I can see them through the window. Look, see for yourself!" I did and Billy was right. "If daddy asks you why we were under the bed, tell him we were talking about what we were going to get him and mom for Christmas." Christmas was just around the corner, and this was the only idea Billy could come up with that seemed halfway possible.

"Okay, I will," I told Billy.

But not being sure that I wouldn't break down and end up telling dad the truth, he repeated the command again. "Now Donna, you've got to stick to this story, no matter what. No matter how hard he tries to get you to tell the truth, don't tell him. I'll get in a whole lot of trouble if you tell him."

"I won't tell him, I won't tell anyone, I promise." I kept

my promise. You're the first person I've ever told."

"Did your dad ask you about it?" asked Dr. Boyd.

"Oh yes, he did. Later on in the day, he told me to come with him. He said he wanted to talk to me about something. He took me in his bedroom, which immediately caused an eerie feeling to go through me, an unconscious reminder of another time when he took me to his bedroom. He sat me on the edge of the bed; I trembled inside. He got down on his knees and very gently said, "Tell daddy what you and Billy were doing under the bed. I won't get mad. I promise."

Edith Rose was in a panic! She too remembered a morning with that same gentle voice. 'It's a trick!' Edith Rose said to me. 'Don't tell him. You know he's lying. He'll hurt you if you tell, he won't keep his promise.' I was so frightened I couldn't speak. I kept trying to catch my breath, I started to hyperventilate. The blackness came, I lowered my head and disappeared. Out came sweet, beautiful Beth. She spoke to dad with a soft, innocent voice. "We were just talking about what we are going to get you and mama for Christmas."

"You can tell me the truth, daddy isn't going to get mad at you, honest." He thought he was talking to me, Beth laughed inside herself and thought, "He thinks I'm Donna. Can't he see I'm much prettier than she is? Don't you know Donna's the one that took her underpants off, not I." And then Beth spoke out loud, "Honest, daddy, we were discussing what we wanted to get you and mom for Christmas. That's all, really."

And knowing that was the only story he was going to get, dad got up off his knees and said, "Okay, you can go play now."

As I walked out of his bedroom, I returned into my own consciousness, as Donna, and Beth asked me, "Who is he to accuse me of doing something wrong? I wouldn't take off my pants for my brother. I'm a lady." I, Donna, was the tomboy; Beth was the lady I could never seem to be. She has a sort of drawl, you know. Not so much a drawl, she just drags out her words, slow and easy. I like to listen to her.

Later, I saw Billy and said, "You told me they were shopping." I was kind of mad at him.

"That's what the girls told me," he responded. "You did a good job, not telling dad," Billy gave me a big hug and it felt good.

"How do you know what I told dad?"

"I would be in big trouble by now if you'd told him the truth."

I found out later that the girls had told Billy that mom went shopping. They didn't say with whom and Billy assumed that because dad's car was gone they had gone together. Mom went with the next door neighbor. I don't know where dad was before he brought the people in the house, probably driving them around to see the area."

"Our time is up, Donna. Boy! You're doing great. Keep up the good work and remember don't hold back, just let go."

Deeply Unaware

"Good morning, Donna. How have you been these last three weeks?"

"I've been doing a lot of thinking. Beth's been on my mind. I remember another time Beth saved the day for me. It was when I was almost thirteen. School was out for the summer, and mom sent me to the store for milk. It was a Saturday at the beginning of summer. "Donna, I need you to go to the corner store and get me two half-gallons of milk. And, bring me back the change. I need it."

"What if there's only a dime left, can I spend it?"

"Yes, you can have a dime. Bring me the rest if there is any."

I felt good walking to the corner store knowing I had three months ahead of me with no school. Being around

Donna Mae Rose

people for long periods of time made me uncomfortable. Not the scary feelings I felt when in the presence of my father, but feelings of confusion and frustration. Walking to the store by myself gave me a sense of freedom, the freedom of getting away from my father. He worked out of town all week and came home for the weekend. We often went to the store for mom. She never learned to drive a car. We wouldn't have been able to afford two cars anyway, even if she did know how to drive.

Dad was acting strange this one weekend, calling me Edith Rose in a teasing way, different than usual. This was the name he used when he was mad at me. And, the difference gave me a feeling that was most disturbing. I didn't know what he was up to. I just knew he was up to something.

"Where are you going Edith Rose?" he said, with a lilt in his voice to let me know he wasn't mad.

"To the store to get some milk." I answered, wanting to say, "What's it to you?" I kept those words to myself.

"Watch out for the boys" was supposed to be a joke. He laughed a little chuckle. I just kept walking out the door, wishing he'd disappear into thin air to never be seen again.

I stopped for a minute and looked at Dr. Boyd, for reassurance I guess, and then went on: "I loved walking into this store, all the candy to the immediate right as you walked in, just sitting on the shelves ready to drool over. I stood at the counter, paying the clerk, waiting to see if I was going to be able to enjoy some of that candy, when I saw my dad come into the store. This was most unusual. Panic began to rumble within me. The knots in my stomach grew tighter and tighter as did an almost uncontrollable desire to run out of the store, to run and run and run. But, where would I go? There was nowhere to run.

He came over to me and in his stern, demanding voice

100

said, "Go get in the car and wait for me." I did as I was told. I was scared and anxious. This man intimidated me so very much. I went to the car and, with the ice cold bottles of milk in one hand, tried to manipulate the car handle with the other. My right foot was on the ground and my left foot barely up in the car. My ankle dangled below the car handle between the opened door and the seat. I was trying to boost myself up with my left leg with plans to put my rear just barely on the seat. The weight of the right leg on the ground was supposed to help me scoot further onto the seat, but in my nervous state, I hit the inside handle with the sack holding the milk. I could feel something cold running down my leg. "Oh, no, the bottle broke!" I said out loud, my heart pounding. I was overwhelmed by the fear of dad raging over how clumsy and stupid I was.

I frantically tried to figure out what to do next, when a lady walked up to me. I thought she was going to ask me if I needed any help, but instead, she said, "Look," pointing to my left leg, "Look, dear. You've cut your leg." I looked to where she was pointing, and it looked as if the back of my ankle was almost cut in half. I think I hadn't felt a thing, maybe, because the ice cold milk numbed the pain. I didn't know I had cut my leg until the lady brought it to my attention. Some sort of calm came over me and I responded to her words quietly, repeating what she had just said to me, "My leg is cut. My dad will be here soon. He's in the store." Something was happening to me; I was unbelievably tranquil. It was like I was floating in the loss of my identity, becoming invisible to escape my present situation. This happened to me often in panic situations, and this was definitely a panic attack. I didn't know I was creating personalities. In my horrendous fear, Beth came to soothe me."

"They came to you on an unconscious level. Now

you're becoming aware of them on a conscious level," Dr. Boyd reminded me.

I didn't respond to his statement. I still had more to tell him about Beth and the incident. "I think that lady was an angel passing by to help me, 'cause she was very insistent about me getting help.

"You be sure and show that leg to your dad, it needs to be taken care of right away."

"I will. Here he comes now," said Beth in her lovely soft voice.

"What did that lady want?" asked dad.

"I broke one of the bottles and cut my leg. She wants me to show you."

He looked down at my severed leg and said, "Oh, God!" He helped me in the car and rushed to the driver seat. We passed our street.

"Where are we going?" I asked.

"To the emergency."

I felt absolutely relieved. To this day, I believe my dad had plans of doing something awful, awful and painful, but was interrupted by the accident. I was actually happy the way it turned out. The accident was way better than what would have happened to me that day. I think they call that a blessing in disguise.

It turned out to be a serious cut. The local emergency staff did all they could and told us we needed to go to the General Hospital in L.A. They told my dad I needed surgery. We went home first to let mom know I was okay. We knew she was worrying and wondering where I was. When she came out to the car, she was surprised how up-beat I was. "I'm okay, really mom. Everything is going to be fine. I just can't move my foot until the doctor fixes it. Will you go with us?"

"Of course, I will. I was scared to death to come out to

see you, but your dad assured me you were laughing and in a good mood. I'll go get my purse and we'll go." I was in an extra good mood. Not only had I escaped from a place of terror, but Beth was with me, giving me a feeling of comfort.

While at the General Hospital (which, by the way, is where I was born), the doctors explained to mom and dad my accident was a grave situation, and there was a possibility I would never walk again. The broken glass had cut the tendon in the ankle area and it took thirty internal and external stitches to complete the surgery. I stayed in the hospital for ten days and spent most of the summer in a cast. Three weeks before school started, the cast was removed. I was back in school that September and walking. When mom could see that I could walk, she told me what the doctors had told her and dad at the hospital.

I don't remember Beth being with me after mom got in the car to take me to the hospital, nor afterwards, when I was up and about. But in the stillness of my being, Beth was with me and we enjoyed Billy's company. He was not only a brother; he was a real friend and father figure. Beth and I both delighted in his companionship. We helped him with the chickens and rabbits, feeding them, gathering up the eggs, and holding the chickens' heads while Billy chopped them off. We also had the honor of taking the guts out. Billy didn't want the water bag to break on him, so we did it for him. We didn't mind; we liked doing the things that Billy didn't like to do. Of course, Billy never knew that Beth was with me. But when she was with me, I was happy in my world with mom, Billy, and her. Billy would take "us" for rides on his motorcycles and shared his bicycle with "us." She wasn't always with me. Sometimes, it was just Billy and me. I loved those times, too. He played jump the fence with only me and we talked together, just the two of us, just Billy and me.

"You cared for both Billy and Beth, didn't you?" asked Dr. Boyd.

"Yes, I did, very much. I was the tomboy and Beth was the lady I always wanted to be, but couldn't"

"Why is that Donna, why couldn't you be a lady?"

"Because I wasn't allowed to be myself. I was only allowed to be a thing for my father. I was supposed to be someone without feelings, without choices, without any thoughts that would go against his wishes. It was Beth who could be herself."

"What about your mom? She allowed you to be yourself, didn't she?'

"Well, I guess. Yes, she did, but my father's way with me was overpowering and left scars on me, deep-seated scars that changed me into what he wanted me to be. Or else! He sort of brain washed me. When I was with mom I felt loved, but she feared dad, too. She couldn't take away the fear from me because of her own fear. Her fear of him overflowed into us kids. We learned fear from both mom and dad. From dad, we learned fear from the way he was with us, and with mom, it was from her fear of him. Fear was implanted in us almost from birth."

"Well put, Donna, well put. Our time is up, a little over in fact. I'll see you next time. Take care of yourself."

"I'll do my best." On the way home I thought about Dr. Boyd and how sensitive he was. He had waited for the appropriate time to reveal "the people" coming to see him.

I went on with my life as best I could. My routine, while waiting for three weeks to pass, remained the same. I worked, visited my mom, and tried to remember the things from the past. Bill and I stopped going to counseling together. I had my "real" friend Georgie to run around with. And we had fun together.

* * * * *

"The three weeks went by pretty fast this time." I said to Dr. Boyd.

"Time has a way of moving too fast, if you ask me." He responded. "How are you feeling, Donna?'

"Fair, I guess."

"You sound a little down. Are you?"

"Yeah, I am."

"Are you up to talking about it? Tell me how you feel."

"What do you mean, how do I feel?" I said angrily. "I'm not supposed to feel; I'm not allowed too. Why do you keep asking me how I feel? Feelings are for people good enough to feel."

"Don't you think you're good enough to feel?'

"Maybe, maybe not. I'd like to believe I'm good enough to feel but when I have a giant of a man telling me I don't count, making me feel like trash, well, it's hard to believe in my goodness."

"Is this why you let your people feel for you?"

"Maybe, I guess. Nobody wants to listen to me."

"I do, Donna. You know I want to listen to you."

"Sometimes, I want to cry and I can't. When I try to bring 'the people' together so there's only me, it feels like pieces of broken glass. When they start getting close to me, I feel like I'm bleeding and I push them away. What's to become of me, Dr. Boyd?"

"Do you feel like crying right now?'

"I think so, yes. I'm choking it back."

"Let it come, Donna, let the tears come. You have cried before and know how relieved you feel when you cry."

"I'm okay, honest." But, I wasn't okay, because I started crying and kept crying until my tears dried up. "It's about my brother, Billy. He was killed instantly. I think I told you this before. I felt so fragile after he was gone, more insecure and shy. I was no longer happy and out going, the way Billy had taught me to be. Beth felt awful when I told her Billy was never coming back. She would come to me in her sadness, talking to me in that slow, drawn out way of hers. We were both devastated. I would listen attentively while she told me what she was going through. I felt great sympathy for her, because I was going through the same thing. I believed my feelings didn't matter, but I could empathize with Beth."

I broke down and sobbed. It seemed like I cried for the longest time before Dr. Boyd spoke.

"Here," he said, handing me some tissue. "I think you do believe you're good enough to feel."

"Thanks. Maybe I do, maybe I do."

"I'm sorry about your loss. Losing someone you love is tough."

"Thank you. He meant the world to me. It was awful not having him around. He was so good to me. I'll never forget him."

"I'm sure you won't. How are you feeling right now?"

"Like the ugliest person on the face of the Earth."

"You're not ugly, Donna. What makes you think that?"

"My father always told me I was the ugliest thing when I cried."

"You've got to stop believing all those things your father told you."

"I know. I'm working on it. I do feel better. I've never cried like that over Billy. I feel like a load has been lifted off me. I should cry more often; it does me a world of good."

"How old were you when your brother was taken from you?"

"Somewhere around fourteen."

"The puberty years, Difficult years at best. They must have been difficult for you."

"It was an awful time for me. I was experiencing strong sexual feelings. They wouldn't go away. It was like a driven arousal. I didn't know what was happening to me. It was a really strange desire stirring in me. I was lost as how to deal with it. I know now it was supposed to be a normal stage in my life, but under the circumstances, this feeling would not take the normal path. It took control of me and it was hard for Beth to continue being with me. She did not share her feelings with me. They never went deeper than brotherly love, but her ability to make believe and pretend helped me through the feelings I was going through. She helped me to pretend that this peculiar thing I was experiencing belonged to someone else, and it worked for awhile. But, the sex drive building in me was no match for Beth; it was a force that would not be stopped, and Beth just up and disappeared. The distorted, abnormal sensation I felt separated from me, as all things did when I couldn't cope. Wanda came forward. She was born of the rape. She eventually took over my body and tried to satisfy herself through men's bodies. Her ceaseless attempts to gain gratification damn near drove me insane — can we talk about something else, please?"

"Of course you can. Let's move to something more pleasant. Tell me some of the fun things you did as a child."

"I can remember some of the good times. Grandpa and Uncle Bob, mom's stepfather and half-brother, came over about once a week during the summer to take us kids and mom to the beach. Dad was out of town working. Mom brought food and drink for us. I enjoyed going to the beach; I loved the water. But, I hated it when it was time to go home. I'd ask mom if dad was going to be home when we got there. The answer was usually "no." On Fridays, however, the answer was "Yes. It's Friday and he'll probably be home when we get there." I tried to stay happy as we sang songs on the drive back. As we got closer to home, we would get quiet. Once we were in our driveway and I could see dad's car, my happy times were over. I had returned to Hell and dreaded the world I was about to enter.

Marge and I played jacks and checkers. We played house; that was really fun. We used those snap clothes pins to make a mouth-and-ear piece, and then we put it on a used vegetable soup can for the hang-up part. We really got into pretending. Sometimes mom would let us wear her dresses, but that was only when dad was out of town. It was a wonderful way to get away from our reality and the cloud that hung over us.

Mom always celebrated our birthdays in some special way, and each holiday was celebrated in some way. It got pretty hectic at Christmas. Dad always blew his stack and went into one of his rages. It knocked some of the excitement out of us, but we managed to glean some joy in spite of his rotten attitude.

The older girls and Billy listened to the radio in the evening, after dad went to bed. When I got older, I listened to *Stella Dallas*. I could hear the entire program if I ran all the way home after getting off the school bus. I remember listening to Inner Sanctum once or twice with the rest of the kids. You know, that program with the old squeaky door. Billy would put a sheet over his face and creep toward me making a WHOOooo sound and scare the daylights out of me. I would scream and run to mom, who was usually in the kitchen. The girls laughed to their hearts' content. You know, Dr. Boyd, now that I think of it, I bet they wanted to get rid of me and it worked. When my dad was out of town we were so happy, so free and full of laughter. Even mom was more relaxed. The constant worrying she did while trying to keep things under control disappeared during these great times without dad around."

"I saw the happiness in your eyes when you talked about the good times. You expressed it very well."

"I think I'm getting to know myself a little better, understanding more of what is going on."

"Yes. You are acquiring knowledge about yourself."

"I know I'm not insane, and I'm not as afraid as I used to be. My desire to be whole is what keeps me going. I want to know what it's like to be a single person. You know what I mean, a person without so many personalities."

"I don't think you could have a better goal. You're crossing over into the real world, a healthy world. You're doing a great job, Donna. You really are."

"Another thing I liked to do was to spend time alone. I loved to just be quiet and go within myself. Consciously, there didn't seem to be anything happening, but now I know there was a lot going on. I played jacks by myself and colored in my coloring book. My favorite thing was to play with my paper dolls." With the words "paper dolls," I felt a dread coming over me.

"What is it Donna. Are you remembering something? Stay focused."

I nodded and said, "Something painful. Not physical, emotional."

"Are you ready to share it with me?" asked Dr. Boyd.

"Yes, I can. I want to."

"Okay now, take it slow and go only as far as you want."

"I remember it was a Saturday, and my dad drove in from being gone all week. He told my mom he wanted her to go for a ride with him. He picked up Happy and went to the car to wait for my mom. I was on the front porch playing with my paper dolls. Sometimes, I would spend hours with them. Mom came over to me and told me to get my sweater because we were going for a ride with daddy and Happy. When my dad saw mom bringing me with her he said, "Why does she have to go with us? Can't she stay with the older girls? I just wanted the three of us to go."

"The girls need to do their homework, and they don't want to put up with her whining and crying while I'm gone." This explanation infuriated him. He pulled out of the driveway like a speed racer, telling my mom, "All I wanted to do was take Happy to get her an ice-cream cone." His tone was so full of hatred.

When we arrived at the ice-cream parlor, dad took Happy and went inside. While they were gone, mom told me, "If Happy offers you a bite of her ice cream, tell her you don't want a bite. I'll get you one as soon as I get some money." When they came out of the store, Happy had a double-scoop chocolate cone in her hand. She never offered me a bite and I never asked her for one. Happy ate it all as we drove back home. I felt so awful about myself. You know, thinking I was not good enough, and because of it, I never played with my paper dolls again. Those paper dolls had given me so much enjoyment."

"That was a terrible thing for him to do. Why do you think you stopped playing with your paper dolls?"

"Because, I learned that after pleasure came pain. And in my mind, the pleasure the paper dolls brought me was the cause of the pain I felt, being left out from getting an ice-cream cone."

"Wow, Donna. Do you see how aware you're becoming?"

"Yes, I can see that. I never felt the pain consciously until now. Edith Rose was with me that day. She was the one feeling hurt, believing her 'badness' directly resulted in not getting any ice cream. I denied myself the feeling of pain and gave it to Edith Rose. Boy! That truly hurt me, I know it now. That was an extremely painful thing to experience. But, you know what else? In harboring my feelings, the split came."

"That's very interesting. You're a bright lady. How old were you when this happened, do you remember?"

"Thank you," I said, feeling mighty proud of myself. "I was somewhere around eight. I know it's close to the end of our session, but can I change the subject? I want to tell you something."

"What do you want to tell me?"

"You won't believe me."

"Try me."

"I've already told a couple of other doctors about it, but they just fluffed it off as a dream."

I'll listen to you Donna, then I'll decide if it's real or a dream. Okay?"

"Okay. Plain and simple, I had a vision. It was when mama came home from the hospital. After the rape, I waited and waited for her. When I saw her walk in the front door, I was so relieved. Nobody will ever know how relieved I was. It felt like a heavy piece of metal had been removed from my shoulders. I was so glad to see someone who loved me as much as I loved her. I went right over and reached out for her to hug me. But dad wouldn't let me.

"You get away from your mother. She can't pick you up. Get out of the way! She needs to sit down. Leave her alone."

When she sat down, she said to me, "Come closer to me, dear. Stand right here next to my chair. She touched me ever so gently and said, "Mama's not strong enough to hold you right now. In the morning when daddy's gone to work, come get in bed with me. Sweetie, will you do that?"

I nodded and said, "Yes." My heart was willing to wait because my soul knew the morning would come, and when I heard the front screen door slam, I hurried to crawl in bed with her. That's when it happened. I closed my eyes for awhile, snuggled up to mom and felt a peace come over me that was absolutely beautiful. When I opened my eyes, I saw a glowing white light. I closed my eyes again, thinking it might be the milkman, but I thought, 'What would the milkman be doing in mom's bedroom.' There was no fear in what I was experiencing. I opened my eyes again and the light was still there. This time I thought it might be Jesus. The light was so bright that it radiated all around this bright figure, the radiance brought me a joy I never felt before. The darkness within was gone. There was no sorrow burdening me, only a feeling that everything was going to be okay. It was as if the light was coming from God himself."

"That is beautiful, Donna, just beautiful."

"But do you believe me?"

Dr. Boyd was quiet for several minutes before speaking, "it doesn't matter what I believe; it's what you believe. That's the important thing: What do you believe?"

"I believe it, I don't understand it all, but I believe it." The session was over, and I felt better than I had in weeks.

While I waited for my next session, I thought about the vision and Dr. Boyd's response regarding it. He was right! It's what I believe that counts. I remember the experience; it was the greatest feeling of comfort I had ever known. I could feel love enfolding me, giving me the reassurance I needed so desperately. I fell asleep those many years ago, and when I woke, I had no recollection of this absolutely powerful, calming incident. Years later I remembered. But as I said, the doctors I tried to discuss it with just fluffed it

off as a dream. It was no dream. I had been awake; it was
real.

* * * *

"Hi Dr. Boyd."
"Good morning, Donna. How have the last three weeks
been for you?"
"Alright, I guess. Actually not too bad. I spent time
with Georgie. We went antiquing; it was fun. Having a real
friend is kind of nice. I think I'm waking up to 'the
people'," I said, getting right to what I wanted to tell him.
"What I mean is I'm noticing time I can't account for. I
know it's when one of 'the people' take over. That's good,
isn't it?"
"That is good; that is very good." Dr. Boyd replied. "It
means that you're consciously becoming more aware."
"I don't like not knowing what's going on in my
absence but I kind of think it is progress."
"It is," he said, giving me the encouragement I needed.
"Can you tell me how you feel right before it happens?"
"I knew you were going to ask me that. Talking about
my feelings is important to you, huh?"
"Feelings are very important. They're a big part of who
we are."
"Well, let's see, my body heat increases, I get warm all
over and then I feel as if I'm spiraling into blackness. It
isn't the black slate, ya maybe it is the black slate. Let me
think a minute." It was difficult to explain. "It isn't the
black slate anymore. It turns into…it's a black hole and I'm
spiraling down. I feel pressure in my head, not hard
pressure, just a…a…a pressure from the feeling of twirling
around. I don't think it takes long, 'cause after the feeling
of pressure, I disappear.

"Do you know who takes over?"

"No. I just notice there is time I can't account for. Strange huh? This is a very strange thing."

"Do you remember ever feeling this way before?"

"Yes. I thought about it over the last three weeks, knowing you were going to ask me that question."

"You're getting to know me pretty well." He said and I nodded.

"It was the first time I noticed a boy, or I should say, when a boy noticed me. He sat next to me one day in the cafeteria during lunch. He was so pleasant to me. He asked me what room I was in. I told him as my heart started to pound. He kept a conversation the whole time we ate. He told me his room number and how close he lived to the school and how nice his teacher was. God! I felt good and shy, all at the same time. This boy really gave me the attention every girl my age wants. I was thirteen. The very best thing that happened when he got up and said, "Here, you want my cookie? I'm too full." As he handed me the cookie, he said, "Maybe I'll see you tomorrow. Bye." He waved to me as he walked off. I don't know when I ever felt so good. It was delightful to say the least, and the butterflies in my stomach were in color, I swear. I couldn't wait to tell Marge. She was in the kitchen when I walked in from school. "There's a boy at school who likes me," were the first words out of my mouth.

"What's his name?" She asked me.

"I don't know, I'll ask him tomorrow. We had lunch together in the cafeteria. He sat next to me and started talking to me. He's really nice and he told me he'll see me tomorrow." I felt so excited telling Marge about this boy. As I gave her the details of that most wonderful experience, I moved back against the stove, pulled out my starched blouse, and continued to finish the story about the boy who paid attention to me.

Marge listened attentively, almost as excited as me. "Where do you know him from? Is he in your room?"

"I never saw him before today. When he got up to leave, he handed me his cookie," I told her, feeling the best a thirteen year old girl could feel. As I leaned against the stove, I felt heat go up my back. I quickly moved away. Mom had put water on for spaghetti and I thought it was steam causing me to feel the heat, but moving away didn't stop the hot burning feeling against my back. I turned around, showing Marge my back and calmly asked, "Am I on fire?"

She hollered, "Yes, yes you are! Yes, Donna, you're on fire!" As she yelled, I started running back and forth in the kitchen. Marge pulled up my skirt and started fanning the fire in an effort to put it out. Mom came in to see what all the yelling was about, and as soon as she saw me on fire, she smothered it out with my skirt.

I was in a panic. Mom set me in a chair. I was kicking my legs, crying and moaning. "Listen to me, Donna listen to me, the fire's out. Let me take a look at you," mom said, with a concerned tone.

"Don't touch it, please mama, pleas-s-s-e don't touch it?" I had been so happy just a few minutes ago, and now I was miserable.

"I'm not going to touch it. I need to see how bad it is." I knew I could trust her, so I allowed her to take a look. "This needs to be checked out right now. We're going to the emergency."

"What will the doctor do to it!?" I asked her.

"He'll put something on it so it won't hurt so much." She said, with that please-don't-give-me-a-bad-time-about-going-to-the-doctor tone.

"Will you go with me, mama?'

"I'll go with you, sweetie." She leaned down and gave me a kiss on the cheek.

I'm not clear who took us to the hospital, a neighbor perhaps. I know it wasn't dad; he was out of town. The doctor put some kind of salve on the burn. He said parts of my back had third degree burns, but I didn't have to stay in the hospital and I was glad. I wanted to be home with my mom. I felt the pain all evening, and when I went to bed that evening, my brother Billy came in to see me. "Does it hurt, Donna?"

"It hurts awful," I answered honestly.

"I'll be right back. I'm going next door to borrow a fan."

He ran out of the house and came back with the fan. He held it up next to my back and it helped a lot. He held it there until I fell asleep. He cared about me and I loved him. I wish he was still here for me to talk to."

"What a nice thing your brother did for you. I'm glad you had him for as long as you did."

"Yes, it was wonderful having a brother like him. It took time for my back to heal, but it was my heart that remained in pain. The power of the pleasure/pain conditioning took over. I was out of school for a week. The first day I went back, I made sure the boy who had made me so happy did not see me.

When I got home from school, Marge asked me about the boy. "Did you see that boy you told me about, you know, the one that gave you a cookie."

"Oh, him? I don't like him anymore." That's all I said, and then went outside to be by myself. I went to one of my favorite places, on an ant hill way in the corner of the backyard. I would sit close to the ant hole and watch them go in and out, wondering if the ant that went in the hole was the same ant that came out. It was here, on the ant hill that the spiraling feelings and the blackness took over. My thinking was affected. I always ended up getting stung, and would go tell mom. She always told me to put some mud on it, which I did. It helped some."

I started to continue when Dr. Boyd said, "Let's stop here. Talk to me about the ant hill. Can you elaborate?"

"Only that I liked to go to the ant hill when I needed to be alone. They were red ants, and I could see deep inside myself when I watched them, the ants I mean."

"What did you see when you went deep inside yourself?"

"I didn't know then but I know now that I could see 'the people' stirring around, that I wouldn't be lonesome anymore. That is until I got stung. A sting would bring me out of myself, and I would leave the ant hill. 'The people' would be gone. I don't know how that happened."

"You weren't really watching the ants. You were probably staring into the hole and went into a hypnotic state. Your unconscious showed you what your consciousness wasn't aware of. Is that when your feelings of "warm blackness" were felt?"

"I think you're right, because right before I could see 'the people,' I would wonder if it was the same ant that came out of the hole that had just gone in. Crazy huh?"

"No not crazy. You were able to get in touch with your suppressed self, the parts of you that had split. This is how you coped with and adapted to your situation."

"How did I do that?"

"I'm not sure. But sheer fear played a very big part in it. Did the fact that they were red ants have any meaning to you?"

"I believe it came from the deep rage inside of me that even to this day is hard for me to express."

"I know there is rage in you and with good reason. Just

think about it, Donna. You believed you had to rid yourself of all pleasure in order to avoid pain. That is called brainwashing, a conditioning that you still need to work through."

"I believe that. The paper dolls helped me get in touch with my suppressed self, too. I was eager to get away from my conscious world. So many painful things happened to me, making me want to be somewhere else."

"You were able to connect with 'your people'."

"Now that I think of it, they seemed more like reflections of me rather than parts of me."

"Maybe that's how you should think of them, as reflections in a mirror. That may help you see them in a different light."

"I could do that. Thinking of them as parts of me is difficult, but as reflections, that will be much easier. Now, I know the biggest injury I received from believing in the pleasure-before-pain...what shall I say...principle was emotional. Avoid pleasure and pain won't come. That's exactly what I believed. You're right. This was the conditioning I learned from my father."

"Good work, Donna. This has been a very productive session."

"Thank you so much. I know our session is over. Bye, Dr. Boyd."

I think I wanted to say "I love you" right then, but I didn't.

The Challenge Of Chaos

"**G**ood morning, Donna. Tell me, how did you spend your last three weeks?"

"Thinking about what ifs."

"What do you mean?"

"I mean, what if my life was different, what if I'd had a normal life and things had been different?"

"Why are you wondering about things like that?"

"I've been thinking about my life. I didn't know how to make friends in an appropriate manner. My emotional and social skills were definitely impaired. I was handicapped in a very real way. I didn't know how to be a normal teenager.

I didn't have dates with boys who would take me to a dance and hold my hand, giving me a kiss good-night when he brought me home. That is a way of life I've never known. I gravitated toward loud mouth, dirty talking boys who asked me if I would fuck them. I was flattered when a boy asked me to have sex with them, not indignant or angry, but flattered.

"You were a troubled child, a deeply disturbed teenager," said Dr. Boyd with compassion.

"I know that now, but I didn't then. I didn't even think there was anything wrong with me. It was more like a driven instinct, an irresistible urge. I wasn't a normal person evolving into womanhood."

"How did you do in school, Donna? Did you get good grades?"

"The school curriculum was easy for me until the eighth grade, and even then, I received good grades in everything except math. When we got into fractions, I was lost. Besides, my fascination with boys was the primary thing by that time. My interest in boys caused an inability to concentrate on the school agenda. My thoughts felt disorganized. The feelings going on inside of me were supposed to be a natural part of growing up but they weren't, not at all. I realize now that, unconsciously, I remembered the rape and the distorted memories of that horrible morning that took me down another path. I separated myself from the puberty years and the feelings that went along with it. This caused an internal battle. The driving force of my sexual feelings was intensely strong, and I couldn't cope with them. These feelings took a dark, black, downhill spiral through a blackness that is hard for me to talk about. As hard as it is for me to admit this, I must tell you that I experienced sexual arousal that awful morning. I know I was a wounded child; I know that now.

It twisted my mind and the thought of it makes me cry for the child that went through it."

"Donna, that child was you, is you, as a woman. Listen to me, feel the compassion for yourself. I feel compassion for you."

I looked at him and believed him. For the first time, I was waking up, or so it seemed to me, to my connection with the child that was me. I didn't say a word to him about it. I took a few minutes to feel the oneness.

"I would have loved to be normal in my childhood, in my adolescent years, and in my young adult years, but I wasn't. So, I'll just have to adjust to what is and get on with it."

"You said you've been married three times. Tell me about your first husband and how you met him."

"I used to go to a place called Simon's, a circular restaurant with glass all around it. It was a hang out place for young people like me. I met a girl named Bonnie while I was there. Sipping on a cherry Coke, she introduced me to George, who eventually became my first husband. The first time I saw George, he was walking towards Bonnie and me. When he got within hearing distance, he greeted Bonnie. They talked for a short time about the illegal car racing that was a big thing in our lives at that time. George would glance at me every once in awhile, and finally said, "Who's your friend?"

"George, meet Donna. Donna, meet George."

I said, "Hi," and George asked me, "Will you go out with me tonight?"

I had not as yet become sexually active, but George would change that. I agreed to go out with him and told Bonnie I would see her later. We offered to take her home, but she said she wanted to stay a little while longer and would find someone to take her home. George and I got drunk on whiskey, and we had sex in the back of his car. No courtship, just "Hi" and "Will you go out with me?" The next thing you know, we're having sex. That's the way our relationship started. We got acquainted after we had sex. We saw each other every day for a week and had sex each and every time. I loved it! And George loved that I loved it. It was lust, not love, but nobody could have convinced us. We just knew we were in love. George worked the oil fields during the day and would meet me at Simon's early in the evening. One of those evenings, we went over to his friend's house. Somewhere in the conversation, George said, "you know, Bud, if I had four new tires to put on my car, I'd take Donna to Arizona and marry her."

"I'll see what I can do about that," was Bud's response.

In a joking manner, I told both of them, "What about me? Do I have anything to say about it?"

George said, "Well, baby doll, do you want to?"

"Without hesitation, I said, 'Yes, I do.' I was grinning from ear to ear."

At this point in telling Dr. Boyd about George and me, I stopped talking and stared off into space. Everything happened quickly. There was no black slate, just a sudden trance followed by, "She's getting very nervous."

"Who's getting nervous?" asked Dr. Boyd, taking note of all that was happening.

"Oh excuse me for not letting you know. I'm Joyce; Donna's gone."

"Hello again. What makes you think Donna's getting nervous?"

"Because I know her like a book. She's trying very hard to face her fears and she's feeling out of control."

"How can I help? Is there anything I can do?" Dr. Boyd asked.

"You're already doing it. She trusts you. Being here for her is what you can do."

"I know Donna is overcoming enormous obstacles," responded Dr. Boyd.

"Yes, she is Dr. Boyd. She's getting in touch with her feelings and she's so scared."

"I know it's scary for her. Can you tell me what she's going through?"

"She's grieving. She's getting in touch with herself, and she grieves for her lost self."

"Will you elaborate?"

"She's frightened and sad. Frightened because she feels her emotions. She believes it's wrong to allow these feelings to go on, and you're telling her that to feel is a healthy thing. The conflict is tearing her up. She feels guilty. Giving up her old belief system, seeing that it's okay to feel, is wreaking havoc with her mind. She believes feeling is what causes bad things to happen to her."

"Can you help her understand that she has a right to think and feel? Her father has brought great harm to her. Can you tell her that?"

"I might be able to, but she feels so sad and deserving of punishment because she could never be what he wanted her to be. She was never able to forgive herself completely, or to stop thinking only of his wants."

"Tell her she is worth more than her father taught her, that she matters and has every right to be."

"There's something else. She's thinking a lot about Wanda lately, and this scares her, too."

"What does Wanda represent to Donna, do you know?"

"If you remember, Wanda was one of the eight people that came out of the spider the morning she was raped. Donna thinks of Wanda as a bad girl because a girl with sexual feelings is bad. One time when Donna was taking a bath and washing herself, down there, you know, her private place, she got a good feeling. A daddy long leg was on the wall coming down toward the tub. She screamed and jerked her head back, hitting it on the back of the tub. Her mom came to see why she was screaming and took her out of the tub to comfort her. Donna told me all this once, and that belief came to her. You know, to feel good would only bring pain. She believed she was punished for feeling good down there. That's just an awful way to grow up, don't you think? She told me she was only eight when this tub thing happened."

"Your right, it is absolutely awful! We need to help her get over that lie. It's not true. It's okay to be happy, to feel pleasure. You've been a big help to me and I want to thank you." There was no response from Joyce. She was gone.

"Whoa! I've been gone, haven't I? Who was it this time?"

"It was Joyce, Donna."

"I'm going to have to get used to this for awhile, aren't I?'

"Yes, you are. Your inward search is extending outward through your personalities. Your determination to resolve this situation is allowing them to come forward," explained Dr. Boyd.

"What do they say to you?"

"They tell me things you can't remember right now."

"Oh," I said, satisfied with his answer. Give me a minute to recall what we were talking about." A few minutes lapsed, "Oh, yeah. I was telling you about George and me. I think we really cared about each other. We liked being together and we wanted each other. It wasn't a one-sided affair. The strongest thing we had in common was the hormones raging in both of us. I was fifteen and he was twenty-one. It was really my first crush. It never should have gone as far as marriage. But it did. Anyway, Bud showed up at George's house a few days later with four new tires. We decided to get married the following weekend. I told mom that a friend of mine was having a slumber party, "Please, please mom. Let me go to the party. I promise I'll look for work on Monday. Maybe I can find some babysitting jobs or house work, something to bring in some money. Pl-e-e-a-a-a-s-s-s-e-e-e, let me go."

"Alright, I'll let you go. Now listen to me, Donna, you are going to find something to do first thing Monday morning." She tried so hard to be stern.

"Thank you, thank you, thank you," I said and gave her a big hug and kiss. "I love you, mama. I love you." We watched Tennessee Ernie Ford and had a snack. Life was good. Dad went to work, but he didn't do the out of town jobs as much as he used to. Marge and Happy were in school, and Dorothy, Louise, and Ray no longer lived at home.

And so, we went off to get married. Bud and his girlfriend went with us to be our witnesses. Driving to Arizona gave me the feeling of being free as a bird. We were happy as a lark. We satisfied our urges without judgment. It was a happy time for me.

We had some problems regarding my age, which was fifteen. We went to Phoenix first, but that didn't work. The police told us that without proof of my age, it wasn't likely anyone would marry us. He suggested that we might have a chance if we went to a little town at the other end of Arizona. I don't remember the name. What I do remember is seeing buildings made out of rock as we came into that town. And this is where we married. We were on our way back to California as Mr. and Mrs. George Nathaniel Dickson, when I wondered what my dad would say: "What is my dad going to say? We have to let mom and dad know we're alright. Stop at the next phone and I'll call Doris." Doris lived across the street from my house. "Doris, it's me, Donna. George and I got married. We're on our way back right now. We did it in Arizona. Will you go tell my mom I'm okay and that I'll phone her when I get closer to home."

"You're crazy Donna. Your dad's going to kill you. Where do you get your guts?"

"He'll probably have it annulled and then kill me," I responded. I began to feel afraid of what he was going to do. I told George, "George, I can't face my dad. I'm petrified."

"Don't worry. I'll be right there with you. We'll face it together." said George, pulling me closer to him.

On the phone, mom told me he was mad but trying to control himself. We decided it would be best if George and I came over in the morning. I was more than glad to put it off. "I don't want to see him, George. He has such an awful temper."

"That's all he has, baby doll. He just yells and cusses, and he's got you all buffaloed. Your mom stays and listens to all his shit." He reached for my hand and I reached out for his. "Everything's going to be alright. Let's not ruin this day."

"Okay. I love you."

"Did George know your mom and dad?" Dr. Boyd asked.

"George had met mom and dad three days after I knew him. He told my dad, "I love your daughter, Mr. Watson and someday I'm going to marry her." His straight, up-front way of talking pleased my dad.

"It damn well better not be soon. She's too young," responded my dad.

I reminded George what he had said that day. He

looked at me and swallowed with an exaggerated gulping sound before saying, "I'm telling you, baby doll, it's going to be okay." And surprisingly, it was.

When we walked into the house, I went right over to mom and gave her a big hug. Boy! It felt good to see her. Both George and I went over to dad and sat down on the floor in front of him, where he sat in his favorite overstuffed chair. "Hi, dad. I'm really sorry for worrying you and mom." I waited for him to tell me I wasn't living with George, that he was having the marriage annulled, and that was that!

Instead, he looked at George and said, "She's your wife now and you better take good care of her."

"Yes, sir. Oh, yes, sir. I will. I'll take very good care of her." We were both amazed and relieved.

Dad looked at me and said, "Your mother says this just might help you grow up. I'm damn mad at you right now, so it's best you don't stay too long. Come back in a few days, when I'm cooled off."

"I will dad." At this point, George and I got up. I leaned towards my dad and gave him a gentle kiss on his cheek. Dad had mellowed out as he got older, but he still knew how to pitch a fit. He just didn't do it as often. But, him not getting mad? Wow! This was the surprise of a lifetime.

"You two get out of here." He said. I know he was pleased with the kiss I gave him.

"Whew!" I said, as we jumped in the car. "Was that easy, or am I dreaming?"

"Come here, you sweet thing, and give me a kiss. We made it, Mrs. Dickson, we made it."

"And for the first time, I had felt my dad's love toward me as a daughter. We had just experienced that most wonderful kind of love between a father and his child. It was the way I had always wanted it. It is a memory I will keep with me forever. I guess it was difficult for my dad to express love in a healthy way."

"It seems you're right about your dad. So, who wanted out of the marriage?"

"I did. I grew tired of the monotony. When I could talk Bonnie into ditching school we would spend hours together at Simon's. On several occasions I ran into Bud. He told me he wasn't going with Amy anymore.

Bud asked me, "Do you want to ride around with me for awhile, just you and me?"

I think Bud was flirting with me, the wife of his best friend. "I'd like to, really, but I can't today. Maybe another time." I said, giving him big eyes and doing a little flirting of my own. I wanted to go with him so bad, but I didn't. Not that time.

George and I got a place of our own, a bachelor's apartment. At first, that was all we needed, a place to eat and a bed to make love in. But as time passed, I grew tired of George's love making. I was restless and wanted to be free. I had a crush on Bud and I wanted to be with him. Bud was all I could think about. I would go to Simon's hoping to see him. When he did come in, we would ride around all day until just before George got home. Bud would take me to my little apartment and drop me off to my dull existence. Up until this time, nothing sexual happened. One day, I asked him if he would take me grocery shopping, and he did. He brought me home early, so he could help me put the groceries away. Then he said, "You have a crush on me, don't you?"

"Yes, I do." That's all I said. He brought me to him and kissed me square on my mouth. The excitement of wanting someone new raised the passion in me. We went to my bed and did some heavy necking. I told him, "I want you Bud!"

"I want you, too," he said sitting up in bed. I thought

he was going to take his clothes off. Instead, he said, "When you're not with George anymore, let me know." He left my apartment, got in his car, and drove off.

I left George a few days later. I just up and left while he was at work. I was home with mom once again. She told me I just wasn't mature enough to be married, and dad said, "At least, you're not pregnant." I was pregnant; I just didn't know it yet. Our marriage began and ended in less than three months. It was early October when we were married. I was back home with my folks shortly before Christmas.

"I got a feeling our time is up, am I right?"

"You are exactly right. Have a nice three weeks."

* * * * *

"I'm in a bad mood today." I said as I walked into Dr. Boyd's office.

"What's going on with you, Donna?"

"I don't know. It's all this heavy stuff coming down on me. This multiple personality disorder gets to me now and then. Sometimes, I feel like I'm less resistive to this bizarre thing happening to me. And then, I'll have a day of hopelessness, but before the day is over, I'm positive again. I seesaw back and forth. My hopeless times leave me feeling vulnerable. Not being able to understand what's going on causes me to see only the evil of it all. I'll feel weak and helpless, and then I'll turn around and see myself as a whole person, able to visualize beyond this horrible condition I'm in. I know I need to expose them all to be free, but sometimes it seems such a difficult task."

"I don't have to tell you that it is a difficult thing to overcome, but you're doing it. Don't be hard on yourself. One day at a time, Donna, take it one day at a time."

"On top of everything else, my personal life is in

shambles."

"What's going on with Bill and you?"

"Long story short, it's just not working out. We don't go to counseling anymore. We're like two strangers living under the same roof. I was so sure it would work out."

"Is it definitely over between the two of you?" Dr. Boyd asked.

"He's been offered a job on a dairy in Oregon."

"Are you moving with him?"

"He wants to go visit with the people that hired him to see what it entails. He asked me to go on the trip with him. I've never been to Oregon and getting away from everything sounds super good to me."

"When would you be leaving?"

"I'm not sure it could be as early as this weekend."

"I imagine it would be quite difficult to keep a healthy relationship going, under the circumstances." Dr. Boyd changed the subject. "What happened to you and Bud, did you marry Bud?"

"Oh, no! Bud and I were hot for each other. There was no love involved. It took awhile before I ran into him at Simon's. I wanted to see him so much, but he just didn't come around. And, I started to feel sick. I slept late in the mornings and took naps in the afternoon. Mom could see I wasn't feeling good. She asked me, "Donna, when was your last period?'

"I don't remember. I think it's been awhile." I had started my period at the end of my fourteenth year, just several months before I met George. "I've only had three periods since I started, and they're painful. I'm glad they're gone." Being pregnant never entered my mind.

"You need to go to the doctor and see why you're not having your period. You might be pregnant."

"Will you go with me?"

"Yes, we'll go together."

And sure enough, I was pregnant. "What am I going to tell your father?" said my mom out loud, more to herself than to me.

"He's going to be mad, isn't he?" I said to her, squeezing her hand in a loving way.

"He probably will be," she said softly, "He probably will be."

"Wouldn't it have been nice, Dr. Boyd, if she could have said, 'the three of us need to sit down and work this out'? Instead, I heard him yelling and raving through the night. Mom told him as he got ready for bed. He was cursing at her, saying, "Those girls must like pain. Goddamn it, mother! What are we going to do with these kids of ours?" I could hear every word he said, and as usual, mom took all the hell he dished out. It actually seemed to be a ritual between them. He blew up; she calmed him down. She had gotten better and better at it as the years passed. He could release his anger with mom, knowing she would stay with him. Even if she left, he knew he could talk her into coming back. Mom was so patient with him, with every one of us, we were her family and she did the best she could, the best she knew how.

Dr. Boyd nodded as I told him about the game my mom and dad had played most of their life. He didn't comment about it but instead said, "What do you think he meant when he said you girls like pain?"

"What he meant was that my oldest sister, Dorothy, was also pregnant. My son was born September 11, two weeks before I turned sixteen. Dorothy's daughter was born a month later. The difference was that Dorothy was with her husband and was twenty-three. She didn't live at home. Mom reminded dad of this, which helped him calm down a little. When dad lost his temper, all logic went out the

131

window, and this is when mom would help him come down from the rage. Only then could he see things in a much calmer manner.

When she came into the living room, I said, "Mama, you poor thing. He's so mean and you just stand there and take it."

"You just never mind about me. I'm fine. Your dad has had a lot of responsibility raising all you kids. He wanted things to come out right and worries a lot." She went out to the back porch to do some laundry. There was something exceedingly special about my mom. She was number one on the list for providing unconditional love without effort. It was as natural a thing for her to love as it was for her to breathe.

As soon as I got over my morning sickness, Bonnie and I went to Simon's. I hadn't gone much of anywhere since I left George, except for the week I tried to find Bud. And this night, I found him. There he was, sitting there, and my heart jumped into my throat. I walked right over to him and he gave me a big kiss on the mouth. "Rumors have it you're not with George anymore."

"You heard right. Did you hear I'm pregnant?"

"I heard that and see the rumors are true." He put his hand on my little round stomach and said, "I won't have to worry about getting you pregnant. Will I?"

He looked at me from the top of my head to the bottom of my feet. I knew that tonight, Bud and I were going to have sex. I looked down, like I always did when I felt shyness come over me. "I'm four and a half months along," was all I could think to say. I surely did have a crush on him, but it was something more than a crush that made me want him sexually. A strong drive pushed its way into my consciousness, an overpowering urge. You know, Dr. Boyd, I named that urge "Wanda" many years later. For now those uncontrolled, unconscious, unexpressed feelings seeped into my conscious awareness. and I knew Bud was the one who would satisfy those urges tonight. And he did. We went to a motel and had sex. When we were through, he went and got us some coffee. We talked about the failure of my marriage, smoked cigarettes, finished our coffee, and talked some more.

"I won't be here for long," Bud said. "I'm working out of town, I don't like it, but I need the money."

"How long will you be here?" I asked him.

"Only three more days. We'll get together before I leave."

"Okay," I said, not really caring if I saw him again or not. I don't believe he cared either. We didn't see each other before he left. I saw him at Simon's a couple of times after he returned, but it was over. No more crush on Bud. Eventually, as my pregnancy advanced, I was content to stay home with mom to wait for my baby to be born.

The natural tendency to detach myself from others, made it easy for me to stay home and do nothing, that is, except drink coffee with mom. I was more than willing to isolate myself from the outside world, a world so difficult for me to cope with. Others saw it as wanting to wait until my baby came. It was so much more than that, more than even I knew."

"Well, goddamn, isn't she an intelligent wizard?" someone said.

"Who do you mean by 'she'?" asked Dr. Boyd, knowing what had just transpired.

"Oh, excuse me all to hell. I didn't introduce myself. I'm Wanda, you know, the wild one. And the 'she' I'm talking about is the know-it-all, psychological one you know as Donna."

"You sound angry. Are you?"

"Yeah, I'm damn mad and why shouldn't I be? My mean old, hateful father raped me. And, I know Donna thinks I'm nothing, and that makes me mad. I've lived with anxiety all my life. I never knew when that son-of-a-bitch was going to come after me. The pressure to live up to his expectations made me crazy. He brain washed me; he controlled me; he tortured me. Let's see, what else am I pissed off about? Oh, yeah, he told me he was just trying to love me. He's the one that's nuts, now that I think about it. He told me I was his woman, his woman? Jesus Christ, I was a little girl! I was just a little girl. He made me submit to him. What in the hell was I supposed to do?"

"You know it's okay to be angry. You have every right to be."

"It isn't all right to be angry. Just ask my dad."

"It was not okay for him to treat you like he did."

"Do you want to hear something else?" Wanda asked and Dr. Boyd nodded. "Donna put me down in that black hole. She's trying to separate herself from me."

"Could it be she did that to stop herself from getting out of control?"

"Beats the hell out of me! You're the psychiatrist."

"Maybe Donna was trying to get away from pain."

"I know she felt the pain, too," Wanda remarked. "Just tell her to stop psychoanalyzing me."

"She's trying to understand herself," he responded.

"Well understand this, we both felt the pain and we both felt the stimulation."

"What do you mean?"

"Some of the things dad did to us felt good, we got excited. But it was confusing, too, because he told us not to tell anyone. That let us know we were doing something wrong. Was I doing something wrong?"

"You were afraid not to do what your father told you.

You did nothing wrong; your father was the one that was wrong. Can you see that what I'm saying is the truth?"

"Yeah, I see what you're saying. I got to go, nice talking to you, doc. I'll tell you one more thing before I go. Donna totally trusts you, or I wouldn't be here now. She's afraid of me and doesn't regard me as part of her. I guess we just don't understand it all right now."

"That's right. It'll all come together soon. Are you leaving now?"

"Yes, Edith Rose is coming to talk to you. Bye, I'll try to come back again."

"Hello, my name is Edith Rose. I'm one of the people who lives in Donna Mae."

"I'm Dr. Boyd. Did you say you live in Donna Mae, not Donna?"

"Yes, that's right. Donna Mae made us. It was Donna who put us in the black hole."

"How old are you, Edith Rose?"

"I'm six and a half. How old are you?"

"Well, that's not important," said Dr. Boyd with a smile on his face. Can you tell me more about the black hole?"

"It was very dark until Donna opened it up a little. Now there's some light coming in. I like it better with the light. It makes me feel less afraid."

"Why do you think she let some light in the black hole?"

"Because, she's feeling safer since she's been talking to you."

"How many people live there with you?" asked Dr. Boyd, wanting to find out how much Edith Rose knew.

"All of them. And, we wait to see which one of us gets to come out."

Dr. Boyd, with a grin on his face from the answer Edith Rose gave, asked her, "Do you know how to count?"

"Yes, I do. I know how to color, too, and I don't get out

of the lines 'cause I try to be a good girl."

"Even if you go over the lines, it doesn't make you a bad girl."

"I always try to be a good girl. Sometimes I don't know what being a good girl means. Daddy didn't think I was a good girl. I'm sorry I'm so bad," she said, hanging her head.

"You're not bad. You didn't do anything wrong. Nothing that happened with your daddy was your fault. Your daddy was the bad one."

"Do you think you like me?"

"I know I like you. You're very sweet and you're not bad. Do you believe me?"

"Mama always told me I was a very good girl. I believed her, so I guess I believe you."

"Good. What your mama told you is the truth."

"I want to come back and see you, can I? I tried to do what he told me to do."

"Yes, please come back. Don't forget what your mama and I told you. You're a good, sweet little girl."

"I won't forget." Little Edith Rose was gone.

I was sitting in the big comfortable chair when I came back, my head in a fog. But, I knew where I was. "Give me a minute to clear my head."

"Take as long as you need."

Several minutes went by before I asked, "Who was it this time?"

"Wanda and Edith Rose."

"Wanda? What was she doing here? I don't like that."

"You sound angry, Donna. Are you angry?"

"No, I'm scared of her."

"What is it about Wanda that scared you?"

"She just scares me. That's all. Maybe because I think she'll take over again. I never want to live like that again. I feel guilty about the way Wanda lived…we lived…I lived…that was me that behaved like that. I should be punished. She liked to have sex with different men. No, I did that! I should be punished."

"You seem to be confused as to whether your separate from Wanda or not. Are you?"

"Well… I…we…Oh God! The last three weeks have been terrible for me. My memories of the trauma have been haunting me. I know that remembering will bring me to my healing, but I also know that it's frightening to feel my people. And, that's what I've been doing, feeling my people."

"Tell me about it, Donna, share it with me. Can you? Will you?"

"I'm trying to share it with you right now. It's difficult. It's such a struggle to bring it all together."

"Tell me what you can," he said, in that understanding, gentle way.

"The names Edith Rose and Wanda keep rumbling in my mind. They appear to me as if they're trying to tell me something. I accept them in my consciousness, and then they disappear. Little by little, I would let them stay with me for awhile, and then one time Edith Rose spoke to me." I stopped at this point and looked to Dr. Boyd to say something.

"Go on, Donna. I know this is almost impossible for you to believe, and understandably so. I know recalling the past is painful. Talking about it will eventually bring clarity."

"It's very painful when they come to me. I get nauseated and that sick feeling stays with me for days. My well-kept secret seems to be exposing itself. I realize this is a good thing. Edith Rose spoke to me. It was like she was introducing herself to me. She said, 'My name is Edith Rose. I'm six and a half. Now that you told Dr. Boyd about me, I can begin to get well from this sickness I got from what daddy did to me.'"

"Oh God! I'm getting sick to my stomach." I put my arms around my stomach and bent over, shaking my head back and forth.

"Take some time to catch your breath. Remember what I told you about breathing."

I sat up, took several deep breaths, and let them out. I gained my composure and went on, "That wasn't all she told me. She said, 'I was born with you. I don't ever remember being without you. I stopped growing after that awful morning with daddy.'"

"You gathered up a lot of information and that's good. How are you feeling right now, Donna?"

"I'm not sure. Bewildered would be a good word to use. I lost my fear of the big black spider, and the black slate has disappeared. Actually, I think I'm feeling fine."

"You are truly experiencing a breakthrough. I am so pleased." Dr. Boyd was unable to keep his obvious feelings of pleasure to himself, and I was amazed at his genuine interest and concern.

"I guess that inner door into the darkness of my mind is opening, slowly, but nevertheless opening. I feel as if I'm being led through the darkness toward the light."

"That's a good way of putting it, Donna. That black hole, as you call it, is no longer dormant."

"I must say, I do feel much better. But, don't get too happy, 'cause I'm not sure I can talk about Wanda."

"You did say Wanda's been on your mind, didn't you?"

"Wanda is a difficult subject for me. I worry about her taking over again. I remember Wanda being in control of me, using my body, degrading me. How could I forget? She could leave the internal world I had created for my people and enter the real world. It was a struggle to overcome her. And now, I fear that talking about her might even be dangerous. I don't think I'm willing to chance it."

"I don't believe you need to worry about that ever happening again. You don't think that irrationally anymore. You're much too knowledgeable. Your once-destructive thinking caused your behavior. You're much more informed to live like that again. You don't have to be afraid of Wanda anymore. Let go of the guilt, and the need to be punished will disappear. Believe me, Donna, your future will not be like your past."

"It's not just feelings of guilt. I feel sad, unlovable, and worthless. I want to believe you. I really want to believe you."

"Well then, believe me. You have to make the choice." Dr. Boyd said sternly.

"Wanda has been coming into my consciousness. Here, I discovered that Wanda and Edith Rose are closely intertwined. Wanda told me something that is so disgusting, so repulsive. God, I hate what she told me!"

"What did she tell you Donna?"

"Like Edith Rose, she introduced herself to me, in this way. 'I am Wanda, my father's woman. Edith Rose is my daughter. My father made love to me once, and I fell in love with him. I have forever wanted to return to him. No other man could satisfy me, because it was my father's affection that I really wanted. I took over your mind and body for awhile, and when I was in control, I was able to comfort Edith Rose and relieve her of her guilt. But, those feelings would return again and again. She, too, wanted to go back to that morning to undo the wrong she believed she had done. She wanted to win her daddy's approval. As for me, I just wanted to have him love me again."

"This is too unbearable Dr. Boyd. I need to change the subject."

Donna Mae Rose

"No, let's stay with it for a little while longer. Let's not put a judgment on it. You mentioned you felt a sexual arousal during the rape."

"I know I said that. I surprised myself when I said it. It is true, I was stimulated by it. That's a terrible thing. I feel really bad."

"Now remember, we're not going to put a judgment on it. Okay? Your father taught you to feel guilty in feeling pleasure. Somewhere in your mind, you accepted it as true."

"Yes, he did. I remember the feelings and changes I went through during my teens. I experienced a great deal of anxiety during those years. The physiological changes taking place intensified my already nervous state. It felt scary, yet strangely familiar. It reminded me of that morning and of the sexual arousal I experienced. Of course the memory of it was on an unconscious level."

"It caused pathological problems that caused you to act out in a compulsive, addictive behavior. I won't go into details, Donna, but I will tell you this, Wanda knows your dad was a high-grade bastard. The counseling we're accomplishing helps your people as well as yourself. I'm putting it this way because this is the way you see it right now, and that's what is important. The thought of your people are seeping into your consciousness, and you're coming together in your thinking. You're doing a marvelous job. We need to stop here Donna. Our time is up. Great job!"

140

A Light In The Dark

"**G**ood morning, Donna. How's the last three weeks been for you?"

"Well, let's see. It consisted of working, sleeping, eating, working, sleeping, eating, oh yeah, coffee with my mom and an occasional time out with Georgie."

"I thought you were supposed to go to Oregon with Bill."

"I did go but that was just for a weekend. We left on a Friday morning and got home late Monday night."

"So, tell me, how did it go?"

"The time away was good. Oregon is beautiful but our relationship is not. I won't leave you right now. I need you more than I need Bill. Our relationship is a struggle and I've got a struggle of my own that needs to be dealt with.

What with my mind being in a state of absolute disorder most of the time, I just can't work on my marriage right now.

The rejection of my people is no longer possible. They surface into my consciousness and introduce themselves to me. Not as strangers meeting for the first time but as people who have finally decided to force me to admit to their existence. They don't want to be denied any longer. They want to be noticed, to be accepted. I know now, Dr. Boyd, they have always been interwoven in every area of my life. The only difference now is my acute awareness of their manifestation."

"The awareness is good, Donna, very good. You know that."

"Sometimes I wonder. This mess I'm in is such a painful thing. The constant confusing maze keeps me on edge. It's unsettling, irritating and I get afraid. The uncertainty of it all is exhausting. But, I do know that the ugly truth has to be revealed."

"What are you feeling right now?"

"That I'd like to runaway and forget this whole damn thing. It's a horrible night-mare that won't go away. It's taking so long. Why can't this thing be over?"

"It will be over. Trust me, someday this will all be behind you. Remember to keep your eye on your goal."

"I try to do that, I really do, but sometimes my concentration is so fuzzy that I can barely remember anything."

"Can you remember what you talked about in our last session?"

I thought for a few minutes and then, "yeah, my getting and being pregnant, my one-night stand with Bud, and what a jerk my dad was with my mom. I feel sad and boxed in."

"What does being boxed in feel like?"

"It feels dark, like I'll never see sunshine again."

"Donna, you can't change the past but you can accept it and move on. It's not a good idea to keep running. I know you wish your people were not there, but they are. You must have faith in yourself and your ability to overcome this affliction. Draw on that courage of yours, make it happen. You can do it."

As always, I needed to hear that. "I know your right, I truly want to be able to think for myself without so many other people in me thinking differently than I do."

"It can happen, Donna. It will happen. You're tired and vulnerable right now. It will pass. Again, I repeat, someday this will all be over for you. Remember, there's only one way to walk, and that's straight ahead; and, there's only one way to stand and that's on your own two feet."

"Boy! You really know how to give a lecture, and a damn good one at that. I want to believe you."

"Make your goal your priority, let it be larger than life."

"To reach my goal is my life. Okay, I can do it, that is, as long as I've got you to lecture me." I smiled at the doctor, and he smiled back. "Can I change the subject, you know, move on?"

"Absolutely!"

"I'd like to tell you about my son, the one born to me two weeks before I turned sixteen. He had cold black hair and lots of it. He was the spittin' image of George, with those high cheekbones and the Indian coloring. I named him Ray George, the Ray was for my dad, and, of course, the George was for my baby's father. I don't know why I gave him my father's name. I guess I was still trying to please him. My baby was never called Ray. We always called him Georgie. He cried a lot, so much so that mom had us take him to the doctor. I never did get all the details as to what was wrong. I left that to my mom. Caring for an infant was the farthest thing from my mind. I know the doctor gave him a prescription for Phenobarbital. The doctor said it would help him sleep. It did help him sleep for longer periods of time, but he was never a relaxed baby.

The psychological effect his birth had on me was destructive. The pain of his birth unconsciously set off the memory of the rape. It started an inner conflict too big for me to cope with. Wanda stirred so wildly in me. I could feel her coming into my consciousness. It was my self-destructiveness coming out, in bodily form. The blackness came after the terrifying fear made its presence. It engulfed me from within and without. The mythical belief I had conjured up as a young child, pain follows pleasure, overwhelmed me.

"Oh God! Oh God! Oh my God!" I cried out. Silently I said, 'I feel the pain, I feel the pain. Why does it have to hurt so much?' On an unconscious level, my thought was, 'Is this the pain of all pain, to make up for all the pleasure I've never been punished for? There has to be a way out, there just has to be!'

"There is. Let me take over." Wanda was talking to me from deep within my unconscious, "Letting me take over will stop your pain. You won't feel it anymore, I will."

"I was baffled. I didn't know what was going on. I knew I was in labor and that was it. I felt confused, dizzy, disoriented. I let Wanda take over, and the pain seemed to go away even though the labor continued, and, in time, my baby boy was born. Wanda was out and in control, and obsessed. My sexual activity up to this point appeared normal, but there was nothing normal about it. Yeah, I had had a crush on George and then Bud, but the experience of sex had given Wanda power to evolve. When the pain of child birth came, the door opened completely and the constant preoccupation with sex was a driven, persistent thought.

I couldn't wait to get out of the house, to be with someone. When Georgie was six-weeks old I asked mom if I could go out. "I'm so bored. I won't be too late."

"I don't know, Donna. Where is it you want to go?"

"Just out. I'll call Bonnie and see if she's going to Simon's. I need to get out for awhile."

"If you make sure Georgie's asleep before you leave, I guess it'll be okay."

"Did you give him his medicine yet?" I asked mom.

"No not yet. It's only seven. He doesn't get it 'til eight."

The hour I waited seemed to take forever! I fixated on what I wanted to do, but knew Georgie had to be asleep before I left. I called Bonnie,

"Hi. how you doing, little mama? Boy! It's good to hear from you."

"I'm a little mama alright. Are you going to Simon's tonight?"

"I wasn't planning on it. Why, do you want to go?"

"I want to. I need to. But I don't want to go alone."

"I'll go with you. What's your plan?"

"Come on over here and see my baby, then we can walk there together."

"Okay, I'll be over in an hour."

"That's perfect. Georgie will be asleep by then. You can take a peek at him and then we'll take off. See you in an hour."

I got Georgie ready for bed and held him while waiting for eight o'clock. Bonnie showed up in about an hour and a half. And with pride, I showed her my son. He was important to me, but something else was the driving force in my life and it was making me crazy.

Mom took the main care of Georgie. I am so grateful, Dr. Boyd, for all she did for us. I know now I wasn't being a total brat, as some of my family thought, nor was I being completely irresponsible. Not just a rebellious teenager. There was probably some rebellion in my behavior, but mostly, I believe, I was, as you say, deeply disturbed.

After giving Georgie his medicine, it took an hour for him to fall asleep. When Bonnie came, I showed her my baby boy and we left for Simon's. I hadn't felt so free since George and I eloped. Before the evening was over, I had picked out the man I wanted and he flirted with me. He got up from where he was sitting, walked over to me, and asked, "Do you mind if I sit next to you?"

"Sure, it's okay. Come on, sit down." We exchanged names and had some small talk, while psyching each other out. "Do you work, go to school or are you rich enough to stay home and live the life of Riley?" I asked him.

"Right now I live with a friend, I'm looking for work, and no, I'm not rich at all. How about you?"

"I've never held down a job, I don't go to school, and I'm not rich, not by a long shot."

"What do you like to do?" he asked. "Do you like to go to the show?"

"Yeah, I do, sometimes. Do you?"

"Once in awhile I do, when it's a really good movie. Would you like to go to a motel? And if the answer is yes, will you go with me right now?"

"Yes I do and yes I will. Let's go."

"Okay!" he said, with a somewhat surprised tone in his voice.

I asked Bonnie if she needed a ride home; she didn't. She wanted to stay at Simon's a little longer. She said she would find someone to take her home. And so, the animal instinct arose and, without thought, took charge. We stopped at a liquor store and he bought whiskey for us. We went to a motel, had sex and satisfied our out-of-control impulses. We drank whiskey straight with a water chaser and smoked cigarettes. We were relaxed with each other. We had put no judgment upon ourselves. We did what we wanted. There was not one feeling of having done something wrong. Not from me, anyway.

"Where you from, I haven't seen you around?" He asked.

"I had a baby a few weeks ago. I haven't gone anywhere for a long time. I live with my parents," I answered. "How long you been going to Simon's?" We were making an effort to make conversation, to acknowledge each other.

"Just a few months. I was born in Colorado. You from here?"

"Yeah, born and raised right here in good old California. What time is it?"

"It's almost one. Why, you got a curfew?" He asked and then laughed.

"Like I told you, I live with my folks and told my mom I would be home by twelve. When you live with them, there are rules to follow. We need to scoot on out of here. Will you take me home?"

"Sure. Can we go out again?"

"Why not," I answered. "I'll see you at Simon's."

He took me home. I did see him at Simon's, but I never went out with him again. Once was good enough for me. This was the pattern of my life for almost a year: one man after another." I paused, recalling those dreadful days. I got up from my chair, went behind it, and started pacing. That feeling of wanting to run was all over me."

"Donna, Donna! Don't run away from this, stay with it. You know how much sharing this with me will help. Please, come sit down!"

At the sound of his voice, I stopped pacing. I stood

there, gazing off, without really looking at anything. In a few minutes, I said, "Give me some time, Dr. Boyd. I need to get myself together." He nodded his head in agreement and waited for me.

"I had absolutely no regard as to what could happen to me. It was more of a detachment from anything or anyone, rather than disregard. They were not men that I liked or disliked, only things to ease my obsessive behavior. And, to avoid the unaware pain. After being with a man, I would feel so good, so relieved, but it would last only a couple of days, then the same old stress reaction would appear again. I guess in reality there had been no real satisfaction. I was totally lost in the maze of my inner life and the pain that surrounded it. I was blinded from the truth of my desolation. As the uncontrollable urge increased, I would seek out another man to relieve the obsession and the cycle started all over again. I lived in a world of illusion. I was emotionally unavailable to anyone, especially myself.

"Oh, Dr. Boyd. Help me to get through all this."

"I'll help you. You're helping yourself. Look, you're back in the chair and ready to go ahead. It looks to me you've got your courage back."

"It's been a long, destructive road. Maybe I am getting my head on straight. Dr. Boyd, those were awful years, I never, never want to live that way ever again."

"You won't. You're too aware to let that ever happen again. You're committed to resolving your problem."

"You know, I can be so down and afraid, feeling hopeless, then something happens. It's strange. I turn around and I'm feeling good again, courageous and ready for whatever is ahead of me."

"You have a strong desire to be well. You're receptive and insightful. I'm impressed.

"Thank you for saying that. I appreciate your faith in me."

"When you face your situation head on, progress is made."

"Facing Wanda is extremely difficult for me. She frightens me."

"Without a shadow of a doubt, Donna, you will never live like that again."

"Sometimes, Dr. Boyd, I get lonesome and I turn to my people for company. Is that okay?"

"Yes, of course it is. What you're telling me is you're aware of them. Are you aware of all of them?"

"Yes, I think so." As I said this, they all started to come into view of my mind.

"Yeah, and she tells you all about me, so you won't like me. That bitch, with a capital B. Oh, I forgot... I'm Wanda."

"You came to see me again. Good. Donna tells me what she knows so she can get well," said Dr. Boyd.

"Okay, you have your opinion and I have mine. Anyway, thanks for letting me blow off steam that last time I was here. It was good to have somebody listen to me. My mother pisses me off. Where was she when all this stuff was going on? It burns me up. She looked the other way and we suffered for it. Yeah, I'm crazy, whose fault is that? What would have happened if she had left and stayed away? We would have had a different life. But no, she had to keep coming back, so many times. Jesus, I wish things could have been different."

"You're feeling very angry right now, am I right?"

"Damn right I am. Am I to blame for what my father did?"

"Absolutely not! Talk to me about your anger."

"I don't understand why I tried so hard to please him. I

was so obedient to whatever he wanted to do to me. Why is that?"

"Your obedience was based on fear. You were a child that knew only fear and shame from your father's behavior toward you. Don't blame yourself. You did what you did because of your feelings of danger and apprehension of pain."

"Well, maybe," Wanda said thoughtfully. "What about my mom? She was never mean or hateful. Can you give me some understanding about her?

"Your mom was as terrified of your dad as you were. But she was more afraid of the unknown. Her life with your dad, as frightful as it was, was also predictable. She knew what to expect and learned how to cope with it."

"Oh," Wanda said, stopping for a minute to take in all that Dr. Boyd had said. "But she didn't protect me. If she had left him..." Wanda didn't finish, looking at Dr. Boyd for the answer.

"She didn't leave him. What happened happened, and now it has to be dealt with."

"What about Donna? She's ashamed of me, isn't she?"

"She's ashamed of the way her life was lived during those obsessive days. And now she's handling it in a constructive way, in a way that will help her move on."

"How do you feel about how she, ah... we... I lived?"

"I'm glad she wants a better way of life."

"You're okay, doc, you're really okay." And just like that, Wanda was gone.

"Hi, Dr. Boyd, it's me, Edith Rose. How are you doing?"

"I'm fine. How are you doing?" he asked.

"I just wanted to say hi and tell you I used to read the funny papers to Marge and Billy."

"That's interesting. Can you tell me more about that?

I'd love to hear what you have to say."

"They couldn't read and I could. They're older than me, too," she said, enjoying her time with Dr. Boyd. "I could read before I went to kindergarten."

"You could!? How did you learn to read?"

"I used to sit on my mama's lap, a whole lot. She would read to me and I remembered the words."

"That's wonderful. You're an important young lady. What else can you tell me?"

"I used to play on the ant hill with Donna. We watched the ants go in and out of the hole, and they would sting us. Mama told us to stay away from that old ant hill, but we didn't mind her. We liked to watch them. We hate spiders; they're so scary. I know Wanda, too."

"You do? What do you know about her?"

"I know Donna keeps her and me separated from the others."

"Separated? How does she do that?"

"All of us are in the black hole, you know, something like an ant hole. But she keeps us apart from the others. It's a safe place, where she can watch us all the time. She says she wants to keep a close eye on us."

Dr. Boyd leaned forward in his chair and said, "Thank you, so much, for telling me about the black hole. Can you tell me what it looks like?"

"You can't see it from the top of her head," Edith Rose meant from consciousness. "But inside, it's like… it looks like… I can't think of what to call it. It's like what a caterpillar stays in while it's changing into a butterfly."

"You mean a chrysalis?" he asked Edith Rose.

"I remember!" Edith Rose said with a happy lilt in her voice. "It's a cocoon. Is that the same thing as what you just said?"

"Pretty much."

"That's it then. It's a cocoon."

"Thank you for telling me about the cocoon. Thank you for sharing this with me. I appreciate it."

"That's okay," said Edith with her head down in a shy manner. "You're welcome."

"I think we need to let Donna come back now, but first, is there anything more you want to share with me?"

"Can I tell you something about my daddy?"

"You certainly can. What is it you want to tell me?'

"You already know my daddy was mean. He was emotionally abusive." Edith Rose said this with pride because she knew what emotionally abusive meant. She looked at Dr. Boyd with a sense of importance and then went on, "I tried really hard to stay out of his way. But if daddy had made up his mind to be mean, he always found a way. Now this is what I want to tell you, Dr. Boyd. I remember walking by him while he was sitting in his chair reading the paper. When I got right in front of him, he put his foot out and tripped me. I fell and got up as fast as I could. He told me, 'See, I told you! You're clumsy and stupid.' He just seemed to hate me."

"I'm sorry he did that to you. You're not stupid and you're not clumsy. Can you trust me enough to know I wouldn't tell you anything that wasn't true?"

"Oh yes, I can do that. I trust you."

"Good. Then I repeat, you are not clumsy and you are not stupid. Say that back to me, will you?"

"I'm not clumsy and I'm not stupid. I'm going now. Bye."

"Whoa! Give me a minute or two, Dr. Boyd. It's me, Donna." While waiting for the fog to clear, to fully come back to my conscious state, I felt no fear knowing I had switched with someone. "I see I'm sharing again today. I hope they left me some time to talk with you."

"Yes, there's time enough left. A couple of them came to see me."

"What do they say to you?" I asked.

"I'm not going to share that with you. You'll remember someday, when it's time."

"The old confidentially thing Huh?"

"That's a good way to look at it. You said you thought you knew all of your people."

"I think so, yes. Why? Do you want me to name them?"

"No. What I'd like you to do, when you get home, is write all their names down on this piece of paper." He handed me a sheet of paper with an oval-shaped thing with lines coming out it.

"What is this?"

"Write all the names of your people in this drawing. Number each one as you write their names along the lines of my drawing in the order that they came."

"Okay, I will," I said, looking a little puzzled. "I don't understand but I trust you."

"Your trust in me is helping you to let go of the fear and allowing yourself to connect with your people. Feeling safe is important. Allowing your people to express themselves is one of the keys to seeing who *you* are. It seems to me your people want you to know them. What do you think?"

"I think you're right." Up to now, it's felt like psychological warfare going on within me. It's been terrifying, but the fear seems to be subsiding. I'm not as afraid of them as I used to be."

"Your fear has been keeping you from the very thing you want."

I took the time to think instead of going off emotionally. "A lot of my behavior was done without thought. I was like a robot and that's not living at all. I want to live life in a healthy way. I don't want to be impulsive anymore."

"That's good, Donna. Your life has been very complicated, still is. How do you feel in regards to your people being a part of you?"

"I still see them as reflections of me but it's as if there's an invisible barrier that keeps us from being one person. You said it right; my life is still complicated."

"You're facing it more, Donna, and that recognition will help the integration take place."

"I am so grateful for you, Dr. Boyd. I've gone to so many doctors, and none of them could see the real problem. And now I have hope. I know I have a long way to go but I'll get there, I just know I will."

"Now there's an attitude that comes from a person that sees herself as worthy. Your self-esteem has improved considerably."

"I know it. It feels good. I'm beginning to see things differently."

"Overcoming the fear and accepting your truth is real progress."

"Your words of encouragement help a lot. I appreciate it. I've been thinking about Carol lately. I remember one day while I was in the front yard, I let out such a blood-curdling scream that my parents, who were in the backyard, thought I had surely been hurt, even hit by a car. I often had screaming bouts but this time it was ferocious. I had stopped screaming in my crib because of what he did to me, but it didn't stop me from screaming in other areas of our place. I screamed because Carol, like my bottle, would disappear and fear would come to me. In fact as I got older the temper tantrums increased. And this day, it was the scream of all screams.

When my father saw I wasn't hurt, that it was just

another tantrum, he told my mom she'd better stop me from ever screaming again or he would. My mom spanked me a good one. I don't ever remember her spanking me before. I learned that day that screaming was not allowed anywhere. I stopped the screaming but Carol was stronger than ever. After this incident I became more withdrawn, because when I stayed very quiet, Carol would talk to me. It wasn't talking like you and I talk, it was more like a gentle presence, very soothing, and it relieved the anxiety in me. There was quietness between us, a sense of being that didn't need words to express. We just knew we were in perfect agreement. She gave me comfort. Whenever I sensed her near me, I was so happy that I would giggle and we would laugh together. It was a warm and compassionate feeling. I hated going to school, because the disruption of school activities kept us apart. At home there were lots of times for Carol and me to be together. I was quiet in my happy world with her. Then that awful morning came and Carol went away. The pain was coming from everywhere and all the people came to me that morning, but Carol was gone, as was my quiet world.

"That must have been a wonderful experience for you to feel Carol that way." Dr. Boyd responded, keeping my mind on the joy of Carol and away from the pain of that morning.

"Oh, yes! It was. So many times, I would experience different feelings all at the same time and it made me very confused. But with Carol, it was just us. I never giggled out loud when my father was around to hear me. I didn't want him to see me being happy, because he seemed to love to make sure my joy was taken from me."

"When you felt all those different feelings at the same time, did it frighten you?"

"Very much."

"Your inability to process what was going on in you, as well as the dynamics in your environment as a child, was frustrating and confusing."

"Yes, that's exactly right. Even now, sometimes, the inability to understand all that's happening to me is difficult for me. But usually, if given the time, I will eventually work it out in my head."

"As a child, it, of course, was harder to understand than it is now. The confusion of your father saying, 'Do this, do that, or you'll be sorry,' must have brought on a bewilderment that overwhelmed you."

"Right, and when he said, 'Do what I tell you and you won't get hurt,' and I would do what he told me but would get hurt anyway, it baffled me. I would be lost."

"Is it possible, Donna, that you lost sight of what was reality and what was fantasy? Children do fantasize and maybe in your childlike way you build a place within your mind, in an effort to feel safe. What do you think? Could this be what happened?"

"Maybe that's what happened. I really don't know. I am aware that children use their imagination, but I'm not sure if that's what happened. I know I wasn't allowed to be myself. And, I know I didn't want to be punished. I tried everything I could to keep my dad from doing the hurtful things he did to me, both physically and mentally. Emotionally, it caused me a great deal of damage. Even the times in between were full of anxiety, almost as painful as the actual abuse. The waiting for the 'next time' was agony. Just seeing him glare at me was enough to set me off. To avoid him was almost my every thought. Not a nice way to grow up."

"Not a nice way at all. I wanted to ask you, Donna, did your mom always help you raise your son?"

"Until he was nine months old, Georgie's dad wanted

his brother and wife to raise him. I was running wild, so I agreed. I was not very faithful in staying connected with him. I don't see him at all, haven't for years. But I do believe it was the best thing to do for my son."

"Under the circumstances, I believe that it was, Donna. It's time for us to stop. Keep up the good work." We both got up to leave his office and he put his arm around my shoulders, walking out with me. I always felt a wonderfully warm feeling when he did this. "You're coming together, and it's wonderful to watch. See you next time."

Hidden Agenda

"You're looking gloomy this morning. Are you going to talk about it?"

"Bill's gone. He took all his things. I feel sad. I care about him a lot."

"Maybe he'll be back soon," said Dr. Boyd.

"I don't think so. This thing with me must be difficult for him. I believe he's gone there to live. He wants me to go up there to live with him, but I can't leave you right now. I need to get well. Relationships seem impossible for me. Bill is my third husband. I told you about George."

"Yes, you did. Dick was the name of the second one, right?"

I nodded.

"How long were you married to him?"

"I went with him for fourteen months. We were married for fourteen years, and I was single for fourteen years before Bill. Don't ask me to explain that setup, it just happened that way. Dick and I were truly in love at one time. Falling in love with him stopped me from running around with different men. I met him, wanted him, and had him. I thought that was all there was going to be with us, but I was wrong. The thing that set it apart from the others was our strong attraction for each other. We went out every night for a week, and I knew we fit together like two peas in a pod. A feeling of love evolved between the two of us and our relationship continued. We were inseparable from the start.

What made it truly grand was that this love flowing between us was stronger than any sexual need I had for other men. I was able to stop the one-night stands. I was aware only of Dick and our love for each other. I lived to be with him. I thought about him constantly, and, being so absorbed in him, pushed back any thought and feelings I had of the sexual addiction that secretly clamored to be in control. Toward the end of our fourteen months of dating, we talked about getting married. I wanted to marry him because I loved him, and because I was experiencing fewer, more subtle moments of the urges that had once preoccupied my entire being. This desperate need would make its way into my consciousness, and I would immediately push the feeling back, thereby denying their existence. Not knowing all that was going on in my subconscious made it impossible to live a normal life. I believed that if we married, I could control the sexual impulses. It wasn't going to be that easy. I was still secretly driven by an obsessive hunger.

It was only several months into my marriage that the conflict started up once again. It was a battle between two personalities, the one who wanted to be the faithful wife and the one who had to return to a life she couldn't do without. I struggled with this dual personality for three years. I was baffled as to why I wanted to cheat on Dick. We loved each other. He had changed his life for me, and I thought I had changed my life for him. We lived with his parents, because neither one of us were working at the time we got married. I had never worked before except to help my mom with the ironing she did for other people. We both got jobs soon after we married. I got a job at Ajax Hardware Company and Dick found a job at a typewriter company. He worked there for years.

After feeling antsy all the time from my inability to concentrate on much of anything except to satisfy my sick need, I started cheating on Dick. I would find ways to get away from him. I sent cards to myself inviting me to baby showers, Tupperware parties, insisting on my night out with the girls. Whatever I could come up with, I used, and it seemed to work. Or maybe, it gave him an out to do what he wanted. He had busied himself with playing pool and bowling.

The people I surrounded myself with were without morals; we were self-centered, caring about no one but ourselves. We knew nothing of commitment or of being trustworthy. Infidelity happened all around me. Even my mother in-law, or should I say, especially my mother in-law, Birdie and I ran around together. She loved going to bars, and we went together whenever we could find a reason to sneak out on our husbands. It didn't matter to her that my husband was her youngest son. It didn't matter to me either. I tried to live the honest, committed life and failed. As the obsession became stronger and stronger, I gave up and went with the sickness that was mightier than me. For one thing, I didn't give it a thought that something could be wrong with me. I just went along, following my instincts. I was a prisoner of a world I knew nothing about.

One of the nights Birdie and I had managed a night out, we went to a bar called "The Place." There was a new band playing and the bandleader flirted with me, and I flirted back. During the intermission he had drinks sent over to our table. I walked over to him and said, "Thanks for the drinks. I haven't seen you here before. How long are you going to be here?" I asked, flirtatious and seductive.

"For two more weekends, then we'll be moving on. My name is Earl, what's yours?"

"Donna," I answered. "It sure would be a sad thing if we didn't know each other a little better before you left. Don't you think?"

"I think it would be a dirty shame. Want to go somewhere when I'm through for the night?"

"Sure," I answered. Knowing he would be leaving was a plus for me. I'd go out with him once and then stay away from "The Place" until he was gone.

The drinks kept coming the rest of the evening, for both Birdie and me, compliments of Earl. He even dedicated a song to me. I was having the time of my life. I didn't know why I liked living this way, only that it gave me a high that is indescribable.

Wanda knew why, and she was in control. It seemed as if I was making the choices through the mind of a very sick person.

Birdie said, "If you're going out with Earl, you better call Dick and give him some reason for being late."

"What about you? What shall I tell George if he answers the phone?"

"Tell him I'm on my way. I'm leaving after I finish this drink."

I called Dick. He wasn't there; my father in-law

answered. "George, will you tell Dick I'll probably be late coming home tonight? A bunch of us are going out for breakfast when the bar closes, and then we might go over to my girlfriend's house for awhile. Birdie's not coming with us. She'll be home in a little while. Tell Dick not to worry. Someone will bring me home or I'll spend the night with my friend. "

"I'll tell him when he comes in. Did you say Birdie is on her way home?"

"She'll be home soon. She's finishing up her drink."

Earl and I went to a motel, but this time I resisted being with this man, not like it used to be, without any thought. I would get a vague desire to run out the door, then it would pass. The uneasiness of not wanting to be with this man, along with the sense of being held against my will, caused a feeling that someone else was in my body. Wanda and I were in the process of connecting with each other. Then it happened! Deep within my subconscious, I actually talked to someone: 'What are you doing with this strange man? I have a husband. I don't want to be doing this.' The apparent intruder that seemed separate from me ignored my words and continued having sex with Earl. When it was over, we dozed off and night turned into early morning.

I woke up with the bandleader next to me. I felt disoriented. My world had turned upside down. I wondered why I was here instead of in bed with my husband, my dear one. I got up to look in the mirror to see if I looked as bad as I felt. And, what I saw shocked me into a confusion that remained with me for several days. I saw two faces staring back at me, but only one body. There was a reflection of me, and there was someone else. She looked just like me, only she had black hair. We had never, ever been together as strong as at that moment. "What are you doing with this man?" I asked her. She disappeared without saying a word.

She had also been frightened when she saw the two of us in the mirror. There was no fight in her. She had been exposed and wanted out of this peculiar situation."

"That had to be a confusing, scary predicament, seeing someone with black hair and you with blonde hair. Goodness, Donna, how did you feel?"

"Bewildered, disoriented, confused, and yes, scared. I got out of bed and put my clothes on. I had no idea where I was; I only knew I wanted to get out of there as fast as I could. But then, Earl woke up and lifted his head and could see I was dressed. He asked why I was dressed and said, "I'm not through with you yet. Take off your clothes and get back in bed." It was a demand, not a request. And not knowing why, I did as I was told.

Like an obedient child, I did as I was told. 'What is going on?' I thought, 'Where is that other woman, and why am I being so passive?' It was Edith Rose who was being passive. She seeped into my consciousness. It was sheer fear that made Edith Rose undress and get back in bed with Earl. When Earl made the demand to come back to bed, the memory of that horrible morning with Dad surfaced, and Edith Rose was there looking for the woman I scared off. Both Edith Rose and I wanted Wanda to help us, to protect us. And because of Edith Rose and me, she returned to get us both out of this jam. I didn't want to betray my husband, and Edith Rose was having a panic attack that could only be calmed by the one person who had been with her since that awful morning. Wanda became the dominant one and got back into bed with Earl. They had sex.

Wanda had come to our aid. I was in shock. I had been awakened to a most desperate situation. Wanda was through with him. She had been with him once; that was enough for her. She had come to our rescue, and when the sex was over, she left. Earl told me to get dressed and he would take me home. Those were grateful words. It all seemed so unreal to me. All I wanted was to get home to feel some sense of security. I told Dick that the girl who was supposed to take me home was too drunk to drive the night before, so we stayed over until she was able to take me home.

My subconscious had reached my consciousness and awakened in me the split. For the first time, I had been exposed to the one with the black hair and Edith Rose as separate entities within my being. The revelation of these two was the most shocking thing I have ever discovered about myself. Up to then, that is.

A vague dissatisfaction lingered with me as I tried to live the life I wanted with Dick. Everything I came to know that morning with Earl was quickly forgotten. I had put it out of my conscious mind, but unconsciously, I began to compensate, to create a plan of action to stop the out of control behavior that I abhorred. In an effort to hide the ugliness that dwelled within, the plan to control Wanda and to prevent the outside world from knowing what lived inside of me began to take shape. I believed I had to hide this terrible secret, at all cost. 'No wonder daddy couldn't stand me. He must have known my secret all along,' I thought.

I learned that Edith Rose was gentle, affectionate, naïve and shy. She had clung to Wanda since the rape, and she experienced the nurturing she loved through the different men Wanda had been with. She also needed someone to hide behind. She had been through a horrendous ordeal that morning. After all, she was not quite six and a half when it happened. The fear in me made the decisions in my life, and I desperately wanted to be like everyone else. I saw Edith Rose as an opening to subdue Wanda. Finding out how sweet Edith Rose lessened my anxiety. She was not a nymphomaniac. Realizing this fact gave me the edge over the addiction. I was better able to control my shame by allowing Edith Rose to experience herself in the unconsciousness of my soul. What I'm about to tell you, Dr. Boyd, came from the logic of a twisted mind."

"What you're telling me, Donna, is that you have become so connected with these two personalities that you understand what goes on in your subconscious."

"It's unbelievable to me."

"It's not so unbelievable when you understand about the subconscious and the conscious. Tell me about it, Donna. I'm not here to judge."

"Okay, I will. Dick's brother, Lindsey had been coming on to me, and I with him. This started several years after my marriage to Dick. It remained only flirting for a long time, but when I discovered the two personalities in me, the plan was to go ahead and have sex with Lindsey to allow Edith Rose to experience the comfort she needed. Giving Edith Rose the upper hand would give Wanda less power. When Wanda exposed herself that, in itself, lessened her power, and I would rather have Edith in charge rather than Wanda. Wanda's power scared me.

"I didn't know what I was doing on the conscious level, it just looked like I was highly sexual and that Dick wasn't enough for me. I know now that my reality set me on a destructive path. I tried to hide my ugliness, and my choice led me into an affair with Lindsey that lasted two years."

"Why didn't you get counseling?" asked Dr. Boyd.

"Because, I didn't want to admit there was anything wrong with me. Even though I wanted to be a good wife, I didn't want to expose the life within. It was alright if someone found out I was sleeping with Dick's brother, but heaven forbid they should find out about my distorted secret life. Wow! I told you this was twisted. Keeping the secret was most important to me. Actually, I hardly consciously gave the life I lived much thought beyond wishing for it to be different. Lindsey's and my sex life gave us that high that comes from doing something forbidden. He gave me the feeling that what was going on between us, in that moment, was the most important thing in the world. It was easy to be with him, because his mother, my mother in-law, knew about our affair.

I didn't know how to change things. My consciously unknown world blocked my way. I feared that others might find out what was going on in my head. What was I thinking? What was the reasoning behind this way of doing things? I thought I knew. Nothing seemed to matter but to keep the secret, but the concealment of the secret was the very thing I needed to reveal. Neither my behavior, nor my dishonoring Dick, seemed a major concern. Keeping the secret, no matter what, was my priority: 'Don't tell anyone, or something bad will happen,' were my unconscious thoughts. Now I know why; it was because someone had told me a long time ago that I better not tell or I would live to regret it.

Wanda didn't like the confinement of fooling around with only Lindsey. She tried to rattle me. I was restless at times, and sometimes, I had a knot so big in my stomach that I thought the ache would never go away. But, I was able to call the shots, and she never beat me down. I pretended to be a good wife and ignored the other side of my life. There were so many ugly, scary, negative, and destructive thoughts that kept running through my mind. I was lost and unable to make my world happen the way I dreamed it."

"Donna, you certainly have had a struggle most of your life. It looks to me, that through the years you have kept up the fight, and it's helped you to become more and more insightful."

"I can see that, too, even though I didn't realize I was struggling, that there was even a fight going on. I eventually grew tired of the way things were. I lived with so much guilt and was unknowingly hounded by the many little egos trapped inside of me, each with their own needs and wants and opinions. I had no idea why I was so unstable or why the constant nervous stomach wouldn't go away. All this unrest, for some reason, led me to remember going to church as a child. I experienced good feelings during those church years.

I converted to Catholicism. My father in-law was a devout Catholic and was most pleased when I showed interest in his church. It seemed as if my conversion was on its way. I made a complete turnaround. I became strong enough to stop the affair with Lindsey. My marriage seemed to be going in the right direction, and I was, at last, living a moral life. I believed the life I had always wanted was happening. The happiness I felt was too loud for me to notice the underlying, unresolved issues. When a slight depression would set in, I would brush it aside as the impatience I experienced waiting for the day Dick and I could be married in the Church. There was some delay because of my previous marriage. We needed permission from some higher up in the Church. "This will take some time," said the Father.

"That's okay. I can wait." I said with excitement in my voice.

"The thing is, Donna, while your waiting you'll be required to remain celibate. According to Church law, you're living in sin with Dick."

Feeling somewhat discouraged, I said, "How long will it take? Three or four months?"

"It can take much longer than that, at least a year,

maybe more."

Even though my heart sank at his answer, I tried to remain hopeful. "I'll talk to Dick about it tonight." As I walked away, I knew I would never be married in the Church. I knew Dick would not consent to being celibate for that long, and I knew I would not lie to the Church. Somewhere within my soul was a person with morals. I continued to attend Mass but the energy of interest was no longer there.

The world came down on me once again. I wanted children but just couldn't get pregnant. Pressure began to build in me. Our marriage was going into our eighth year without children. I talked to Dick about adoption; he agreed. From this decision came a situation that brought about another personality. Joyce Jordan entered my internal world. She became my companion. She was strong and capable, and I was weak and unstable.

My sister Marge came to me one day and told me there might be a chance of my getting a baby through a friend of hers. The friend's husband had had an affair and got the woman pregnant. The woman he had the affair with was also married, and her husband had had a vasectomy. The woman confessed her affair and her pregnancy to her husband. Her husband told her he didn't want to lose her, but he would not be able to accept raising another man's baby. The woman agreed to give up the baby in order to keep the marriage together. When the baby girl was born, the biological father revealed to his wife what was going on, and they decided to raise the child. But when the wife saw the child, she knew she could not care for the infant without constantly being reminded of her husband's affair. She explained her feelings to her husband. And knowing how much I wanted a child, she talked it over with her husband and agreed to let the newborn come to me.

The beautiful baby girl became our daughter at seven days old. We named her Susan Marie. She was the love of my life. I was in my glory, yet I was extremely nervous, much more than any new mom would be. Now I know that the pleasure/pain thing I believed was a big part of my nervousness. But at the time, I only knew that she was special cargo, and I wanted everything to be just right for her. I just thought I was being extra cautious so as not to make any mistakes.

The biological father worked at the General Hospital, where he had access to blank birth certificates. He was going to fake a birth certificate for us to avoid the legal red tape of adoption. We never got that far. My world fell apart, my happiness short lived. When Susan Marie was fourteen-days old, Marge came to me with some very sad news. The biological mother wanted her back. She couldn't let her go as she thought she could, and when her husband realized how miserable she was, he told her to bring the baby home and that he would do his best to love her as his own."

"That's not all, Dr. Boyd. The police were looking for Susan Marie and had the wife of the biological father in jail, because she refused to tell them where the baby was. Good God Almighty! How do I get myself in these messes?"

"You certainly have had a lot of disappointment. Think of it as all behind you now. You're on your way to the good side of your life. How did you handle giving up Susan Marie?"

"I told Marge to tell the police what was going on and where the baby was. I was so hurt, but I knew it was the right thing to do. I had to go to the police station to sign a statement that declared I wasn't involved in a black market scam. As I was leaving the police station I began to feel the pain of it all. The pain would come and go like labor pains. My outer world began to shatter and the world within waited to see which one I would choose to relieve me from the tremendous agony I was in.

Once again I heard the words, 'I'll get rid of the pain if you give me the power.' It was Wanda, seizing the opportunity to return to her old lifestyle. I refused her offer. Instead, a new personality emerged. Joyce had been created for this particular job, and she was one of the dearest of my people. Her full name was Joyce Jordan, Joyce for the joy she would bring me and Jordan for the Jordan River that I had learned about while going to the Catholic Church. She was also the only one given a last name.

The pain of it all left me weak and vulnerable. The Church had let me down, my baby was gone, and my desire to cheat on Dick was stronger than ever. I slept all day, did very little housework, and was just plain miserable. My youngest sister came over and suggested I start counseling. She gave me the card of her therapist, and to my surprise, I called and made an appointment. Somewhere within, I had decided once again to rid myself of these obsessive thoughts that I had personalized in Wanda. I had a port of entry through this first doctor. I was over twenty-six when I started therapy. Boy! What a journey it's been!

As time went by the sessions helped me a lot, but I hadn't as yet talked about the urges in me. Finally, I said, "Dr. Weber the reason I started coming here was to stop the urges I have to cheat on my husband. I already have and I don't want to start up again."

"Were you promiscuous before you met Dick?"

"Yes, very," I answered. "I'm not proud of it. In fact, I'm extremely ashamed of it."

Then he said to me, "Between now and our next session, I want you to think about the first time you learned about sex."

"Oh, I've always known about sex," I answered as a matter of fact.

"No you haven't," he said. "No one is born knowing about sex. Someone told you or showed you."

After leaving his office I became restless and agitated. I was in a mental fog all the way home. It was four days later when flashes of pictures started jumping into my mind: 'Daddy, no!' My emotions skyrocketed, the fear in me intense. I put my hands up to my face to shrink from what I thought I was seeing. I wanted the images to go away. I shook my head until it disappeared. But a few hours later, the flashes would reappear. I went into shock at the sight of what I was seeing. It was my father and me, in his bedroom. We didn't have any clothes on. Oh my God, No! I could not believe it, would not believe it. I felt drained. I couldn't wait for my next session.

Finally the time came and I tried to the best of my ability to explain what happened.

"Let me ask you some questions. Will that be alright with you?"

I nodded.

"Are you telling me your father raped you? It was in the morning and you were a child. Where was your mother?"

"Yes, that's what I'm telling you. My mother was in the hospital."

"Do you remember how old you were?"

" Almost six and a half." At last it was out. His taking the lead was the help I needed to put the pieces together. I remembered a little more but was never able to recollect all the details. It didn't seem to matter. I remembered enough to move beyond the uncomfortable place I had been prior to the sessions. As I continued the sessions with Dr. Weber, the compulsive urge to have sex with strangers disappeared. I began to feel that sense of freedom I had always loved, and I believed I had conquered the monster within. I felt strong and confident.

But as we know now, Dr. Boyd, that feeling of freedom wouldn't last. But at that time, life was at it's best for me. Dick and I managed to stay together. We bought a three bedroom home. It was an opportunity for a brand new start. Unbeknown to me, Joyce helped me in my efforts to be a wife I could be proud of. She honored me, where as Wanda had caused me humiliation. Joyce could see the good in me, and because of it, I became more positive as time went by. But, the desire to have children still burned in my heart. Then something wonderful happened. Through the marriage of my oldest sister, Dorothy, I became a mom.

Dorothy's husband Jay had custody of his little boy and needed someone to care for him. Little Russell came to live with me on a room-and-board basis. We bonded instantly. I loved him dearly and still do. After caring for him for about six months, Jay was willing to let Dick and I adopt him. We went through legal adoption, and the whole procedure went without a hitch. I knew it was meant to be. I think of Russ as my very own, and my desire to be a mom was completely satisfied.

I continued counseling with Dr. Weber until his one-year internship ended along with our sessions. For awhile, things went pretty well, on the surface that is. Underneath, my people played havoc on my mind. I went in and out of a depression that eventually wouldn't go away. I experienced separation anxiety. I missed Dr. Weber and decided to call him: "Hi, Dr. Weber. It's Donna. Do you remember me?"

"Yes, of course I do. Are you okay?" he asked.

"Not really. Is there anyway I can talk with you? I sure need to! I've been so depressed lately."

I think maybe he heard the desperation in my voice. "I

have a minister friend that has a church pretty close to where you live. I'll ask him if I can use his office. If it's okay, I'll come out that way and counsel with you. How does that sound?"

"It sounds great!" And, the sessions started up again. I was delighted. Yet deep within me, there was another feeling, a feeling of dread, a desperate fear reminding me of the pleasure/pain syndrome I had been conditioned to. Another thing was happening. When I remembered my father raping me, on an unconscious level, my personalities tried to reach my consciousness. Their struggle to survive had taken a giant step. The unknown in me had no idea they even existed.

In the second month of our counseling, Dr. Weber informed me he would no longer be available. He said his busy schedule would no longer give him the time. "I talked to my minister friend, and he says he would be willing to counsel with you. Are you interested?"

"I don't think so."

"If you change your mind, don't hesitate to call him. His name is Pastor Anderson." And with that, he got up, gave me a big hug, and said, "Remember, Donna, it's always darkest before the dawn."

And it did turn dark for me. I was despondent for several months. I pined for Dr. Weber, as if I had lost a dear one after a twenty-year relationship. I was needy, clingy, and I had built a golden calf made in the image of Dr. Weber. I finally decided to give Pastor Anderson a call. We set up an appointment and I took my self-pity, the empty feeling in the pit of my stomach, and the ache in my heart and dragged myself to his office. I went to him several times and the confusion subsided. When I realized what a jerk I'd been regarding Dr. Weber, I also realized that what Dr. Weber and I had worked through in our sessions had not been in vain. What he had done for me would not be wasted. On the way home from my last visit to Pastor Anderson, I decided to stop the therapy and instead attend his church. I studied the bible and began to feel much, much better. For a while. My secret personalities had a power of their own. The secret itself provided the power, and they would not leave me alone.

The church Dr. Weber introduced me to was a great source of strength for me. I felt clean, so when the depression set in once again, I was baffled. I didn't have a clue as to why things kept turning sour on me. Once again, my world caved in on me and I fell apart. My house became a filthy mess. I left dishes in the sink for days and I didn't care. Indeed, I barely noticed. It had been months since I had counseled with Dr. Weber, and the clammering in my head only got louder and louder. My personalities wanted their freedom, each wanting to live in the consciousness of my mind."

"She came back again. Dr. Boyd, she came back again!" I said feeling anxious just telling him about it.

"Which one Donna?" he answered, sounding very calm, which is what I needed.

"Wanda, it was Wanda. After all the hard work of trying to get rid of her, to get rid of my urges, she came back. She talked to me, in a high-pitched arrogant voice. 'I'll always be here. You'll never get rid of me.' She said it over and over. And then, she would laugh the most vicious laugh. I hated her. She took my body without my permission, just like my father had done. I hated her so much that I lit cigarettes and put them out on my arms and thighs, where she had let so many men enter. She took my dignity away. Do you understand, Dr. Boyd? She took my dignity away from me!"

Dr. Boyd didn't say a word. I started to cry softly. "She

took my dignity away, and I was the one who experienced the humiliation…the degradation. It's such an embarrassment."

"Donna, dear, all I can say is let it go. Let it all go. It's over, it's done with. You're choosing life now. That's what matters right now. You're choosing life."

"I hope so, I really do. I don't want to be invisible anymore. I don't want anymore forgotten secrets. I want to be free from all this."

"You will be, you will be."

"I feel such shame. Sometimes, I can feel the rage along with the shame."

"Let me tell you the good thing about all this: some of the shame and rage your feeling is coming through your personalities, and that means you're connecting with your oneness with them. Do you understand?"

"Yeah, somewhat," I said. "I really hated it when she came back again. Yet, hating her gave me strength and enough sense to call Dr. Weber.

"Hello, this is Dr. Weber."

When I heard his voice, the stress blew out of me like a popped balloon. "Dr. Weber, someone's talking to me and laughing at me," I said hysterically.

"Donna, is this you?" I didn't think to tell him who I was.

"Yes, can you help me?"

"Calm down, Donna, calm down a little and we'll talk." I calmed down somewhat, and he said, "Can you see this other person who's talking to you?"

"No. She's inside my head," I answered. Hearing his voice continued to calm me. My heart had been pounding loud and clear, but became quieter as he talked to me.

"Where is Dick?"

"He's at work," I answered.

"Donna, I want you to listen to me very carefully. I want you to stay right where you are. I'm going to call Dick. He'll be home soon to help you. Now, don't go anywhere. Can you give me Dick's work phone number?"

"I won't go anywhere. I'll stay right here 'til Dick gets home. I promise." I gave him Dick's number and kept my promise.

Dick came home and put me in a mental facility. It was called Resthaven, located somewhere in Los Angeles. I was heavily medicated the whole time I was there. I was antsy and my concentration was practically nil. Most of the symptoms came from the medication given to me. It was a reaction called Extra Pyramidal Symptoms (EPS). EPS is the portion of the central nervous system responsible for coordination and integration of various aspects of motor behavior and bodily movements. When EPS is adversely affected by an antipsychotic drug, the symptoms characteristic of its function will appear, which are restlessness, inability to sit still, pacing, stiff mechanical gait, tremor, and fine quivering motions due to alternating rapid contractions, especially of the arm muscles. There are other symptoms involved but these are the ones I contracted."

"You must have read up on the medication they gave you."

"I did, after I got out. Whenever Dick or mom came to visit me, I could not hold a conversation or sit for more than a few minutes at a time. I would have to ask them to leave fifteen minutes into their visit. Mom even brought my dear little son, Russ with her once. I felt so bad asking her to leave after such a short visit. All I could do was pace back and forth. She said she understood. She is an angel, always patient, always gentle.

Not knowing it was the medication that caused the

reaction, I felt hopeless. I don't remember much of anything about those days. I don't remember talking to any other patients, and I vaguely remember talking to a doctor once during my entire stay there. On my ninth day there, I called Dick and told him I hated the place, to come and get me. I missed my son and I missed the familiar surroundings of my home, my family, and my friends. Within a few days of being home, the medication started to leave my system. I felt much better. I also found courage through church. I began to gain some inner strength and hope that maybe, just maybe, I could conquer this thing that would not leave me alone. I wanted to be healthy, and I wanted it with a passion"

"You don't have to tell me about your passion for wellness. You've got a strong dose of it."

"Boy, those were awful days. No matter how hard I tried I ended up at square one. It was like climbing up a high hill, and just as I would get to the top, I would roll back down to the bottom."

"You've done a powerful job, in spite of it all. Your personalities had to be exposed before you could get to the top of that hill and not roll back down."

"My life has been a roller coaster ride, one day feeling good, the next down in the dumps. But at least Wanda's under my control." As soon as I said this a frightening thought ran through my mind. "Has Wanda been trying to seduce you!?"

"No. Her passion right now is anger. Donna, we need to stop. Our time is up. Do you have that piece of paper I gave you last session? Did you write down all the names?"

"I do and I did." I reached into my purse and handed him the paper. "Thanks for all you've done for me. I appreciate it."

"We do it together. You are a survivor, Donna,

definitely a survivor."

"I know I could not do all this without you."

"Well, thank you." he said as I handed him the paper.

Painful Prison

"Good morning, Dr. Boyd. Those last three weeks just whizzed by for me. I can't say it's been all good or all bad, just fast."

"Do you want to tell me about the bad or the good?"

"Neither right now. There's something that keeps nudging me on. I think maybe that's a good thing. The unseen forces within keep nagging me on."

"She's gone, Dr. Boyd. It's me Joyce. I know she's been staring off into space lately. She's disturbed and turns to me when something like this happens."

"Can you tell me more about how she's feeling?"

"For one thing, writing down the names on the sheet of paper you gave her upset her a lot," answered Joyce.

"What upset her?"

"It was that oval-shaped drawing with the lines sticking out of it. She kept staring at that piece of paper until she turned inward and sensed a conflict. Something was opposing her existence, and she wanted to exclude herself from the clashing going on. She stepped back and let me come into her consciousness."

"Is she excluding or rejecting herself?" asked Dr. Boyd.

"She felt unreal and just backed off."

"Will you tell her for me that she doesn't need to feel afraid of who she is?"

"She sees herself as being safe when she disappears," explained Joyce.

"It's not easy for her, I know. She needs to be patient with herself," said Dr. Boyd.

"She feels different from others, I mean, from the people outside of herself. She still tries to deny the people within her, because it's something she doesn't want. I'll tell her what you said about being patient with herself, but not right now. I have to wait until she stops feeling unreal."

"Tell me about her feeling unreal," said Dr. Boyd.

"She wants to feel unreal, sometimes, to be nothing. She is fearful of 'being.' She says it feels so good to just 'be,' but then the fear sets in and the conflict of that pleasure/ pain thing begins to torment her. She can't seem to shake the belief in that."

"That fear is imbedded in her. It must be a terrible thing to live with," he said with understanding.

"Occasionally, she'll go for a long time without fear and seems to be over it, but then it comes back and takes over. It drains the life out of her and she crashes."

"Let's talk about you and what you know about her people. Will you do that for me?"

"Sure. Let's see. What I know is that Carol is always three, Beth was the same age as Donna when Beth came to be. That was twelve. Beth turned thirteen when Donna did and remains thirteen to this day. Susie was a teenager when she appeared and aged each year on Donna's birthday, but Susie is much younger then Donna. Then there's me. I was twenty when I became one of her personalities, and I'm always twenty years younger than Donna. Wanda's the same age as Donna. She's compulsive and mentally disturbed. I'm mentally healthy. Mary, Laura, and Mildred are ageless, what I mean is, they have no age. There like... um... like thoughts. Yeah, that's it. There just like thoughts in Donna's mind. Mary is destructive and very negative. Laura protected the place all of us stayed before you came along. She's gone now because she's not needed anymore. Mildred protects Donna when she enters consciousness. When we're all integrated, Mildred will be gone, because like Laura, her purpose will have been completed. Mary's the one to be careful of. She tries to get Donna to kill herself. She used to be harmless, when Edgar protected Donna from her. But now, in Donna's weakened state, Mary frequently comes into Donna's consciousness and tells her to solve her problems by ending her life."

"Where is Edgar now, when Mary comes around?" asked Dr. Boyd.

"He is starting to back off. He knows Donna needs to become aware of Mary in order to work through the self-destructiveness."

"I'm very impressed with your awareness of what's going on. You are well informed, and it's a big help to me," remarked Dr. Boyd.

"Thank you," Joyce responded in a dignified voice before continuing, "Edith Rose formed from the morning of the rape, she was six and five months. She never aged until you came along, and now, she is starting to grow up. Last but not least is Donna Mae. She was born with Donna on

September 25, 1931. Right now Donna Mae is extremely repressed because of her feelings of unworthiness. She's actually the one who brought the people into existence. After that morning Donna Mae formed from the split along with the others. She was brought down so low that she didn't want to be seen anymore."

"I have learned so much today. It seems they have all been given different abilities and different things to deal with." said Dr. Boyd with great delight in his voice.

"Yes, and as the changes are taking place, Donna becomes terribly confused. I am glad to be of any help I can." said Joyce proudly.

"Her very existence is threatened," said Dr. Boyd, as if thinking out loud.

"Truth be known, Wanda is the one who feels her existence is threatened. She feels rejected by Donna. She says Donna is trying to get rid of her."

"It's not Wanda she's trying to get rid of; it's the obsessive behavior. Wanda will remain, but the behavior will change into a healthy sex life. Can you tell her that?"

"You want me to tell Wanda or Donna?" asked Joyce.

"You two talk about everything together, so tell Donna. And tell her we will find the value in each personality, even Wanda."

"I'll try to tell Donna, but you know her big problem is fear, unrelenting fear at times, and it's hard to get through to her. What can we do about that?"

"What we can do is take the time to work through all the fear until it subsides enough for her to think things out. And when this happens, the fragmentation she's experiencing will begin to integrate. We have a long way to go, but I'm confident we will get there."

"That is very reassuring, Dr. Boyd. I must go, but before I do, there's one more thing. I forgot about John, both him and Edgar came to be that same morning. He is Edgar's companion," said Joyce hurriedly and was gone.

"Hello, Dr. Boyd. Guess who I am."

"Let's see, you're wearing black slacks and a pink blouse. I would guess, Wanda, but you usually wear all black."

"You're right, I am Wanda. The pink blouse is because Carol is with me, and her favorite color is pink. Edith Rose and Joyce are with me, too, but Carol got to pick out the pink blouse."

"How are things going with you?" asked Dr. Boyd.

"If you're asking if I am still pissed off, the answer is yes. I never realized how angry I was 'til I started talking to you. My father used me for his own sick satisfaction. He didn't care about my needs. He forced me to be what he wanted me to be, and by the time he got through with me, I was so twisted I couldn't see straight. Then when Donna discovered me, I was put away in that dark place with Edith Rose and separated from the others. Actually, it's not so dark once your eyes get used to it. It's lighter than ever, because Donna is peeking in. She's been allowing herself to, as she calls it, open up the spider door. More and more, she's curious as to what's behind it all. It scares the shit out of her to open it completely, gut-wrenching scared to be exact. I think she's afraid of herself. Maybe she thinks of herself as the big monster behind the door, or to be more exact, maybe she's afraid I'm the big monster and that if she opens it too wide I'll get out. I don't know what she thinks. I only know I've never been able to be myself, and that really makes me mad. Then there's Joyce. She calls me mentally disturbed. The know-it-all Miss Joyce. She doesn't know everything, she just thinks she does. Anyway, this whole thing is a catastrophe, if you ask me."

"It is indeed a catastrophe, and in time, we're going to

sort it all out. Your anger is justified, you know. Taking the time to talk about your anger means taking the time to feel and that's good, that's very good. What about your mom? Where are you with that?"

"I guess I'm still mad at her. If she could have seen the damage being done to us kids, maybe things would have been different. In spite of everything, I do love my mom but hate the way I had to live when I was a child."

"I believe your mom did the best she could, under the circumstances. And, I want you to know that you're every bit an equal with Joyce, not only Joyce but with all the others. Do you believe that?"

"I want to, I really want to believe I'm an okay person. I seesaw back and forth, and more times than not, I go back to believing the worst about me. I believed him when he told me I was his woman…and that morning, when he told me he just wanted to love me, between both those things, I just didn't know what to think. So, here I am, living with God knows how many personalities and only God knows when it will all end. When will it all end, Dr. Boyd?"

"I don't know, but I do know it will end. You must keep remembering you were only a child. There was nothing you could do."

"Why is Donna trying to get rid of me?'

"Listen to me closely: she only wants to get rid of her sickness, her addiction. She's not getting rid of you, she's working on becoming a healthy person and that will include, not exclude, you. Do you understand?"

"I think so, sort of. After I think about it awhile, I'll probably understand it better. Thanks for listening to me. I need to go, must share my body, you know."

"Hi, I'm Carol. Edith Rose told me to make sure to tell you my name. Do you like my pink blouse?" asked Carol, touching her blouse with all her fingers and looking down at it. "Pink is my favorite color. Donna had pink pajamas on when I started to be a person. I was the first person she made."

"I'm glad to meet you," said Dr. Boyd, "And, your pink top is very pretty."

"I can't stay very long. I wanted to see you because Edith Rose told me how nice you are. She likes you a lot."

"I like her a lot, too," said Dr. Boyd.

"Donna bought me a doll and she lets me play with it when there are no real people around. I always mind her."

"Is that the little nurse doll?" he asked.

"Oh no, that belongs to Edith Rose. We both have one. Mine's a little baby doll with a pink dress. I love her. I think I better go. Edith Rose wants to say hi. Bye."

"Good bye," said Dr. Boyd.

"Hello, Dr. Boyd. It's me, Edith Rose. Carol wanted to see you. I told her to go first, and then I'd take my turn. A lot of us came to see you today, 'cause Donna's not going to be here."

"Good morning, Edith Rose. I wondered why I was getting so much company today. Thanks for explaining that to me. Tell me, do you have a doll to play with?"

"I have a nurse doll. It has a nurse's uniform on. Donna bought it for me one day on her way to work. We stopped at a second-hand store. She bought one for me and one for Carol. We play with them when no one's around. Can I talk about my daddy?"

"You can talk about anything you want," responded Dr. Boyd.

"I thought he was going to be nice to me that morning, but he wasn't. He tricked me. He wasn't nice to me at all. He was very mean. Sometimes, he would stick his foot out when I walked by him and trip me. He would laugh and tell me how clumsy I was. That wasn't nice, was it?"

"That was not nice at all. Your daddy was wrong to be mean like that. The mean things he did to you were not your fault. Do you understand?"

"Yes, I wasn't the bad one, he was."

"Right. You do understand. You don't need to feel guilty, okay?"

"I won't feel guilty anymore. I promise."

"Good! No more feeling like your bad, and no more feeling guilty," said Dr. Boyd.

"Mama was always nice to me. I love her so much. She is sweet and gentle, and she hugs me a lot. I wish my daddy could be nice like that."

"That would have been nice for you."

"I think I need to go now. I like talking to you. I'll be back. Okay?'

"Okay," he said, and Edith Rose was gone.

"This is the damnest way to live! Do I have to be punished because Donna's got something wrong with her? This is not the way it's supposed to be. I want it to be only me. Why do I have to share a body with someone, anyway? It's not right, it's just not right. Oh, yeah, I'm Susie. Hello, Dr. Boyd."

"Hello. Are you upset about something?" asked Dr. Boyd.

"I am. I sure am. I came here to get Donna out of a mess, and now I'm in a prison and can't get out."

"You say you came here to get Donna out of a mess?"

"That's right. She was about to collapse when I came along."

"Can you tell me about it?"

"Sure I can. I'll have to go back a ways if we got the time."

"Tell me as much of it as you can. Don't worry about the time."

"I always worry about the time. I'm here one minute

and gone the next. It's so very annoying. Anyway, I'll get back to the story of how I was created. Donna got the number of a doctor Happy had started seeing and made an appointment with him. Of course, he wanted her to talk about the experience with her father. Well, that started a downhill decline in her health. She felt the anger towards her father, and in turn, that caused the panic. It is imbedded in her not to feel anger of any kind in regards to what her father did to her. She couldn't cry either. That old bastard taught her well. Donna withdrew into that nothingness, as is so easy for her to do.

This doctor, Dr. Elders is his name, put her in the hospital. It wasn't Resthaven; it was a place somewhere in Beverly Hills. He wanted her to have shock treatments, and she signed the permission papers. She told me about those shock treatments. That's not for me. Boy! That is spooky stuff. The electroshock involves the passage of an electrical current through the head and brain to produce unconsciousness and convulsions. The spasms of the convulsions are suppressed by a muscle paralyzing agent. You probably already know all about that." Dr. Boyd nodded in confirmation. "She stayed in the hospital until the treatments were complete. Donna said she started to feel better. She once again became strong and full of hope. It lasted for a year before she descended down into the depths again.

"Becoming herself has been a very difficult thing . It doesn't come easy for her."

"Learning to know oneself requires the different stages that occur during childhood and adolescence. It's a day-by-day process that needs parents who allow the child to evolve at her own pace. The environmental experiences provided, along with support and healthy stimulation, are vital in the child's life. This was not the case in Donna's upbringing. A child needs to be free from fear, to feel safe and to be able to be who she is without guilt. She was forced and molded into something she's not. It's not hopeless for her, not by a long shot, but much more difficult than most. Her personal will was taken from her, and now, she's attempting to find out who she really is."

"You really know your stuff. Donna did have to suppress her feelings, so I think what happened is she found herself a place to hide inside her head and let her personalities live for her. Maybe she felt too unworthy to feel or live in her consciousness. Donna liked the darkness, no one could see the real her. She believed she was safe, yet she lived with anxiety all her life."

Dr. Boyd smiled, acknowledging Susie's wisdom. "Good observation, very good," commented Dr. Boyd. "As a child, one learns self-worth, or lack of it. Donna became what she thought she should in order to be accepted. We are what we're taught, and a child's deepest desire is to be accepted and loved simply for being herself."

"I guess we understand her pretty good. It still doesn't stop me from wanting to be on my own. So, here we go with the rest of the story of how I came to be. Donna eventually hit bottom again and was put in the same hospital where she had the shock treatments. She hadn't seen Dr. Elders for several months. When she felt good, she'd quit going to a doctor. Dr. Elders wasn't available at the time because of an eye infection. After talking to Dr. Elders, his replacement suggested to Donna that it might be a good idea for her to stay at the hospital for awhile. She told me how beautiful and peaceful the place was. She said it was like being on vacation. There were no shock treatments this time, and she was allowed to do just about anything she wanted. Being on time for meals and making bedtime curfew were the only requirements. She needed the rest and said it was a blessing to be in such a tranquil place. She described the landscape to me; it sounded like a little bit of heaven. There were lots of trees and green, green grass. Donna said the grounds were very well cared for.

During one of their sessions, her doctor at the time told her, "Donna, when you leave here, you need to continue with your therapy. You have serious problems that need to be worked through, and it will take time." She told him it was too far to travel back and forth to his office in Beverly Hills. "I can give you a name of a therapist. He's an MSW in Whittier that will be much closer for you."

"Okay. Give me his name and I'll get in touch with him when I leave here," Donna told this doctor. When she got the phone number, she left. She was supposed to stay for two more weeks, but only stayed for eight days."

"How did she get home?" asked Dr. Boyd.

"Her car was in the hospital parking lot. The MSW, I think, means he was a social worker with a master's degree. She was on her way to her moms, because her marriage to Dick was over by then. There wasn't a chance in Hell for it to stay alive. The fear of Wanda was always with her, and Dick had become preoccupied with bowling, golfing, and shooting pool. She said she liked staying with her mom. Staying with her mom was good for her: 'It gives me someone to be with that truly loves me. Mom's never judgmental and has the ability to accept people right where we are in life, and that alone is a comforting thing.' That's what she said about her mom."

"Let me stop you for a minute. When you speak about Donna's mom, you say 'her mom.' Tell me about that." He leaned forward in his chair with great interest.

"I never think of Donna's mom as my mom. I came alive due to the dilemma that occurred between Donna and the MSW. That whole thing ended up a disaster, and the pain of it all brought me into existence. It always feels like Donna is my mom, and Dr. Lopez, that's the MSW, is my dad. That's just the way I see it. I only call her Donna because I've been taught to, ever since my beginning."

"I see," was the only comment Dr. Boyd made and leaned back into his chair.

"Something's happening to me, Dr. Boyd." said Susie with annoyance. "Someone is pushing their way through. I hate this! I hate this! It's not supposed to be this way."

A period of silence occurred, and then with head lowered, a voice came, "I can hear every word she's saying. It's me, Donna."

"I didn't expect to see you today. How are you feeling? I hear you've been under the weather."

"I feel like I've been drugged. I'm tired and weary. My stomach is queasy. Everything I eat backs up into my throat. Other than that, I'm doing fine. And, oh yeah, I'm totally stressed, worn out, and I feel as if I've been up for seven days and seven nights straight. So, are you sorry you asked me how I'm feeling?" I said, with humor.

"Your sense of humor seems to be intact," he said grinning that little grin of his. "I'm not sorry I asked you. What happened to make you go away?"

"I think it was that piece of paper you gave me, with that oval shape circle on it. I kept looking at it and I felt weighted down. As I stared at it, the inner part of the oval turned cold black and the lines you had on it, sticking out from the body part, looked like legs and they started moving around. I saw all my personalities in that black thing, and it freaked me out. The undertow of the burden set before me rushed into my throat, and the sounds of my personalities began to chatter among themselves. The revelation of what was going on inside of me, once again, surfaced up into my consciousness and a deadly fear gripped me. I dropped all resistance and opened myself up to the plight of my existence, accepting that which was mine to deal with. It took some time for me to get myself together again. And here I am, not in great shape, but nevertheless, I'm here to tell you the rest of what Susie was telling you."

"This looks like another breakthrough for you, Donna."

"I hate it when it comes so fast. It knocks me off my feet and takes awhile for me to come back to myself, whatever that means."

"It means you're becoming yourself. And, did you come back to tell me about another painful situation?"

"That's it exactly. Do we have time?"

"We'll take the time. Give me a minute to let my secretary know we'll be a little longer." He buzzed his secretary and told her.

I took over where Susie had left off. "I didn't make that appointment. I told myself I was okay, that I didn't need to be in therapy anymore, that I knew enough about my past and about myself to handle whatever came along. Consciously, I felt capable. I didn't know I would not be able to live a stable life until my personalities were known to me. I lived in an unknown prison, a painful prison. I decided to get a job.

"Mom, I'm going to see if I can find a job. Living on welfare doesn't give me enough money to be on my own. I'd like to get an apartment for Russ and me."

"I think that's a good idea. It would keep your mind busy, too. Do you know where you're going to start looking?"

"It will have to be near the bus line. I can't rely on that car of mine. It's broke down more than it runs. I want to be close to you, 'cause you're my best friend and I love you." I gave her a big kiss. "I'd like to work at that place that takes care of retarded infants. You know, that one I told you about, it's called Snow White Nursery Home." When I came home after applying to the nursery home, I was full of hope. "Guess what, mama, I'm so excited. I might have a job soon at that place I told you about!"

"That would be wonderful. I hope you get the job. I know you'd be good at taking care of those babies. You got a phone call, a Dr. Lopez. He left his number for you to call him. He says it's important that you call."

"Dr. Lopez? Who's that?" I said out loud. Then it dawned on me, "Oh yeah, it's that doctor I was supposed to start seeing when I left the hospital. That was three months ago. I forgot all about calling him."

"I think it would be a good idea if you made an appointment with him. He seemed really concerned and eager to help you."

"I feel okay, mama. Maybe it would help. I'll think about it." And I did think about it. It felt so good to believe I was doing fine without going to any doctor, but with Mom's encouragement, I called and made an appointment.

I went to him for three years, and I'm not kidding one bit, but that last year was a living hell. Unable to think for myself, I became an extension of him. He was a man that believed he had all the answers, so in his eyes, I didn't need to express any opinion of my own. I was back in that old familiar territory, the one that was not allowed to be my own person. I was lost once again and he became the dominant one in my life."

"In reality, Donna, you were still controlled by your father. Dr. Lopez was the outward expression of the inner fear of your father. Psychologically, your father was and, to a certain degree, is in you. This is something we need to work on."

"That may be true, but there was, ah, ah, *is* that part of

me that melted in the presence of one so sure of him self. As much as I hate to admit it, I liked being told what to do. I loved not thinking for myself."

"That is learned behavior and is difficult to break down. You were brain washed as a young child, and now in a very real sense, you need to be de-programmed."

"It sure hasn't been an easy task," I said, shaking my head in agreement.

"It's not easy at all," responded Dr. Boyd.

"Dr. Lopez always seemed to turn our sessions into conversations about sex. Like he would say, 'you need to get on with your life. You have a job you like and that satisfies you, but there are other ways to be satisfied.' I had gotten the job at Snow White Nursery Home and told him about it and about how much I liked it.

"You need to find someone who can give you emotional security, someone who understands you," he would say, "And it can't be just anyone." This is the way the sessions would go. I tried to talk about my son or my mom, what I wanted to do, and my idea of what my future should look like. But inevitably, he would somehow find a way to direct the conversation back to sex and how I needed to be with the right one. I guess I just wasn't getting it, and after two years of going to him, he said, "Donna, you need to be with someone who knows and understands you, sexually. Do you know who I mean?" I looked at him without answering, so he continued, "Haven't I given you understanding? Haven't I given you emotional security? Donna, you need me to show you what making love is all about." I was in shock. I was so disappointed in what I was hearing that whatever emotional security I thought he had given me came crashing to the ground. I didn't want to believe what I was hearing.

I had come to believe we developed a kind of

relationship that a daughter and a caring father share. And now, he had just told me he wanted to go to bed with me. Not only that, he wanted me to believe he would be doing me a favor. An uneasiness flowed through my body. I became restless; I couldn't sit still. The unknown stirred within me. Now, it's clear what happened. Wanda wanted to run into the arms of a stranger, not particularly this man, just any man and only once. Edith Rose felt the pain of betrayal again. Mary wanted me to take my life, screaming in my ear to end "all this turmoil" once and for all. But I didn't hear her, I only felt her because Edgar, the one whose function is to protect me from Mary, was doing a suburb job of keeping me from her. John was there, too, the one created for Edgar, to keep him from being lonely. All this was going on in my head at the same time. I was frantic!"

"Donna, Donna, stop for a minute. You're scared just telling me about it. Take some time to calm down. Take deep breaths." said Dr. Boyd, recognizing the fear in me.

Dr. Boyd was right. It was as if I was living the nightmare all over again. I took deep breaths and eventually calmed down. "The difference in telling you this time, is that I am aware of my personalities. Boy! I was so unaware back then."

"Can I interrupt you with a question?"

I nodded.

"Can you say something more about John and Edgar? Will you talk about these two personalities?"

"It's too uncomfortable to talk about them. Two males inside of me, that's just too unbelievable. I believe it, but I can't be relaxed with it. Maybe later, when I'm better able to accept them."

"That's fine, Donna, I understand."

"You know me. I need time to process all the amazing

stuff that pops out of my head."

"Don't worry about it. I jumped the gun and know it's confusing to you, for me to do that. You go on with what you wanted to tell me."

"Dr. Lopez devastated me when he told me I should go to bed with him. Any progress I had made vanished with him informing me that I needed to have sex with him. Instead of telling him no, I said, 'I want to go home now. I'll think about it.' I did not want to go to bed with him but I could not say no either.

The whirling in my head, the ache in my stomach, and the sadness in my heart started me spiraling downward once again. I ended up in the hospital. I no longer had insurance, so I went to the psychiatric ward at the L.A. General Hospital. I tried to concentrate but couldn't. I could only focus on Dr. Lopez. I made a desperate attempt to get in touch with him. My dependency on him was so intent that all I could think about was connecting with him again. He called, and when I heard his voice, it was like hearing my master. I felt relieved. I asked him if I could continue counseling with him and he said yes. I felt as if a load of bricks had been removed from the top of my head. I relaxed knowing I would see him again. What was this thing that had a hold on me? I didn't know then but with your help Dr. Boyd, I think I now know."

"What do you think you know?" He asked me.

"I took on the guilt of not wanting to be with him sexually, like I did with my father's advances. My thinking was in such disarray that I felt like a nothing for denying him. I felt victimized by the belief that he was more powerful than me, that I was not an equal and that he was the one who knew better than me as to what should happen in my life. He did have the power, Dr.

Boyd, to do great harm to me. He was supposed to be the wise one, the one to teach me how to live a healthy, productive life. Instead, I ended up with feelings of self-blame." I looked at Dr. Boyd to see if he agreed.

"You're becoming smarter than me," he said, smiling in approval.

"Well, I don't know about that. Let's just say I'm getting smarter than I used to be. When I was released I returned to him. I tried several times to discuss his proposition to have sex with me, but he would deny ever asking me. He said I was a very sick person and had probably misunderstood him. I kept seeing him. He set up appointments for once a month. Waiting to see him from one month to the next was unbearable. If it hadn't been for my son, Russ, and my mom, life would have meant nothing to me. They had become the two most important people in my life. Dr. Lopez was an obsession.

During one of my sessions, I again brought up the subject of us and sex. Again he denied it. "No, Dr. Lopez, you don't understand. You're right. We should go to bed together."

"I don't know what you're talking about, Donna. You need to quit this nonsense." The tables had turned. I was so confused that I became irrational. I started begging him. I would call him between appointments and ask him to have sex with me. On my days, off I would sit in the parking lot across from his office and wait for hours on end until he came to work. When he pulled into the parking lot, I would run over to him and ask him to be with me. What torture I put myself through. This went on for several months. He finally told me if I continued this kind of behavior he would stop our appointments altogether. It was too late; I was beyond stopping. I felt tormented, and in my eyes, he was the answer to stopping this anguish. The only way I believed it would stop would be to do what he had asked me to do. I continued harassing him until he told me he would no longer see me. I was totally controlled by the fear in me. The behavior increased. I'd promised I would leave him alone if he would just take me back as a patient. He absolutely refused.

One afternoon, I waited for him for hours to come out. When I saw him, I ran over and started begging for him to take me back as his patient. He clenched his fist and hit me in the stomach. I fell against the fence behind me. He hurriedly got into his car and drove away. I ran to my car and followed him until he was out of sight. When I could no longer see his car, I pulled over to the side of the road and sat there, staring into space. I remember getting dizzy, and then she came to me: "Let him go. We don't need him, he's a jerk. I'm here for you. We'll see this thing through together."

Susie is her name. She is vivacious, out-going and happy-go-lucky. She is a delightful personality, and I love her very much. Susie is a loveable teenager, and I am her mother. The pain stopped when she came. I was like a drug addict, and she helped me through the withdrawal and the emotional dependence I had toward Dr. Lopez. Susie is rebellious and arrogant at times, but she is also one of the most charismatic of all my personalities. She was just what I needed to get me through that ordeal. I never did see Dr. Lopez again, I never tried to. Consciously, it seemed the desperate need to hang on to him simply went away. Now I understand what was going on, on a subconscious level."

"Donna, I don't know what to say except that you are quite remarkable. What a life you've had. And now, you're changing it. How does it feel to know that you will never live like that again?" Dr. Boyd's remark made me feel good all over.

"It feels damn good. It feels even better than that. Thank you for letting me stay late." I truly appreciated this man.

Accepting The Many

"**D**onna, what's wrong? You're white as a ghost. Did something happen to you?"

"I remember something!"

"What is it?" said Dr. Boyd in a gentle, quiet tone.

"A terrible, terrible thing."

"You've told me terrible things before. Can you share it with me now?"

"It's just so awful. It's humiliating, degrading. I feel so awful about myself."

"Whatever you tell me, Donna, I will never believe you're awful. I've seen your struggle through the years and that struggle comes from a good person. Let's talk it through."

"Oh God, oh God! Why, why, why?" My head shook back and forth.

"Are you in pain?"

"Emotionally yes."

"Donna, you know, talking through the things that have been painful for you helps. It's been like a cleansing for you."

"It...it...it was during the time I was going to Dr. Lopez, dealing with all that garbage. I was weakened by all the stress. Everything I did seemed to take serious effort, yet miraculously, I held down a job, a job I loved, raised my son, and finally got an apartment. I should have had a good image of myself, but instead, because of what was happening with Dr. Lopez, my self-esteem was about as low as it could get. I started going to the bars. I dyed my hair black, thinking it would be fun to change the color of my hair. But, it was Wanda with the black hair. I met Al, a six-foot tall bartender with a gangster look about him. Wanda had found an opening through the low self-image I had of myself. But, this time someone else was with her. It was Edith Rose and they... they... oooohhhh, Dr. Boyd, help me!"

"Take your time, slow down. Remember deep breaths. I'm right here, Donna. Can you hear me?"

"Um, um, I do hear you... it was a humiliating life they lived. Edith Rose said she needed to be punished, that she was a bad girl and deserved to be hurt." I had to stop. I sucked in deep breaths, one right after another. Dr. Boyd could see the struggle going on.

"Let's stop right now and talk about Edith Rose's feelings, her feelings of being bad." He got my mind off of that which was too much for me right then.

"I know she's not bad, Dr. Boyd, but at that time, I didn't know anything except that as a child, I had feelings of being bad, and that through Edith Rose, those feelings would come back to haunt me. I was awakened to those childhood feelings during my sessions with Dr. Lopez. Memories from the past re-lived in my emotions. Those horrendous, irrational fears stayed with me constantly while I was counseling with him. I did what I always did in these situations; I detached myself from my consciousness in an effort to survive. I think I can tell you now what I need to say. I need to get it off my mind.

Both Edith Rose and Wanda met Al that first night at the bar. Al was the bartender, and was smitten with Wanda. He bought her drinks all night. Edith knew that men liked Wanda, and that Al would get jealous of other men looking at her and buying her drinks. Near closing time, in a demanding voice, he told Wanda, to "Wait for me until I get off. When I'm through with work tonight we're going to my place, so don't leave with anyone else." Al thought he was calling the shots, but Wanda had already decided to go home with him and Edith Rose always submitted to a demand.

Wanda and Al had sex together, which meant nothing to either one of them. Wanda went into the bar every night after that first time with Al and waited for him to get off work. He would take her to his apartment, and they would have sex, which was most unusual for Wanda. Edith Rose was prompting her. About the fourth night, Al asked Wanda, "Would you consider becoming a prostitute?"

Wanda gave him an emphatic "No!" No one ever said no to Al without paying the price. He was just like my father.

The abuse started that night, during sex. Al slapped Wanda in the face, hit her in the ribs with both his fists, and said to her, "Don't stop moving up and down little girl. If you do, I'll ruin that pretty little face of yours." He meant it and Wanda knew it. But, it was Edith Rose who would come out each night in Al's apartment, and the "bad girl" would get her rightful punishment.

"Why do I keep coming back to this shit? I'll get the hell out of here when this night is over and never come back." These were Wanda's words, baffled as to why she returned to Al so many times.

Edith Rose stirred and answered Wanda, "Because of me. He knows I'm bad and I deserve his punishment."

"No! Edith Rose, we don't need this. As soon as this night is over we're going home to mom."

"No, Wanda. I need to be punished, we need to stay."

I stopped talking and lowered my head. Dr. Boyd knew exactly what was happening. "Donna, stay with me, don't leave. Can you hear me?" I could hear him, but I made no effort to answer him. "You can do this, Donna. I want to hear the rest of what happened to you. Use your personal will."

My head returned to an upward slant. Dr. Boyd kept talking to me, "This is a choice you can make right now. Draw on your inner strength. Donna can you hear me?" This time I nodded and stared at him for a few seconds before telling him the most degrading, painful humiliation any of my personalities ever went through. "Edith Rose grabbed the power from Wanda and stayed with Al for six weeks."

"Dishing out pain during sex was the way Al enjoyed intercourse. He continued slapping her in the face and doubling up his fists to punch her in the ribs. But, the most painful thing he did was through anal copulation. He put Edith Rose on her stomach and put his hand over her mouth. Then he put the tip of his penis into the entry of her anus, and with full force, he would ram the rest of his penis all the way in."

Again, I had to stop talking to Dr. Boyd. I put my hands over my face and said, "Dr. Boyd, I don't want to stay here with you. Let me go, please. Someone else will finish!"

"Listen to me first, and when I'm through, then it will be your choice. I will accept whatever you decide to do. Okay?"

"Okay."

"I know you have unrelenting fear in you right now. I know this is extremely hard for you to tell me, and I also know that you've already been through it, a long time ago. And now, you're only telling me what you went through. Let me repeat, you're telling me what has already occurred. It's over. I believe in you, in your strength to come through with this terrible, painful situation. If this is as far as you can go, if you're recognizing your limitations, then I will respect your decision, whatever that may be."

I looked at this man that I had come to love and thought about what I was going to do. In a few minutes, feeling shaky, I went on. "He thought he was doing all this to Wanda, but it was Edith Rose that screamed under the hand that muffled the sound of the agony she endured. She truly believed she deserved the pain. Wanda would disappear when the pain came, she wanted out of there. She didn't like the way Edith Rose was able to take over. Wanda had already had him more than she wanted. Once was enough for her. It was Edith Rose that bled when Al did this to her. I think becoming aware of how sick I am is hard for me to deal with."

"That was then and this is now, Donna. You've come a long way. You're not that sick anymore. Dr. Lopez debased you until you thought nothing of yourself. And, Al did the same thing."

"My low self-esteem was more like a self-hatred. I believed I was unworthy of anything good. Those were awful, awful times."

Dr. Boyd and I were quiet for several minutes. We

soaked it all in. Then he asked, "How did it end, Donna?"

"How did it end? Let me think…after that last night with Al my car broke down, and it was too far to walk to the bar. I had gotten behind in my rent, so I moved back in with my mom. I continued working, which seemed to be a saving grace for me. Working with those babies took my mind off of myself. I was exhausted when I got home from work. It was all I could do to give Russ some of my time. Mom always fixed dinner for us. I would watch TV for a while before going off to bed. My fatigue was far more than tiredness from working. I was an emotional basket case, yet in all this weariness, the driving force that had given Wanda and Edith Rose so much power slowly subsided.

After the trauma I experienced with both Al and Dr. Lopez, a major shift took place. I changed for the better. I was more positive. I saw the potential in me, and I saw the need to be healed. Once again, unbeknown to me, the power of Susie was giving me these wonderful feelings about myself. I came out of the dark, the confusion was leaving me, and I knew what needed to be done. I needed to be quiet for awhile, to give way to my thoughts. I asked mom if she would take care of Russ while I was gone, and of course, she agreed. I took two weeks off from work and, because I didn't have the money to take a luxury vacation, I admitted myself into the state hospital.

While in the hospital, I gained some clarity. I realized my blessings. I had a compassionate mom, a son who meant everything to me, and a job that I really enjoyed. These were things to be truly grateful for. The desire to heal was strong in me, but there were many unknowns to me at this time. Believe me, Dr. Boyd, I had no idea all this was ahead of me."

"And you're doing a great job. Working through all this

is a giant step for you. Soon, all your personalities will be working as one."

"Maybe I can find some kind of harmony in all this chaos. You think?"

"I know it for a fact."

"You know, Dr. Boyd, while I was in the hospital after that Dr Lopez and Al episode, I put Wanda and Edith Rose in a clear dome within the dark place, unconsciously that is. In my mind's eye, this was the way I could keep a close watch on the two of them. Crazy huh?"

"No not crazy. It was your way of coping and, in your mind, staying safe."

"I guess," I said somewhat bewildered. "I know I left the hospital with a sense of hope and inner strength. I decided to enter college to satisfy my thirst for learning. I went to Mount San Antonio College (MSAC) and discovered they had an eighteen-month program that included a state board exam upon completion of the program. I was excited! I was going to become a licensed psychiatric technician. I enrolled in all the night classes being offered for this particular program. I knew eventually I would have to give up my job at the nursery in order to finish the daytime schedule. I was okay with that.

The time went by and I was content to live as I was living. My little narrow world of working and coming home to my mom gave me a safety net that was absolutely necessary for my emotional stability. I was around my father for only a few hours a day. What with my evening classes and day job, and his early-to-bed habit, there was little time for us to be around each other.

I felt proud that I was able to cope as well as I did. I became aware of my learning capabilities, and it thrilled me to know I could learn what was being taught to me. I was proving to myself that I was not a dumb bunny. I had created a sheltered life for myself. I felt safe and loved the feeling.

Two of my most positive, uplifting personalities, Susie and Joyce, stirred within my mind and would help me through my college days with flying colors. I made the Dean's List every semester. And now, here I am with you, Dr. Boyd, learning to overcome a mountain-high stumbling block."

"And I might add, you're going to make it, just like you finally received that state board license."

"You really think so? I pray I will become as free as a bird someday."

"Donna, your personalities are memories of the past, separated for the purpose of coping in your most difficult world. You're still wounded, but the healing of your wound is taking place. You will be free. You can bank on it. You can design your own future. I believe you've reached a point where the old coping mechanisms no longer work for you. You're intelligent, and I think you realize your personalities must integrate."

"I kind of know that. They've walked into my life, all my life, and now I need to walk into theirs and tell them, "No more!"

"That's great news, Donna. I am so happy for you."

* * * * *

The mystery of the complex, shattered world I had weaved for myself began to unravel. Ceasing to struggle brought me out of denial into acceptance of the awakening of my nightmare.

"Dr. Boyd, I feel so self-conscious about these personalities in me. It makes me feel like a freak."

"Has this been the reason for some of your resistance to them?"

"I think so. I've tried so hard, most of my life to be normal. But I can no longer hide the fact that I'm not. It's not easy to admit having MPD. In fact, it's embarrassing."

"Maybe if you talked about them it would help."

"What is there to talk about? They are here, inside of me, and I'm trying to face the fact of all this."

"Tell me what you know about them, about you and your involvement with them."

"I know I'm the one each personality has to come through, and that I'm the spokesperson. I detached Donna Mae from myself because, in my mind, she was not allowed to have her own identity in the real world. She then created the personalities in order to live through them."

"Do you know how she did this?"

"In all honesty, I don't know. What I do know is that we project what we see in our minds onto the screen of life. What she perceived in her world is the reflection of her own creation, and I created my own world with an illusion I accepted as real. The belief that I had to hide Donna Mae was my survival kit. I lived in constant fear and my belief system somehow helped me find a way to maintain my sanity. Does this make any sense to you? None of it makes sense to me."

"All behavior has a purpose, and you're telling me what your purpose is. It made sense to you at the time, but now you're seeing it as not so sensible. That is good. Your reality is changing."

"I, meaning me, Donna, is the conditioned one. My function was to hide my personalities and keep Donna Mae from the outside world. This conditioning took time, it happened day by day, bit by bit. My feelings of not being worthy of existing in the sunshine of this beautiful universe was the result of this conditioning.

The morning of the rape, I became adverse to pleasure.

The pleasure was the attention, the gentle touching, the kind voice, and sweet words to me. Then came the pain! The experience of that morning with my father conditioned my mind into thinking, 'Don't go seeking pleasure. Remember, there is always pain after pleasure.' I had come to my dad in childlike trust. Then the split! Donna Mae went in to hiding. I, Donna, was the one to conceal her. I think she sleeps among the rest of us, waiting to be whole." Dr. Boyd looked at me in complete agreement. My mind went to the others.

"I would like to tell you something about John and Edgar. As embarrassing as it is, I must admit these two young men do live in me."

"Tell me about them, Donna. It will be good for you to talk to me about them. Just the fact that you brought them up is a healthy sign."

"I feel a restlessness, a resistance to tell you about the young men in me, but I'll do my best." A few minutes of hesitation occurred before I proceeded. "Ah, their ages are unknown. I only know that they are both young, and John is younger than Edgar. Edgar protects me from Mary. In all her efforts, she was never able to overtake Edgar. He always lived up to his purpose, even though we had a close call. You remember, don't you? That was when you put me in the hospital."

"I remember, Donna."

I had to stop talking for a few minutes. Dr. Boyd remained quiet, knowing I needed to gather my thoughts, to process what needed to be said.

"Edgar is always good to me. I like him very much. He is able to reach the soul of me. He helps me get through the rough times by encouraging me and quoting bible verses to me, like 'All things are possible, only believe,' and 'I can do all things through Christ who strengthens me.' He is a dear friend. I am feeling uncomfortable right now. I feel silly."

"Do you feel silly or do you see these moments with Edgar as a private matter?"

"I think it's the latter. They're special times we share, and I find it difficult to share them with you. But I know its best, so I will. Edgar and I communicate in the nicest way. Sometimes I am so upset about everything—my personalities, my internal world, the ever constant conflict, my inability to cope, but most of all, the ugliness I feel because of it all.

Not one of my other personalities can comfort me like Edgar can. He comes to me in an ever so tender way and says, "Don't be upset, Donna. Everything will be okay, you'll see. Someday, you won't be sad all the time. Someday, you'll smile and feel the sunshine in your heart. I just know it." Things seem better after I've been with Edgar. He cares for me and loves to protect me. It's his job and he does it well.

John is different, he likes being a part of my internal world and enjoys being a companion to Edgar, but unlike Edgar he also likes the external world or I should say he liked the external world. Once, John strayed off his path and scared the hell out of me. He was able to reach my consciousness. He spent time with me when I was with my girlfriend, Georgie. He got a crush on her. At first I didn't understand what was happening. I caught myself looking at her face, she had beautifully flawless skin. Another thing I noticed, it was always me that opened doors. And, I preferred her company to Bill's.

It took several months before I realized one of the men was reaching my consciousness, using time I couldn't account for. I talked to Edgar, and he told me that John had been leaving him alone periodically, and entering my external world. I knew it was true, because I could feel the strong attachment John had for Georgie. *I had to stop him!* If he was ever able to take over my body on his own, as some of the others had, and if he found a girl to respond to his feelings of sexual attraction, I would be in a mess. Now for John to go with a girl would be perfectly acceptable, but in the process of using my body, it would be a homosexual act. And without a shadow of a doubt, I am not homosexual. My search was to find my real self, and for John to take over would not be a part of my real self. So what I did, Dr. Boyd, was in a language that only my personalities understood; I told John, in no uncertain terms, that his world was with my other personalities, especially with Edgar. I told him to accept what was, that his only purpose was to keep Edgar company. He didn't like what I said, but he also knew he would never become strong enough to take over my body. There was no reason for him to. I didn't need him anywhere but with Edgar.

He made only two more attempts to be with me when I was with Georgie. Once, when Georgie and I had finished breakfast at Marie Callender's, we both reached for the check. My hand touched Georgie's, and I could feel John stir within me, wanting to be with her. His last attempt was when Georgie and I were antique shopping, which we love to do. Georgie stepped into the shop first, and as I was coming in, I tripped over the rug at the doorway. She turned around just in time to put her arms around me to prevent me from falling. And John was there, enjoying the caress. After this he disappeared from my conscious world, submitting to his function of just being with Edgar."

Dr. Boyd made no comment about what I had just told him, except to say, "I see you're able to make decisions now rather than remain passive and let anything that comes your way happen. It seems you have a good relationship with Georgie."

"Yes, I do. She's my real live girlfriend. When I first found out about my personalities I told her and she didn't think I was nuts. We have fun together. I'm quite a bit older than her, but that doesn't seem to matter to her. We also work on the same unit. And yeah, I guess it does look like I'm beginning to use my personal will, sometimes." I changed the subject. I wanted to tell him about Laura, "I know something about Laura…"

"Donna. Donna, you've stopped talking. What's going on? Can you hear me?"

I could hear him. I wasn't changing personalities. I just couldn't explain to him about Laura. I could think it to myself, but for some reason, I couldn't find the way to verbally share it with Dr. Boyd. Laura was one of my protectors, especially designed to protect the cocoon where my personalities stayed. She never caused any disturbance within me, and when it was time for her to step aside, she did it with ease. Laura was wise and patient, and just at the exact time, not a minute before or a minute after, did she walk away from her purpose. Only when Dr. Boyd came into her life, and she knew I was in good hands, did Laura walk away. She drifted away into my being. Laura never spoke a word and never came into my consciousness as a single entity, yet she had a very important role to play. Laura left with the satisfaction of a job well done. But all I could say to Dr. Boyd was, "Laura is gone."

"Gone? Where, Donna, where did she go?'

"In to my being. We're one now. We are no longer separated."

"That is magnificent, Donna, absolutely magnificent!"

I saw the pleased look on his face and said, "It's a scary thing for me to give up the way of life I have made for myself. I have believed for so long that it was a safe, protective lifestyle."

"Could it be, that now, as you evolve you can see the prison you've made? That you recognize the limits you've put on yourself?"

"I can see that to a certain point but still hold back from going all the way. My personalities have always been there for me to turn to. And even though I know in reality it's a pitiful life, that I am unable to live life fully, I feel too fragile and vulnerable to give them all up. I know I have to deal with what is in order to move on to a better place."

"Your honesty will help you get there. Your willingness to continue will bring you more understanding, and understanding will bring clarity."

"Even though I have relaxed into a life that I accept as temporary, these people are very real to me." Dr. Boyd shook his head in agreement. "Susie and Joyce have weaved their life into my life. They were involved when I went to college. They go to work for me when I am too overwhelmed to go. I know they keep my appointments for me." Again, Dr. Boyd silently agreed with me. "They socialize for me, and even participate in my real-life family. Susie is full of life. She projects the youthfulness I never experienced because of Wanda. She's not like Wanda at all. Susie is healthy, sexy, vibrant. She is able to reach through to Wanda. They talk with each other. Wanda tells Susie about her sexual escapades, bragging about the days when she was in control.

"I was a wild thing, when I was in control." Wanda said to Susie.

"I guess you were alright. From all those stories you told me. Boy! That was wild."

"I found out I was looking for something that was never meant to be. I'm not as bad as Donna thinks I am."

"Did you like being with all those men?" asked Susie.

"Not really, it was more like something I had to do, rather than something I wanted to do."

One day, Susie broke some news to Wanda. "Do you know your father is dead?"

"Oh my God no! What did he die from?"

"Cancer, he died from cancer. Are you upset?'

"I am upset but I'm glad you told me. Thanks." Then she told Susie, "I'm relieved too. I grew weary over the years trying to accomplish the impossible."

"What were you trying to accomplish?" Susie asked her.

"I was trying to experience the love that came to us that morning. But Donna has told me that it wasn't the kind of love that should happen between a father and his daughter. I feel the sorrow in me, yet I also feel the freedom."

"I was a little afraid you'd be mad at me for telling you about your dad."

"No not at all. Let's change the subject. I've noticed Edith Rose doesn't seem to suffer as much as she used to, and I'm glad for that," Wanda commented.

"Why do you think that is? Is it because of the doll Donna bought her?"

"That could be some of it, and the visits with Dr. Boyd. Edith likes that man. She senses the gentleness in him. I see it too," Wanda informed Susie.

"I have to go, Wanda. I'm going to work for Donna tonight."

Susie was full of life, definitely a character, and even managed to have a short affair. He was a handsome six-foot black man, and a hunk of a man if I do say so myself. The chemistry between them was as hot as a blazing fire. I realized Susie's ability to take control was happening more and more. I also knew she was man-crazy, but unlike

Wanda in that she wasn't driven. She was just a teenager with strong feelings for the opposite sex. She was uninhibited and believed, like most of her generation, that having sex was a natural part of life. One didn't need to feel guilty about it. Susie also wanted to experience for herself that which had up until now been only stories Wanda told. In order to curb Susie's overactive hormones from becoming outwardly active, I decided to find a second job. I also needed the extra money. Life had been financially easier when Bill and I were together. Georgie already worked a second job, so I asked her, "Georgie, what do you do for your second job?"

"It's a facility for retarded men and women," she told me.

"I need another job. Do you think they'd hire me?"

"Sure, they're always hiring."

I put my application in, and the lady at the desk offered to show me around. As we entered the dining room, the woman pointed to a man and said, "That man over there is our day supervisor." By the time I took a look to where she was pointing, Susie had already spotted him. She just pushed me out of the way and I was gone. Susie was experiencing a sexual arousal and was ready to find out for herself what Wanda was talking about. She walked over to him and said, "Hi, my name is Donna." She hated to use my name but knew it was the way it had to be. "I'll be working here soon."

"Hello to you. My name is Rick. Be sure to ask for the day shift."

"I sure will, you can bank on it."

The office lady moved Susie along to complete the tour of the facility. I became frightened from the sexual arousal Susie was feeling. When I felt the arousal penetrate my consciousness, I wanted to avoid the pain that always followed pleasure. I made every effort to gain back the control, but neither my attempt to keep Susie in the subconscious, nor Joyce's intellect could compare with the strength of Susie. Her desire for Rick took dominance. She was so like Wanda in her desire for sex. She was as seductive and could look even sexier than Wanda ever did.

Susie started to work a week later. She also found out that Rick was living with a woman who worked at the facility as an aide. Susie was not about to let that stop her. She worked with Rick every chance she got, and they were drawn to each other.

"I'm going to brake up with Cheryl," Rick told Susie. "We've been together for a year now, and as far as I'm concerned, it's not working out at all."

"I've only got one thing to say about what you just said. If you ever want to ask me out, the answer will be yes." Susie wanted to let him know she was interested. "I work at the State Hospital from 3pm to 11pm, call me anytime. Here's my phone and unit number."

"You'll be hearing from me," Rick told her. He did call Susie a few days later. They talked for awhile then he said, "Will you meet me at La Fiesta's later on tonight?"

"Of course I will," she said, without a moment's hesitation. "I get off at eleven, I'll meet you there."

"Okay. Good deal, I'll see you there. Don't work to hard. Bye." He was as excited as Susie.

"Bye, Ricky. We'll have a margarita when I see you." She got off the phone and went straight to Georgie, "I've got a date with Rick tonight. How about that?"

"Wow, that didn't take long. You better tell me all about it tomorrow."

"I will. Let's meet at Marie Callender's before work tomorrow."

Susie went to La Fiesta's after work. Rick didn't show.

She sipped on a margarita for about an hour, waiting and watching the door. Finally she said, "I've been stood up."

The next morning she called Georgie, "I got stood up last night."

"You did!? What happened?"

"I don't know, haven't the slightest idea. I'm really curious as to why. I don't go to the facility for a couple of days. When do you go in?"

"I go in today for four hours. I'll ask Rick why he didn't show up."

"Let me know as soon as you know. Are you going to have time to go to Marie Callender's before work at the hospital?"

"Yeah, I get off at one. I'll meet you at 1:15, or there about."

I was there waiting for her when she came in. The look on her face told me something had happened. "Donna, Rick got shot last night. He didn't stand you up. He couldn't be there."

"Shot! What happened?" Susie was astounded as to what Georgie had told her.

"I'm not sure, but I think it had something to do with his girlfriend. He's in the hospital," Georgie said, a little calmer than when she had first told Susie.

"Oh my God! Georgie, let's go see him! Can you go with me tomorrow?"

"I can go with you," Georgie responded. "Let's go around 10:00 in the morning. We'll go in my car."

"I'll be ready." We finished eating and talking then we went off to work. Rick had been taken to the General Hospital in Los Angeles. As soon as Susie saw him she went right over to him and kissed him on the cheek. "What happened, Rick?"

"Give me another kiss and I'll tell you." It was obvious

that Rick was glad to see Susie. Without hesitation, she gave him another kiss, this time on the other cheek.

"Cheryl got into an argument with a woman in the apartment next to us. The first day we moved in, Cheryl and her had a disagreement. They never got along after that. They were always arguing about one thing or another. I tried to get Cheryl into our apartment, but before I could, the woman's boyfriend, husband, whatever he was to her, came out of the apartment with a gun, acting crazy. I scrambled like hell to get away, but before I could get into my place, he shot me in the back. So, here I am."

"Are you going to be okay?" Susie asked.

"I'm going to be okay, baby. Don't you worry. I'm going to give you what you want from me as soon as I get out of here."

"How do you know what I want from you?' Susie asked, looking at him with eyes full of passion. "What about Cheryl? She's not going to let you out of her sight."

"Cheryl and I broke up. I am a free man. Come here, I want another kiss and this time put it here." He was pointing to his mouth.

"I will oblige you, sir." And what a kiss it was! Susie thought, 'Boy, he's handsome. I wish he could call me by my right name.' "Will you be here long?"

"No, I don't think so, maybe for another week. I'll call you when they release me." Susie and Georgie stayed for a little while longer, discussing their work, then they left.

"I can't wait to be with him, can't wait," Susie said to Georgie on their way home.

"Tell me all about it when it happens, promise?" Georgie said enthusiastically.

"I promise, scout's honor."

A week went by and Rick called Susie. "Hi, Donna, guess who?" he said, with a cheery voice.

219

"Rick, where are you? You said you'd call and you did. I'm so happy to hear your voice."

"I'm at my mom's. Of course I called you, baby. I said I would, didn't I?"

"Is it alright to come see you when I get off duty tonight?"

"Of course it's alright. I'll be waiting for you," Rick told her.

"What about your mom, will she care?"

"It's okay. Don't worry, come on over. I don't live in the house. I'm living in the garage. I'm going to fix it up into an apartment. It's going to look good when I get through with it. Now be here, baby. I want to see you. I need to see you."

"I need to see you too." Susie thought her shift would never be over, and when it ended, she drove straight to Rick. He stood in the doorway of the garage. She walked up to him, and they walked together into his makeshift apartment. He kissed her passionately. Susie was delighted. He pulled down the garage door and led Susie to the sofa. They sat down and he started kissing her all over her face. Susie was in ecstasy. She had forgotten about the personalities, but they had not forgotten her. Joyce was trying to stop her because she knew I didn't like the idea of Susie being in control for that long. I, too, was trying to stop her because I knew it was an impossible situation. I was in torment, Dr. Boyd. I knew on a deeper level that we were all separate entities, but only one body."

"You were coming into the reality of your truth, Donna. This is a healthy sign. This will cause some trouble in the months to come, but I know that in the long run, harmony will come out of the chaos."

"Sometimes it seems harder than it ever has. They're like a bunch of ants racing to reach the top of the hole. You know, trying to come into my consciousness."

Dr. Boyd looked a little surprised at the comment I made regarding the ants. He only said to me, "So how did you bring it to a close?"

"It was difficult because Susie wasn't in torment at all. She was in her glory. She didn't even notice the attempted efforts to abdicate her from the consciousness of my mind. Rick was the only thing that mattered.

While they were sitting on the sofa—doing some heavy necking, hands all over each other, the heat rising—Rick stopped and moved away from her. He said, "Let's not get too aroused. The doctor said I would need time to gain my strength back and absolutely no sex. I'm so sorry, Donna."

'There's that name thing again. I hate it!' thought Susie. She was experiencing her first crush; she called it love. And though she was disappointed, she said, "I can wait, Rick. It won't be forever, but I can wait for as long as we need."

Rick and Susie saw each other several times over the next six weeks and waited. The garage took shape and looked more and more like a real apartment. Susie had quit her second job, because she didn't want to run into Rick's ex-girlfriend.

Finally, the doctor released Rick. "Be sure and come over tonight, baby. Tonight's the night," Rick told her.

"I'll be there. This is going to be our special night."

Rick walked out of the garage when he saw her pulling into the driveway. He picked her up and carried her to a cushy sofa. After giving her a kiss, Rick took her by the hand and led her to the bed. He kissed her softly on the neck, Susie responded by kissing him on the mouth. "You're lucky to be alive, Rick, you really are. And that makes me lucky, too," Susie said, touching his face gently with her hand.

"I give God the credit," he said, kissing her a couple of times with a great deal of passion. "Let's take off our clothes. It's what we both want." They did. Then he said, "I hope I won't disappoint you. This is the first time I've had sex since I got shot."

"It better be." Susie said, in a teasing, cheerful voice.

"No, listen, I'm serious. I don't know what's going to happen. Stay with me, baby. No matter what happens, stay with me."

"I'll stay with you, Rick. I'll stay with you forever."

Rick did not disappoint Susie. They made love. It was Susie's first time, and she was in heaven. It was not Rick's first time, he knew exactly what to do and did it well. It was over all too soon as far as Susie was concerned. They both felt good. Rick was exhausted. Susie was happy.

"This was not my best," Rick said to her. "It'll get better as I get stronger. I'm sorry, my love, I'm sorry."

"Rick, it was perfect. I'm happy and glad to be with you. I can't wait to be with you again."

"Okay, baby, but it won't be tonight. I'm tired and need to get some rest. Would you mind if we called it a night?"

"No not at all." Susie got out of bed, got dressed, and gave him a kiss good-night. "Call me on the unit tomorrow, that is, if you're feeling okay. I'll understand Rick."

While driving home from Rick's, Susie shouted out loud, "Rick I can't wait to be with you again." When Joyce told me about this, I was irritated and restless. Even though I didn't know exactly what normal was, I knew what normal was not and Susie had to be stopped. But how? I hadn't been able to stop her, and knew Susie was becoming powerful. Rick's being black was never an issue for why I wanted to stop Susie. He was a nice guy and seemed to genuinely care for Susie, not because Susie was experiencing sex outside of marriage, no, that was not a concern either. She was satisfying a sexual need with someone she cared about, not obsessive like Wanda. The reason to stop her was clear and simple: Susie was not a real person in the true sense of the word.

While I racked my brain as to how I was going to resolve this thing, I remembered Beth and was reminded of the incident with my brother, how Beth helped me out of that scary time in my life. Most importantly, what I remembered was that Beth was not sexually inclined. All men were brothers to her.

Rick called Susie within a few days after they made love, to tell her he wanted her to come over after her shift. Susie was on her way to be with him, once again. As she was approaching Rick's street, a voice from within said loud and clear, "You're not going to Rick's. Go home, Susie, go home." Susie was taken unaware. She had been so wrapped up in her own world that she had completely denied the existence of the personalities. The shock of Beth's voice did the trick. Susie immediately disappeared to where the others stayed. I had found a way to take her out of the real world, and that power came in the strength of Beth. Susie was gone, and Beth was driving towards home.

Seeing Beth take over was a bit of a surprise. I let her continue until I realized the deed was done, and at that point, I took over the wheel, I was back in control. Beth left without any problem. As I drove home, my understanding widened. I became fully aware that none of my personalities are real. They are blocks of thoughts that take on a life of their own. The clarity of the mythical community within let me know I was a stranger to myself. My personalities had a world all of their own within my soul that kept me from experiencing my life fully, on my own, without them. I was able to grasp the fact that Wanda has an unconscious goal to find peace in a distorted way, and that I had been hopelessly trying to find peace on a conscious level without knowing about the people. We needed to find the balance, to make peace with each other so that the conscious and the subconscious will no longer be enemies, but instead find the common ground. The one goal we all wanted was to live in the light of our oneness.

I saw myself as the overly protective mother that no longer needed to be. The best thing I could do, no matter how scary it was going to be, was to let my personalities reveal themselves but this time I would be aware of what was going on. I needed to validate and recognize my personalities as missing parts of myself. The belief that there is another way of perceiving life is seeping into my consciousness. And trusting you, Dr. Boyd, gives me the courage, knowledge gives me the logic, and my belief in a God that can do anything gives me the faith to go on."

"That is beautiful, Donna, just beautiful."

"Thank you. I happen to believe you're beautiful. The more I yield to the nightmare the less I know it is nothing to fear. To rid myself of the illusion of separation has become my primary goal."

"Donna, you've done more than accept the truth of your personalities, you've embraced them."

"Yes, I believe I have. Our time must be pretty close to over."

"Almost." Then he gave me the surprise of my life. "Did you know I am receiving letters from some of your personalities?"

"You are? How can that be?"

"I have received letters off and on for over two years now."

"Wow! I can't believe it! I know you're not lying. I'm just completely surprised."

"The letters have helped me, and I appreciate the help over the years," he said.

"I don't know what to say, Dr. Boyd. I just don't know what to say." The silence lasted for a long time but we had gotten used to these quiet moments, and I didn't feel uncomfortable when they happened. Finally, I said, "I'd like to read the letters. I think it would help me to better understand myself."

"I don't know, Donna. Those letters were sent to me to help you. Are you sure you're ready to handle it? You're doing so well. I don't want you to become overwhelmed. We need to go as slow as necessary. There's no hurry." He seemed to be a bit resistive to letting me read the letters but I wasn't ready to give up, not just yet.

"There's no hurry, you say. Maybe I don't see it as going too fast and I do feel ready to read them."

"All right. If you feel that sure about it, I'll get my secretary to give you the copies. Can you come back tomorrow to pick them up?"

"Yes. I'll set up a time with her." The session was over. I picked up the letters the next day and read each and every one of them in a single day.

Coping With Reality

"Boy am I glad to see you. Those letters were so puzzling to me. It seems so strange that they could be sent to you without me knowing."

"Those letters helped me get inside your head."

"That letter Joyce sent you, Wow! How long winded can anyone get?"

"She helped by giving me the details of your life before you were able to express them verbally."

"I'm not saying there's anything wrong with the letters. In fact, the writing gave me a sense of connecting with them, that I like. It lessened my isolation with them, deepened the unity."

"What else, what else do you have to say about the letters? Let's talk about them."

"There are only a couple of them that puzzled me."

"Which ones Donna? Let's discuss any of them that bother you."

"Well, most of them were from Susie and Joyce's diary. That was okay. The one about the people of ants, what's that all about? I brought the letters with me. Do you want me to read the one I'm talking about?"

"That's a good idea."

"There was no date on it, more like an information brochure.

THE PEOPLE OF ANTS BEFORE ENTERING THE DOOR.

Carol: function — replaces need for bottle (self-stimulation)

Edith Rose: function — a door to Donna Mae

Wanda: function — to comfort Edith Rose

Donna: function — to hide the people from the outside world. She's dying and knows it. Unable to hide the people anymore, must make decision to enter spider door

Joyce: function — Donna's companion

Susie: function — to take on normal role, can reach out to the outside world. I, Donna Mae, can hear through her.

Mary: function — now strong and will be stronger after spider door. Is negative prevention of pain, (take heed) Really dangerous at times. She will try to prevent me, Donna Mae, from entering spider door.

Laura: function — protector of cocoon. Me, Donna Mae, inside. (real self) need Donna to enter spider door to leave cocoon and live.

UPON ENTERING SPIDER DOOR.

Edgar: function — protects Donna from Mary. Donna denies Edgar, makes it harder for him to protect her.

John: function — companion for Edgar (Donna denies the two males inside her). They're only here to help.

Beth: function — to bring me, Donna Mae, through the spider door

Mildred: function — protector of the dog, difficult to explain this part. Donna is the dog in that she is what she is now because of her training, Behavior modification. Needs to enter the spider door to become human.

Donna Mae, I am Queen ant — I am heart and breath of all the others. Needed to protect self — reason the others came to be.

"And there it is. Now, tell me that is not weird."

"What part if it bothers you?"

"Next to my name it says I'm dying and I know it. I don't know it."

"Do you think you're going to die, Donna?"

"Not in the physical sense, not right now anyway, but I worry about what is going to happen to me when it's only Donna Mae."

"Tell me what you think is going to happen when it's only Donna Mae."

"I find it difficult to express myself. I feel self-conscious. But like I said, it's not a physical death, but a death of one that gives into the greater self. Carol was the first personality. To me this means that Donna Mae was a whole person before my personalities came. And yet, Donna Mae included herself as part of the whole. She sees herself segregated from the rest of us. I believe all the letters were written from the soul level and I also believe that all the honor, respect, integrity, loyalty, and decency are being preserved in the realm of the soul. The value of our worth will be discovered in the process of the integration, which is happening now. I know it's not completed because I still have time I can't account for. That means my personalities are spending time in my consciousness."

"Donna, you expressed yourself in a wonderful way. You just explained your thoughts on the ant theory and their existence. That's not weird. What are you afraid of?"

"I know something good is happening but what will I be when they're all gone?"

"According to the letters, everything seems to be made ready." Dr. Boyd reminded me.

"I know but I still feel nervous, very anxious."

"Could the fear be coming from your thinking that pain will come to you after the success of the integration?"

A light bulb went off when he said this, "I'm sure this is it. Will that ever go away?"

"Donna, that conditioning can take a very long time to get out of your memory. That is a brainwashing that is embedded in you and may be there for years."

"Thanks a lot for that bit of news. Your honesty can be very annoying at times. But, I do appreciate it."

"I don't believe it will remain as strong as it is right now. It will lessen in time, and may even go away completely, so don't be discouraged."

"That makes me feel a little better."

"What do you think was meant by using the terms 'before the spider door' and 'after entering the spider door'?" asked Dr. Boyd.

"I think it means she talks funny, only kidding. I've thought about that, too, Dr. Boyd and I think before entering the spider door means the indecision to open myself up because of fear. After the spider door means that when I do make the decision to finish what I started, those personalities on the list will be the main ones to help me. I don't see my personalities in a spider anymore. It's more like a cocoon they're in, waiting to be free. And I don't believe Donna Mae will consider herself a whole being until the integration takes place."

"You have the answer to your own questions. And, the ant scenario goes way back to when you spent time as a child watching the ants go in and out the ant hole. What do you think?"

"That you're absolutely right. It doesn't seem so weird when I think of it in those terms. The letters helped me realize that Donna Mae and I are merging. When Donna Mae signed her name to the poem I wrote, I knew it for sure."

"Did you bring that poem with you?"

"Yes."

"I liked it very much. Will you read that again?"

SATISFACTION
I do not understand the ways of God,
I only know He knows what's best for me.
He often comes to me in special ways,
And gives me wings to set my spirit free.

Free to fly into His loving arms,
Peaceful and quiet together just we two.
And when my spirit returns to worldly things,
My joy is total and complete because there's you.
Donna Mae

"It was signed Donna Mae but in that moment we were one and the same."

"Thank you for that," Dr. Boyd said. "What about

Mildred being the protector of 'the dog,' can you comment on that?"

"What I think the reference to 'the dog' means is the brainwashing I received as a child. It said, 'She is what she is now because of her training,' and after the integration I would be myself without the conditioning. Meaning, I would think for myself. And now just a little comment on Wanda's letter." I stopped talking and looked away, staring at nothing at all.

"What is it Donna? Share with me."

"I'm nauseated at that letter Wanda wrote. It's disgusting."

"Read it to me, Donna. Get it out in the open, so you can get it behind you."

"Okay, here goes."

Dear Dr. Boyd:

How do I begin this letter? Maybe by telling you Donna is beginning to trust you. And if and when I come to see you, you can know for sure that she trusts you completely. I'll tell you something about myself. I am Wanda, Donna's twin sister. We both had the same father, and I and my father were in love with each other. Incest I believe they call it. On the morning of February 19, 1938 we made love together. There wasn't any pain for me that morning, for you see, loving him the way I do, there was only joy for me in giving him what he wanted. Edith Rose was the one that suffered so much, and a big part of my going to bed with different men was because in someway it relieved Edith's pain. Also I was searching for the happiness I felt that morning, just being with him. I'm losing control now, if you ever see me, you'll know me. I'll be wearing black in mourning for him. Susie told me he's dead.

Wanda

"Reading this, literally makes me sick to my stomach. That letter, Oh God Dr. Boyd, how awful to say I was in love with my father. Why would I even think that way?"

"Because, my dear, you had a damaged mind. But you also had the insight to know you needed help. Are you okay?"

"I'm… I guess I'm okay. The others' letters aren't as disturbing as this one from Wanda. I think I'm going to puke up my guts when I get out of here. I know why you were concerned about me reading those letters."

"Just remember, that letter came from a sick person and you're not that sick anymore. You've done a great job of working through to the healthy person you're becoming. I'm proud of you. You're a real trooper."

"Yes I am. Thank you so much for helping me to see the positive in all this."

"Does that clear up the confusion?"

"It does, almost. The rest of the writings were little bits and pieces of what was going on, and that's okay. Like you say, they helped you to help me. Just one more thing, Donna Mae said something about Susie and Joyce being gone. I have to disagree with her. I've talked to Joyce in the last three weeks. It's been only once but she was still here. I don't know what she's talking about unless Donna Mae knows things on a deeper level, before I do, on a conscious level. And now, I know that you've known what was going on with me even before I knew, because of those letters."

"Yes, I did," he responded.

"The first letter, from Joyce, was dated April 1, 1978 and the rest expanded on to December 3, 1981. Over a period of three years wow, that's amazing to me! How that happened without me knowing is, yeah, amazing."

"It all took time to externalize. And now you are moving from isolation into oneness. The continued unfolding of your experience will bring you to your desired goal. Just keep going Donna, and you will see what I am telling you."

"I want you to know that I sincerely have hopes of being well someday. But I still feel uneasy thinking about them being all gone. I wouldn't have them to talk to anymore. I would be alone. I don't like that idea."

"You're starting to deal with a new situation that you have to get used to. You're out of your comfort zone and that can be extremely uncomfortable."

"You're right. I can feel the changes and I don't like it. I don't like it at all."

"You've been through some pretty tough times and come through it, and you'll get through this one, too. I think you've got things pretty much under control. How do you feel about it?"

"That it's going to be difficult but I know it must be. More than anything else, I want to be whole. I know there is something more to life than living like this."

"I've got a little advice for you. Relax and let Donna Mae come forth. Walk through the fear. Don't deny the fear, and when it comes just let go, let it happen and it will subside. You think you can do that?"

"I'll do my very best." I leaned back and rested in the chair. My head lowered and without any strain, Beth came. The first words that came out of her mouth were, "I'm a princess."

"Who are you, and what makes you think that?" asked Dr. Boyd.

"Beth, I'm Beth. My real father and mother came from a different country. My father's a king and my mother is a queen. They brought me here for the sole purpose of helping Donna. When she doesn't need me anymore, my parents will come get me and take me back with them."

"That story makes me smile," said Dr. Boyd.

"It's no story, really." She didn't get a chance to say anymore. Beth was gone along with her fantasy.

Then came Edith Rose. "Hello, Dr. Boyd, it's me, Edith Rose. You don't think I'm bad, huh?" She kept her head down and looked up through her bangs. "My daddy thinks I'm bad," she said.

"I told you, it was your daddy that was bad for doing what he did," replied Dr. Boyd, validating her presence. "Can you tell me which one of Donna's personalities likes to spend time with Donna's mother?" he said, deliberately changing the subject.

"There was a long pause before Edith answered. She was giving it a great deal of thought. Dr. Boyd waited patiently as he always did. "It's me. She rocked me a lot and read to me and taught me things."

"What kind of things did she teach you?" He leaned forward, showing a great deal of interest.

"She taught me a poem." Edith Rose smiled a big smile and repeated the poem.

"Roses on my shoulders,
	Slippers on my feet,
		I'm my mother's darling,
			Don't you think I'm sweet?"

She did this using all the antics as she said the poem, putting her hands on her shoulders and standing up to bring her hands down to her feet and putting both hands toward herself, looking oh so sweet, on the last verse.

Dr. Boyd was simply delighted. He leaned back in his chair when she was through and said, "That is a great poem your mother taught you, and you said it so well."

"I love her a lot. She likes to touch me," Edith Rose said, then she was gone.

I continued with what we were talking about before the

change: "You know, maybe I can get through this. No, not maybe, I *can* get through this."

"No maybes about it. You can do what you need to do to get where you want to be. I don't doubt it for a minute. Donna, our time is just about up."

"It is? Where did the time go?"

"We spent a lot of it talking about the letters," he answered.

"A lot of the time?" I said, in the form of a question. "Where did the rest of it go? Oh my gosh, somebody came to see you, didn't they?"

"Two some bodies," he answered.

"Will you tell me who they were?"

"Beth was here first and then Edith Rose."

"Well, that's proof, there's still some work to do isn't there?"

"We both knew that. Keep yourself busy, Donna. It will help you during the process of your integration."

"My job is going to be a blessing. I am better off when I'm doing something to keep my mind off of my personalities. See you in three weeks."

* * * * *

I tried to keep busy, but as hard as I tried, I couldn't keep my mind off my personalities. I needed to talk to Joyce, "Joyce, are you there?" Nothing happened, "Joyce can you hear me?" Then with much relief, I heard "I'm here Donna."

"Oh, thank God," I said. "I need to talk to you. Have you heard from Susie?"

"No, not a word," Joyce said.

"I'm gravely concerned about something. I think maybe I might be gone when all of us integrate. Dr. Boyd says everything will be alright but what do you think?"

"Well, I'm not too sure. I think you'll be okay. What Dr. Boyd told me is that we're all parts of the real you and that we'll live through you, but only as one person, and I believe him."

"That's all good and fine. But if all of you are going to live through me, where am I going to be? I'm really trying hard to understand how this thing is going to work."

Joyce, as usual, tried to help me. "I think I'm getting the gist of it. When we're all one, we'll be whole. All the parts of us will stay, only in your body."

"As one individual, is that what you're saying?" I inquired.

"Yes, I think that's it. What I know for sure, Donna, is we can trust Dr. Boyd. He'll bring us all together."

"Yes, he will. Thanks Joyce for listening and helping me understand. Is everything okay with you? I never think to ask you if you're okay."

"I'm sort of feeling out of it for some reason. I've not been wanting to be involved with the outside world lately. I seem to be content to find my place in you and stay there. I just now came out because you needed me. Now, I'm going back to where I belong."

Joyce sounded different than I had ever heard her before. I wondered if this would be the last time she would respond to my call.

Being able to talk to my people directly did me a world of good. I was always a little bit closer to that oneness I was seeking after a private chat with one of them. It helped me get in touch with my feelings.

I needed to spend some time with Edith Rose. There was something I wanted to tell her. "Edith Rose, I'm scared of you."

"Don't be scared of me. I don't want to hurt you," responded Edith.

"I know you don't want to hurt me, but you will if I take you into my being. Don't you understand, little one, that guilt, shame, and ignorance are the stuff you're made of. If I let you integrate with me then I too will feel those very feelings." There I had said it! It was tough to say, but I had to tell her.

"You already feel that way. By denying me all those years, you were denying your own feelings," Edith answered gently.

I, on the other hand, was on the defensive. "*I don't have to deal with this! I'm not stupid! All the doctors I've ever gone to say how smart I am.*" I said, very loud at first and full of pride, then lowering my voice as I went along.

"Okay then," Edith Rose went on, still in her gentle voice. "Let's take a walk back to when you first began to feel as if you were more than one person."

I thought back and couldn't remember ever feeling as one. Having two names to answer to gave me two identities from the start. I was a quiet withdrawn child, with episodes of rage that occurred without any apparent reason. Reality was a difficult thing for me. The way I was perceived by my father caused a shame that caused me to believe I was ugly and unworthy. I believed what my father taught me about myself and accepted it internally. To accept myself as my mother saw me gave me a much better self-image. I buried that which my mother had taught me, as if to protect my worth from being destroyed, but in the hiding, I also buried my remembrance of knowing I am someone to be proud of.

"You're right, Edith Rose, these feelings are our feelings. No! They're my feelings." And once I had owned my feelings, I felt the love I had for Edith Rose. She was not someone to be feared and no longer an embarrassment. I now knew there was no reason for her or me to feel guilty. I felt satisfied.

This whole experience was unnerving, to say the least. Carol and Edith Rose had been my night people. After the day was over and we were all tucked into bed, these two people would come alive. Both of them would bring out the dolls I had bought them. I gave them permission to get out of bed and get their second-hand dolls hidden in the closet. I had been in total amazement for a long time at Carol's return. The fact that I had forgotten her for so many years and then remembered gave me the desire to hold her ever so tight. I never made Edith Rose feel jealous. I would take turns holding them. I didn't want either of them to feel slighted or to think that I cared for one more than the other. As I evolved, realizing I was not responsible for my father's abnormal behavior and had accepted my own feelings, I could see how loveable Edith had been all along. And, Carol had never lost her innocence.

Although my mind was in a whirl, I kept close watch and was aware of lapsed time. This let me know that the missing time meant I was still not integrated all together. I could not get a firm grip into the one-self. I felt Susie's sadness and anger as she was put in her place. She had always wanted to be the only one, but it just couldn't be. I was making every effort to find a way to let Donna Mae come out, while at the same time I needed to feel safe.

It was indeed a most difficult thing to give them up. I fought the change taking place. I shouted out to them all, "You are all parts of me. Please don't think I am denying any of you! This is just the way it has to be!"

The days went by and I did the best I could to keep my cool. I knew the change would mean a new way of thinking, a new way of being. The unfamiliar was profoundly frightening to me. Coming out of my comfort zone was like pulling out everyone of my teeth without any pain killers.

If I didn't know I would be seeing Dr. Boyd every three weeks, I could not have handled it as well as I did. I hung on to the time when I could be in the presence of Dr. Boyd. He had come into my life just at the right time. Working my way through my fears, my shame, and my guilt had been a horrendous undertaking. Uncovering the layers of degradation, humiliation and the hatred for my self was in no way easy. The feelings of ugliness and worthlessness had been a hard, tedious struggle to overcome. It had taken years and I was still not through.

The day came for me to see Dr. Boyd, and I was thankful. There was something very important I needed to tell him.

"Good morning, Donna. You look concerned. Tell me about it."

"The last three weeks have been very long and very difficult. I feel like I'm in that dark space again. My stomachs in knots, sometimes it's hard for me to breathe. I'm nervous and anxious. I think the compartmentalized people living in me are getting less and less. Shouldn't I be feeling better, you know, with us integrating and all?"

"There's a great deal more to be accomplished. It's not like we have a roadmap to follow. It's a step-by-step procedure, just like it's always been. You have a goal you want to reach. We haven't got there yet. There are still some difficulties that remain."

"Well, I'm sick of it! Maybe it's a losing battle. What do you think of that?'

"I think you're feeling a little depressed. Are you?'

"I know I'm feeling crabby. There's something wrong. I feel alone and lonely. I hurt and my heart is heavy."

"Sometimes healing the mind takes a long time, especially when it's been as injured as yours."

"Is there no end to this? I feel so pressured.

Something's wrong!"

"Just relax now, relax Donna."

"I thought I was doing good. I thought I had control of my personalities. The integration has not happened. I don't feel safe without them. Maybe I don't want to be without them. The thought of them disappearing into nothingness is too uncomfortable for me to consider. I can't relax when I notice time unaccounted for. I keep thinking it's going to all go away pretty soon, that I have made the way clear for Donna Mae to come through. But it never happens. Do you know what's wrong, Dr. Boyd?"

"Donna, you sent me a tape through the mail."

I was shocked! I denied sending the tape. I yelled at him. "I don't want to hear you say that!" I looked at him with desperation in my eyes.

"I'm sorry, Donna, but you did send a tape to me, and you identified yourself in the tape as another personality." He looked at me with compassion.

I took some deep breaths and reconciled myself to the fact the tape had been sent. "Which one is it?" I knew in my heart that Dr. Boyd would never lie to me about something as serious as this, or about anything for that matter.

"It was none of the others. It was a new one." He answered gently, knowing this was disappointing to me.

"Oh, my God! I can barely tolerate what you just told me. Give me some time to process what is going on. I don't want to talk about it anymore today. I'm feeling angry, very angry, very afraid, and the emotional pain in me right now is making me dizzy. I feel so tense."

"Donna, I know this is devastating to you. I've seen you work so hard and I know this is a bitter dose of reality for you to accept. But I also know you can come through this. We'll work it out together, you and me. I'm here for you."

"It's agonizing, to be exact. My heart is so sad, Dr. Boyd. This has knocked me for a loop. I'm stunned. I think I'll leave now. I don't have anything more to say."

"I understand," he said tenderly.

"Oh, I do have something to say. I have something for you from Edith Rose and Carol. They won't be coming here anymore. They have merged into my being." I opened my purse and took out their dolls. "They asked me to give these to you. It's their way of letting you know how much they love you. They told me how much love and understanding you gave them. I thank you for that. They needed you just like I do."

Dr. Boyd welcomed the dolls because he's a gentle soul, capable of not only giving love but also receiving it. "I appreciate their gift. I know how much these dolls meant to them. Go get some rest, Donna. "

I was miserably upset, and driving home that day, I looked back at my ever constant struggle through the years. The memories of the pain, the fear and the humiliation of it all, had made it a long hard journey. Yet, I had survived up to now. Could I endure the fact of another personality coming into my life, just when we were accepting each other into integration? It felt impossible and I felt agitated. Nervous energy welled up in me, and as I drove into my driveway, I yelled, "*I want life, I want life. Do you hear me, God? I want life!*" I looked around to see if anybody had heard me; I didn't see anyone. I knew at this moment that life was not meaningless, that to live fully was in the heart of me. Accepting another personality took some time. It was difficult to say the least. Courage was slow in coming. In spite of it all, I found the strength to face whatever lay in the road ahead.

I resigned myself to finding out who this new personality was. By now I had learned that to expose the personality was the way to bring her or him under my control. My willingness to continue to the very end gave me the strength to take the next step. I knew I had been missing time, but I had assumed it was one of the familiar personalities. I never dreamed it was a new one. I decided to diligently keep track of my time. There were short periods of unawareness, not lasting for more than thirty minutes, and for only three days out of a two-week period. I didn't like this time lapse, but whoever it was wasn't able to cause too much trouble.

During the beginning of the third week, I was laying on my bed, staring into space, when I lost control of my body. When I came around to myself, I was leaving Dr. Boyd's building, heading for my car. I seemed to know exactly where it was parked. 'Oh my God,' I said to myself, 'This personality is starting to take over.' All the way home I concentrated as hard as I could, trying to reach the new one. That evening, doing my best to relax, with the help of medication, she came into view. It wasn't a new personality at all. It was Susie trying to disguise herself. Dear Susie, wanting so much to be the one who would conquer the others, as well as me, even if she had to hide behind a phony personality. Once this was revealed, it was over for her. Susie returned to my internal world. I couldn't wait to see Dr. Boyd to tell him the news. I was going to phone him but wanted two extra days to process all that had happened.

As the days went by, my mind cleared from the fear of it all and I was better able to think rationally. I saw the truth of it all. In reality I had never had them to talk to. They stopped me from being myself. They let me breathe for them and they used my body to exist. I was nothing in their eyes, because I was nothing in my eyes. Even with them, I was alone. The cocoon was dark, and I was there by

243

myself. The people were not real, just a mixture of the different ways I perceived myself and the belief in the separation.

I wanted something more than a make-believe world with people who can disappear at the drop of a hat, while another one appears. I needed more security than that. More stability than the shaky world I had created. I saw them for what they were. I had taken parts of myself and fantasized their personalities and made them real. Life size paper dolls. Walking, talking paper dolls.

* * * * *

"Hi Dr. Boyd. I am so happy to inform you, that new personality is not so new. I know who it is. It's Susie. She can't let go."

"Could it be, you and Susie can't let go of each other?"

"What do you mean? I want her to be gone. In fact, I'm going to tell her she has to go."

"Not so fast, Donna, it's not going to be that easy. You're both hanging onto each other! Think about it, right now. Are you two hanging on to each other?"

"Maybe. I really do want all my personalities to integrate. It's difficult, that's all. I do admit, I love Susie's attitude, her bubbly enthusiasm. She's so vivacious. I love her individuality."

"Are you forgetting she's a part of you, a reflection of who you are?"

"I do forget that. More work to be done, huh? Are you up to the task?" I said in a sort of humorous way.

"Of course I am and so are you. I heard Susie in you just then, in that last remark."

I smiled. "Yeah, I noticed it too. Dr. Boyd, there is a sadness to this integration process. I can't explain it anymore than that. I feel so sad and yet I want so much to know the me in all of them."

"I know you do and it's okay to feel sad. It's not only okay, it's understandable. Donna, I need to tell you something. Two tapes have been brought in and given to my receptionist by you."

A cascade of emotions went through me — anger, surprise, discouragement, fear and then determination. "I am not going to stop moving ahead until this is all behind me. No matter how long or how difficult it will be. Did I say anything?"

"Laura said, you handed them to her and told her to see that I got them. Good girl, Donna, for your determination. Remember your goal and stay motivated."

"This sure is tough, Dr. Boyd. I spaced out a few days ago, and when I came around, I was outside your office. You just explained why. I didn't go in because it scared the hell out of me."

"Old patterns are hard to break, but not impossible. You'll get through this ordeal. Feel your feelings when they come, express the feeling and talk it through. I don't have to tell you what you already know."

"Knowing you'll be here for me is so reassuring." I stopped for a minute to see him from my heart and thought, 'Do you know how much I love you? How much I would love to bring my hands up to your face and touch you? Can you really know how much you've done for me and how deeply I appreciate it?' I didn't say any of it out loud, I just let the beautiful feeling of knowing him go all through me. "Now what? What's the next step? Can we listen to the tapes?"

"Let's make this a short session today. I want you to take the next three weeks and, as much as you can, let the fear in you slip away. Allow yourself to feel your wholeness. Then when you come back, if you still want to listen to the tapes, we will. Do we have a deal?" I nodded.

Broken Wings

We listened to the tapes at the next session. When we were finished Dr. Boyd said, "What do we both know about these tapes?"

"That both tapes, even if she introduced herself with different names in each tape, were Susie," I said, proudly.

"Exactly!"

"It is definitely Susie. She sure does want to remain a separate entity."

"And what does that tell you, Donna?"

"I don't know that one. What?"

"I'm wondering if the integration is really taking place. Susie's still separate. What do you think?" he said.

I… think so… Maybe not… Let me think."

"Come on, Donna. What about the integration?"

247

"*I don't know about the integration, okay*!?"

"Calm down. If something else is going on, let's talk about it. Don't feel you're to blame if it's not happening."

"I've got nothing to say about it." I became quiet. Dr. Boyd waited. And then, "*No, no, no, I have not integrated*! I sincerely thought I was, but I'm not. It's a false integration. They have not become one with me, in a sense they are no more. I just have them huddled together. I learned how to control them, at least that's what I thought I had done. I truly believed they were under my dominion." There, it was out. I felt relieved.

"What do you mean huddled together?"

"I, ah, you know, my personalities remain inside of me. I keep a watchful eye over them. Oh! Dr. Boyd, I'm sorry. There is still a danger of them getting out. I try so hard, but it's just not working."

"I told you, Donna, you are not to blame. The healing process is still going on. Quit trying to get them to go away. Trying to get is trying to control. Let the residue of the past shake off, give it more time and just let it happen."

"I will. I'll be more patient."

"All you can do is deal with where you are right now."

"You know, I'm kind of tired. Actually, I feel exhausted. I think I'll call it a day. I have two days off, and I'm just going to do nothing and rest."

"Be good to yourself, Donna. I'll see you in three weeks. Call me if you need."

I was definitely weary. I felt agitated when I left Dr. Boyd's office. The tension in me was mounting, causing an apprehension regarding my personalities and the possibilities of them coming into my consciousness. My concentration and the ability to focus on any one thing became almost nil. I worried mostly about Susie, her self-preservation skills were the strongest of all my personalities. I hadn't felt so desperate for a very long time.

The next morning I called Dr. Boyd's office and asked him if he would put me on disability for awhile. "I'll put you on for six months, how's that?"

"Oh God, that's great. I feel better already."

Not having to go to work made life much easier. Yet, I was feeling a heaviness within me. Realizing what was in me had to change, that saying good-bye to my different selves was a must. Recognizing the situation and knowing what needed to be accomplished gave me the willingness to allow Donna Mae to flow up into my consciousness. Would it work? I didn't know. I was waiting for my appointment with impatience, causing high anxiety.

On the day of my appointment, the phone rang. It was Dr. Boyd's receptionist.

"May I speak to Donna, please?" she asked.

"This is me," I answered. I recognized her voice and my heart pounded.

"Donna, I'm really sorry, Dr. Boyd has had a family emergency. We'll need to cancel your appointment," Laura informed me.

"When will he be back?" I asked, staying cool on the outside, while actually tied up in knots on the inside.

"Not for a week, maybe longer," she said.

"Okay, thanks Laura. I'll call back in a week." I felt terrified. Panic hit me! I had been practically holding my breath for this day, to be with Dr. Boyd. I felt empty, and there was no one to help me. My personalities were nowhere around. I didn't know what to do. There was only me. A desperate thought came: 'I'll take all my pills.' I had just had the prescription filled. I stared into space and heard a reminder, 'It's the easy way out.' Oh God! Oh God! Oh God! 'Okay, I'm going to take the pills.'

I don't remember what happened in between the panic

attack and my decision to take the pills. The next thing I remember was me on the phone talking to Dr. Boyd's receptionist. As soon as I heard her voice I cried, "Laura, help me, please! I'm scared!"

"Don't be scared," She said in a caring way.

"I can't help it. I'm so scared and it won't go away!" I said in a quivering voice.

"I'll call the doctor in charge and he'll be right on the phone," Laura said.

"Okay, I'll wait for his call!" I said, still anxious.

Somewhere in all this, I had mustered up the courage to reach out for help and unknowingly made the call to Laura. A second after I made the decision to take the pills, I must have also become aware that I was worth saving and, at that point, the past no longer held its power over me. I chose life. Waiting for that very important phone call seemed like such a long time. But finally the phone rang.

"Hello," I said.

"Is this Donna Hunt?"

"Yes, yes it is." I said nervously.

"I'm Dr. Cunningham, returning your call."

"Yes. Thank you, doctor," I said, relieved. "I became frightened when Laura told me Dr. Boyd was going to be gone. I don't know why it scared me so."

"Can you tell me how you're feeling at this moment?" asked Dr. Cunningham.

"Listen to me, doctor. I'm close to coming out of my cocoon. I need to talk to Dr. Boyd. He can keep me from harming myself. I don't want to injure my wings! I really need him to see me through all this! I don't know what to do." He must have thought I had gone completely off my rocker. And, maybe he was right.

"How do you feel about going to the hospital for awhile? I think it would be good for you."

"I can't do that right now. My son, he's in the Air Force and coming from Sacramento to visit me for the weekend. I'm trying to keep it together for him. I'm going to pick him up in a couple of hours."

"Would you consider coming in on Monday. Will your son be gone by then?"

"Yes, I would consider that." The idea sounded good to me. I felt calmer just thinking about it. "I would be very willing to talk to you then, when my son's gone. But not 'til then."

"Can you find some time to talk to me tomorrow?" he asked, ignoring my last remark.

"That would be Saturday," I said.

"Yes, I know."

"I can do that. Russ will be visiting with his friends all day Saturday."

"Good, let's say tomorrow at eleven." His voice sounded nice and I knew I needed to talk to someone.

"Eleven is fine. I'll be there."

"Okay, Donna, I'll see you tomorrow.

"Thank you, doctor."

When I went to see Dr. Cunningham on Saturday, I was very emotional.

"Did you get your son home for a couple of days?"

"I did. He's spending today with his friends."

"You were very upset when I talked to you yesterday. How are you feeling today?"

"No better. I'm in the process of integrating with my personalities and I need Dr. Boyd desperately."

"I really think you should go into the hospital, Mrs. Hunt," he gently urged.

"I'm not opposed to that, but not until my son is gone. Tomorrow, I'm taking him to the Hotel Hilton. And then a limousine will take him to the airport," I explained.

"Will you come to the hospital Monday? Just to talk, Donna, so I can see how you're doing." I looked at him with suspicious eyes. "This is not a trick. You won't be forcibly committed, I promise."

"Okay, I'll meet you at the hospital, but if I'm feeling better I want to make the choice to leave or stay."

"That's agreeable with me. Do you have insurance, Donna?"

"Yes, Blue Cross."

"Let's make it for ten-thirty. And please feel free to call me anytime."

"Thank you." I managed to keep my anxiety under control for the weekend. In silence, I coped with the struggle going on inside of me. Knowing Dr. Cunningham was there for me helped calm my nerves considerably.

On the way to taking my son to the Hotel Hilton, I spoke gently to him. "Russ, I need to talk to you about something."

"What is it, Mom?'

"I have been very tired lately, emotionally exhausted. I've talked to the doctor and he wants me to go into the hospital for a couple of weeks. I'm thinking seriously of taking his advice."

"If that's what you need to do, Mom, then do it. I'll tell you like you tell me, be good to yourself."

He seemed so grown up. I assured him everything was going to be okay. We talked about life's complications but agreed that there was good in the world, and we wanted some for ourselves. We kissed as we parted and, as usual, without thinking, I said, "Be good to your self."

"You too, mom. Take your own advice." He had always been a great joy to me, and now as he was leaving, that same joy came to me. I was so glad that I had had the privilege of raising him. In spite of it all, he had turned out to be a wonderful son.

I packed a few things to take with me to the hospital, having decided I was going to stay. I left my suitcase in my car and went in to talk with Dr. Cunningham.

"Come in, come in," he said, looking a bit surprised, as well as pleased that I had shown up. "How are you feeling, Donna?"

"I feel tired, emotionally exhausted, and I'm afraid of being out there," I said pointing my finger toward the outside of the hospital. "I come from hard beginnings. I was fearful as a child and am fearful right now. And, I'm supposed to be all grown up."

"Do you think staying here for awhile will help you?"

"Very much so. I see myself in segments. I can't seem to solve the problems that plague me and feel safe in a controlled environment. It's what I need right now."

"Well then, we'll set it up for you. I've already let them know you might be coming in for awhile. Did you bring any extra clothes?"

"They're in my car. I don't want to be a victim anymore. I know that means more work on my part. I just feel so fragile and vulnerable. I'm so aware of my neediness. I hate this anxiousness I feel. Lately, it's with me all the time. I want it all behind me, once and for all."

"Good attitude, Donna. I'll show you where you can park your car." I signed all the necessary papers and was admitted once again into a mental facility.

The hospital was my battleground, and it was familiar territory. I felt safe, safe enough to let my personalities run free in my mind. I was aware of all of them and let them run their course until they knew it was of no use to try anymore. My hope was that the treatment I would receive while in the hospital would clear the way for Donna Mae to come forth.

The hospital treatment plan consisted of antidepressant medicine, as well as tranquilizers. The doctor explained I would experience hallucinations for the first two weeks, until my system adapted to the drugs. And hallucinate I did. When I woke up in the morning and opened my eyes, I would see one to three spiders crawling on the wall. Sometimes they were red and sometimes they were pink. On several occasions while taking a shower, I would look down at my feet and the water would become pink, like blood mixing with water. I kept staring at my feet until the water became clear. Strangely enough, I wasn't frightened. I would say to the spiders, "Go away, I know you're not real, Dr. Cunningham said so." After the two weeks I became more aware of my surroundings and realized I was in a Psychiatric Hospital. It was comforting. I needed to be here.

Dr. Boyd had returned one week after I had been admitted. His presence was so valuable to me. I was able to relax knowing he was back and would be treating me. I saw him four times a week. It was the highlight of my whole time in the hospital. I felt as if I was finally reaching the end of my personalities as separate from me. The negative condition of my past was just that, a thing of the past. I was becoming hopeful once again.

During one of my sessions with Dr. Boyd, he became ill. He leaned forward in pain and sweat was on his forehead.

"I'm going for help!" I said. I bounced up and hurriedly headed for the door.

"*No, don't! Come back!*" I did as he told me. I wanted so much to get some help for him but knew he didn't want anyone to see him this way. "I'll be alright in a minute," he said to me with his face squinched in pain. It took three or four minutes before the pain subsided. He leaned back in his chair, and without me even asking, he said, "I have a hernia. They want me to have surgery, but I don't want to."

"Why don't you want to?'

"Because I'm afraid I won't get up off the operating table." I knew what he meant. He was afraid he would die while in surgery.

"If you need to go in, you should." I was worried about him. I expressed a little anger. "You sure know how to give orders, but you don't know how to take them."

"Let's get back to you," he said. "How are you doing?"

"Okay," I said, knowing the incident was over and so was the conversation regarding it. "My personalities are really gone this time. I know it, I feel it. I've learned a lot about myself. Maybe my life will be better when I leave here."

"You can create your own future, Donna," he said. I did so want to believe him.

Seeing Dr. Cunningham was also a part of the hospital's treatment plan for me. Three times a week with him and four times a week with Dr. Boyd had given me the confidence for my future. The voices of my people had ceased to be. In my last session with Dr. Cunningham, he told me I would be discharged within the week. I had been there for five weeks. He also told me that Dr. Boyd was going to have the surgery he needed and would not be available for two months. He invited me to continue therapy with him while Dr. Boyd was healing. I decided to counsel with Dr. Cunningham while waiting for my dear doctor to return.

When I left the hospital, I promised some of the people I had become acquainted with that I would keep in touch. I had every intention of doing just that, but the bond between us in the hospital did not remain. Once I was on the outside, I let the past be the past and walked forward with expectations of good things to come. It was near impossible to imagine that the friendships we developed while in the hospital would ever end. We had been in a different world in the hospital, and as we entered the outside world, our need for each other was over.

Nothing seemed the same outside the hospital as it did when I entered. I felt the aloneness. There was an empty space where my personalities once had been, and the thought of not seeing Dr. Boyd for two months pained me. In the first place, I didn't know how to be normal. It actually seemed like a dreary way to live. There had been a certain hype involved in the sickness. What I needed was to complete my therapy with Dr. Boyd. Switching over to another doctor was difficult for me but I knew it was best to continue with Dr. Cunningham until Dr. Boyd came back.

"Dr. Cunningham, I'm so insecure with this new way of living. That old belief system keeps trying to take charge. It's familiar ground and I'm definitely not in my comfort zone. I want to move forward but I'm nervous and uncomfortable. I'm afraid of the unknown."

"It will take time, Donna. It's something you'll get used to as time goes by."

"I'm sure you're right. I thought it would be better, right away. I guess I want instant happiness. But it doesn't work that way, does it?"

"No, it certainly doesn't."

"I'll be glad when Dr. Boyd gets back. It's not that I don't like you. It's just that we've been working on my problem for years now, and I'm really bonded to him.

"I know and I understand," was all he said. I wanted to ask him how Dr. Boyd was doing, but for some reason, I didn't. I just kept waiting for him to return.

I always kept my appointments with Dr. Cunningham. Talking to him did help the waiting to go by. In between sessions, I visited a lot with my mom. She had always been the great comforter. I was still on disability and needed to be. There was a kind of grieving going on with me without Dr. Boyd.

"Good morning, Donna. How are things going with you?" Dr. Cunningham said.

"I'm a little depressed. I'm finding it hard to concentrate. I feel helpless and angry."

"Let's talk about your anger."

"Well… I'm angry, that's all. Strange as it may seem, I'm angry with my people. They're gone and it makes me mad. They always helped me when I was in trouble. I miss them, I miss Dr. Boyd. I'm just plain miserable and uncomfortable with the newness of things. I don't know what to do. I just don't know what to do."

"It will take time to adjust to your integration. It's a new way of being, of thinking. Be patient with yourself and things will turn around for you."

"I tell myself that very same thing. And I'm positive for a time, but then depression sets in again. I try to see where my people used to be and I see nothing. It's like an empty tomb. I don't know what to do." I repeated.

"I know you don't." He really was a nice doctor, but I had the feeling that sometimes he didn't know what to do either.

"I feel scared. I search my soul for Donna Mae and she doesn't seem to be anywhere around. Nobody knows me better than Dr. Boyd. I'll just wait until he comes back to help me. You know, Donna Mae has been in a dark place most of her life. She said it would be scary coming out and she's right. It's the scariest thing I've encountered in a long time."

"Donna, you don't have to search for Donna Mae anymore. You are Donna Mae. Do you understand?"

"Maybe I don't understand… what I mean is, I do understand, I think. I don't want to talk about it anymore until I can see Dr. Boyd."

"Fair enough. What about the positive side? Can you come up with the good things going on in your life?"

"Maybe, if I think real hard." I could hear the resistance in my voice.

"Give it a try. I know there's something you can be glad about."

""'I'm free to be me. What ever that means. how's that?"

"It's a start. What else?"

"I can make plans without my personalities interfering. I don't have to hide behind them anymore."

"Now see, there is good coming from all this struggling you've had to deal with. And, I know there must be many more reasons to be glad."

"Yes, there is, there's you putting up with me while I wait for my favorite doctor." I smiled, realizing how much he was trying to help me.

"I understand, Donna," he said, smiling back.

Finally, the positive side of me was coming through the negative and I began to believe in myself. I accepted the fact that I am intelligent, capable of learning and flexible enough to examine new ideas and use them for my good. I realized my goals, wishes, and interest are valuable. That I am unique and my feelings, opinions, desires, values and thoughts are elements that make up who I am. All my plans and dreams, the ones that will come to be and the ones that won't, sums up my aliveness, my oneness. I was beginning to understand myself as an individual. It was about time. I was fifty-two years old.

Towards the end of August 1982, I was running out of my medication. At my next session with Dr. Cunningham, I let him know I needed a refill.

"I'll see about getting it filled for you. Donna, Dr. Boyd is back in the hospital."

"He is? What's wrong?"

"He's not healing like he should and his doctor wants to find out why."

I didn't know what to say except, "Oh." I was saddened at the thought of Dr. Boyd not healing.

"I'll talk to him about the Ativan," Dr. Cunningham replied.

"Okay," I said. "I'm going to make this a short session. I need to get out of here and process what you just told me about Dr. Boyd. I'm upset, really upset."

I went home and prayed for this man who had done so much for me, and for so many others. Dr. Cunningham called me in a couple of days and told me a doctor had called in a prescription for me. I picked it up and thought, 'Next time I need it refilled, Dr. Boyd will be back and things will be good again.'

These were difficult times. I had been trying to adjust to a new way of thinking, and the changes in my life were not as I thought it would be. I never dreamed I would not be able to counsel with Dr. Boyd during the most important part, which was of course after the integration.

The closeness I had with my mom was the most precious thing in my life. It had always been a wonderful thing, and now more than ever, I delighted in our love for each other. She comforted me when no one else could. I was soon to go back to work, and I looked forward to it. My next appointment with Dr. Cunningham was for the tenth of September. "My God, this is 1982. Where did the years go?" I said out loud. 'Maybe he'll have some news as to when Dr. Boyd will be back. I hope,' I thought.

On the eighth day of September, Laura, Dr. Boyd's

receptionist called me, "Donna, this is Laura. Can you come in tomorrow morning at nine o'clock instead of the tenth?"

"Sure I can. Tell Dr. Cunningham I'll be there," I said.

"Thanks. Now be sure and be there," Laura responded.

"I will."

I was there at nine but Dr. Cunningham wasn't. I waited for him on a little bench right outside of his office. He was fifteen minutes late and had me come right in. He took me in a room other than the one I always went to with Dr. Boyd. "I'm sorry I'm late, I'm glad you're here, Donna." He seemed uptight.

How come you changed your appointment? Are you going on vacation?" I asked.

"No. Something happened."

"What? What happened, Dr. Cunningham?"

"Dr. Boyd died," he said quickly.

"What! I said, hoping I hadn't heard him right.

"Dr. Boyd died," he repeated.

Again I said, "What happened!?"

"He had cancer all through his body." He said this with great compassion.

I could not believe it… then I believed it… then I couldn't believe it. I was overcome with emotion. Struggling to escape the pain, I felt as if I was suffocating. I took deep breaths like Dr. Boyd had taught me. The grief started filling my body; it was intense. "I can't believe he's gone, Dr. Cunningham. I know he is, but I can't believe it. I feel like someone's hit me square in the stomach, full force."

"I know," he said. "It is hard to believe." Stay right here for awhile. I have to see another patient, I'll check in on you as soon as I can." He was being so tender.

"Okay," I said, not knowing what to do. I was dizzy and

nauseated. I leaned forward in the chair and put my hands up to my forehead. I was agitated, restless. When Dr. Cunningham came back in, I said, "I don't think I'll stay here for very long. I need to do something, go somewhere. I'll be alright."

"Make an appointment to see me, Donna. You hear?"

"Yes, I hear, I will." I was in shock and wanted to be with my mom. I don't remember thinking anything consciously while driving to my mother's, except maybe to hurry up and get there.

She was still in bed. I got down on my knees and said softly, "Mama, mama, are you awake?"

"Yes, dear, I'm awake. What time is it?"

I started sobbing, "Mama, he's dead. Dr. Boyd is dead. It hurts so much." I had lost someone dear to me and the pain was severe.

She gently reached out her hand to me and said, "Oh, sweetheart, I'm so sorry. I'm so sorry." I laid my head on the bed and stayed there for a long time, without saying a word. Finally I looked up at her and said, "I didn't want him to die, mama. I love him. He's gone, he's gone." I was suffering and mom was making every effort to comfort me. And that dear soul of a mom was doing a good job. Her very presence and knowing she truly cared for me helped me more than anything could have at that point.

She stroked my hair, "You're a sweet girl, Donna. I'm so sorry this had to happen. You need to be strong, sweetheart. You've always been so fragile. Remember what you told me. You said Dr. Boyd said you were a courageous person. He's right, you are courageous."

Once again we remained quiet. For how long I don't remember. "I feel better, mom. You always help me feel better. I'm okay, really I am. I'm going home to lay down and sleep for as long as I want. I'll be back tomorrow.

We'll drink coffee and talk."

"Okay. dear. I love you."

"I love you too, mom. I'll be back in the morning."

Amid the rubble of my broken heart, buried beneath the rigor that lay ahead, was my wounded spirit and shattered desire to be whole.

"The sorrow inside of me is awful. Truly awful," I said to Dr. Cunningham.

"You're grieving, Donna. The intensity of your pain will lessen. I know it's hard to believe, but it will lessen."

"Oh, God, I hope you're right. I get so afraid."

"It will take time."

"How long?" I asked.

"There's no set time for something like this. It's different for everyone."

"I'm anxious, I'm losing my sense of security, and I'm becoming negative. I don't want that to happen."

"When will you be going back to work?'

"I start this Monday."

"That will be good for you. Staying busy can be very helpful."

"I think so, too. I'm glad you said that. I'm trying to live up to the things Dr. Boyd taught me, but sometimes it seems impossible."

"I know it's hard for you, Donna. I don't exactly know how to help you. I do know time can be the great healer."

"You help me, Dr. Cunningham. Being able to stay in therapy with you is a big help. Being able to talk to someone who knows Dr. Boyd is very helpful. He is beloved to me. He brought me to my reality. His death, oh God, his death is so heavy."

Entering into reality wasn't the joy I expected. I wanted so much to see him. To tell him how special he was to me. That was not going to happen. I tried to let it go, to move on. I wanted to keep only the memories of what he had done for me. It was not easy, confusion and frustration returned to my soul. I was agitated most of the time. I hated my job yet knew working helped ease the pain. It took my mind off myself, at least for a time.

"Hi, Dr. Cunningham," I said with a somber tone.

"Good morning to you, Donna. You look glum this morning. Share with me."

" Same old thing. Being without Dr. Boyd is tough. I wrote a poem to him. Want to hear it?"

"Yes. Very much."

"I thought of you today,
My heart leaped up into a song.
Loving you has still remained,
Only the pain I felt is gone."

"That's lovely, Donna. Do you like to write?"

"I do. I can lose myself in my writing. I only wish I felt the way the poem says. But, the pain hasn't gone. I read the poem everyday, hoping someday it will be real. I wish he could hear it, the poem, I mean."

"You were knocked down to the ground, Donna. It will be awhile before you can get up and move on to a happier place."

"I yearn for that place. I want life to be good."

"Keep believing it will and it will happen."

"Thank you, for saying that. There's one good thing I have in my life. Besides you that is, my mom. I've always needed her, I guess I always will."

"It's wonderful you have someone like your mom."

"Sometimes when I don't know what to do with this sense of emptiness, I think about my mom and things seem to be better."

"You have had a double dose of change to deal with, your integration and the loss of Dr. Boyd. Of course you're feeling empty. This is your own personal trauma, Donna, and the way your dealing with it will be different than the way others might deal with it. Just try to go with the flow and let each day bring you to your healing."

"I can't remember when anything has been so hard for me. I needed him to not only carry me through the integration but to be there with the strangeness of it all. Now what, Dr. Cunningham, now what? "

"I don't have all the answers. No one does. Just keep doing what you think is best for you. That's all I can tell you."

During my first session with Dr. Cunningham, after Dr. Boyd's death, he had me sign a form for insurance purposes. By mistake, I received a form from the insurance company that should have gone to Dr. Cunningham. I opened it up and on the form was written, regarding me, Autistic Characteristics. At my next session, I gave him the insurance papers and said, "Here, I think this belongs to you." That's all I said about it. He looked at them and said, "Thank you." That's was all that was ever said about it.

I looked up the word Autism in the dictionary. It said, "a mental condition, present from childhood, characterized by complete self-absorption and a reduced ability to respond to or communicate with the outside world." There was some truth in that definition but it didn't fit me to a tee.

The next time I saw Dr. Cunningham, he told me he would no longer be able to see me. He offered to help me find another therapist, if I wanted him to. I declined. I was going to try it on my own, at least for a time. No one but me could figure out the things I needed to know. I asked him where Dr. Boyd was buried. I needed some closure.

I went to his graveside and sat down. I sat and sat and

sat, with my eyes closed, in silence. I let my mind gently slip away. I was no longer at the graveside. I was sitting on the shore. The water was the bluest of blue. The lake was a quiet calm that gave me a peaceful feeling. On the other side of the lake I could see someone getting in a boat, a small boat, and he was rowing toward me. He came right to where I was, got out of the boat, walked over to me, and sat down next to me. It was Dr. Boyd, and for some reason, I was not surprised to see him. We talked just like we used to. We were together and I sensed a comfort in me that I had not felt since he passed away.

"Why did you leave me?" I asked him. "I need you so. Why did you go away from me? Can you come back?"

"I don't need to. You have all that you need inside of you. It's all there within your reach."

"I don't understand."

He knew my anguish and he knew my oneness with God.

"Donna, you have the faith, the courage, and the love to bring yourself to the place you want to be. Believe in yourself. I must go now. You will be okay." He was gone and I was back at his graveside. I loved what had just happened. I felt strong. But, it didn't last. I was still frightened of the future without him. I needed some sense of security. This was too much pain, even worse than that morning so long ago.

History Repeats Itself

I thought of many things during this period of grieving, and the memory of my family growing up was one of them. Indeed, we had all grown into adults but we were insecure and unstable, especially where men were concerned. The fear we lived with as children most certainly had a negative effect on our adult lives. The emotional support and security as children were practically nil, which didn't give us much in the way of stability in our adult life. But, I had learned through the years that I didn't need to be a victim. Dr. Boyd had taught me that. I just didn't know where to go without my knight in shining armor directing the way.

He had never said anything about the autism mentioned in the insurance papers. Is this why it had been so difficult for me to comprehend, why it took so long to process what was going on inside of me, as well as outside of me? The awareness of this reminded me that I had learned to adapt by faking what I didn't understand. My natural ability to isolate emotionally, to detach myself from feelings and with draw, had been stumbling blocks to my growth, both intellectually and emotionally. Yet Dr. Boyd had been able to bring out the intelligence and the emotions in me. My attachment to my people was the inability to envision my own self-image without a connection to someone else. Is this why I created "the people" within, to have a sense of myself?

I remembered what he used to say to me, "To be aware is to be able to change." I think maybe he knew how to bring me out of my lack of knowing. I had been hit hard with the passing of Dr. Boyd, yet I made every effort to take responsibility for my behavior and to be the best I could be. It was a definite challenge to go on some days. On many occasions I would wake up and want to pull the covers up over my head. But more than that, I wanted to do what I knew would please Dr. Boyd. I would say to myself, "I must get on with my life and look to the future rather than the past. It's what inside that will make the difference."

I felt ugly without him. He was a strong, confident man and I believed I needed him to complete the transitional phrase. I thought I was destined to be a poor miserable creature the rest of my life. He had brought me to a new place, where I was going to grow and evolve into my oneness with Donna Mae. Then he was gone, just like that! And even though I knew the cancer had taken him away, I felt abandoned, as if he had brought me to a place where I needed him more than ever and then left me a wounded ugly butterfly, a butterfly with broken wings, unable to fly.

I had faced one mountain climbing struggle only to be faced with another. Anger seeped in, anger I didn't know what to do with. I felt totally sorry for myself. I was completely miserable in the present moment. I had been so ready to press on with my future, but I believed that future would only be okay with the help of Dr. Boyd. I had banked on him to be there for me, to help me put the pieces back together. It was tough to know he would never be there for me, not ever again. Whatever I needed to put the pieces back together would have to be accomplished without my Dr. Boyd.

I found comfort in my mother. Her presence in my life had always been a source of support. As always, she set herself aside to give me a sense of importance. She was an expert on selflessness. The love she gave to me, to her family, was filled with life-giving substance. Mom had become ill in her later years and it was time to give back some of that extra special attention. In doing so, it took away some of my own pain. It helped me to do better with the shock of Dr. Boyd's death. But at times, the depression caved in and I would think, 'I am fifty-one and my life is nowhere.' I would lose all desire to reach out and start over. And I felt old, very old. If I remained in this down mood for any length of time I would write. Writing soothed my soul like nothing else could. It didn't completely take away that gnawing ache that comes with mourning, nor did it take away my feelings of loneliness, but it gave me the endurance to go on.

The loneliness caused my mind to stray to my years with Bill, who was now my ex-husband. He was a kind man with an even temper, and I liked that in him. He had been a lot of company for me and very relaxing to be with. Could it work now that my personalities were gone? We had not been together for three years and had communicated very little. When we did get in touch with each other, it was always me reaching out to him. His inability to reach out to me had ended up being a big issue in our marriage. And what about his impotence? I brought myself out of these thoughts and questions with a 'What am I thinking about him for anyway. He's probably happy as a lark and wouldn't want me back even if I was willing to go back to him.' The idea got lost somewhere in my mind, and I went on with my humdrum life while trying to be as up beat as I could.

"Being positive is what's going to get me out of this," I said one day, giving myself a lecture. "You know, Donna Mae, some realities are grim and some are wonderful. It goes without saying that the grim reaper has, without a shadow of a doubt, passed by your life and even stayed for awhile. But all realities good or bad can all be faced. You've learned that by now. So get on with your life and accept the facts of your life, good and bad." And with that, I looked upward and said, "How am I doing Dr. Boyd." From that conversation with myself, I came to the conclusion that miracles happen to those who believe them. I would turn my life around if it took the rest of my life. I could and would change from a dysfunctional person to a functional, productive one. I was determined! Dr. Boyd had always said that my tenacity would take me to my desired goal. I decided to believe him.

The next morning after the little pep talk to myself, I decided to call Bill. I fixed a pot of coffee and gave Bill some serious thought. He loved the farm life, so if we were to work it out at all I would have to go to Oregon. He was a farmer through and through. His favorite outfit was bib overalls, a plaid shirt and cowboy boots. Again I remembered the good things we had had together. We had been comfortable with each other from the start, which was a plus in my books. And my personalities had integrated, surely that would help our situation. But what about his impotence? Could that be taken care of? If I could overcome my personalities, then together, Bill and I could work through his agenda. These were my thoughts. What I didn't know, was the monster from deep within called the fear factor. Fear of the unknown, fear of the pleasure/pain syndrome, had already raised its ugly head. The root of all this fear had already started a life of its own. The small seed of the old belief system was on its way to creating another family of personalities, and the determined-like weed would lay dormant for several years.

I called Bill. The phone was ringing. It rang three times, then somebody on the other end answered.

It was a woman's voice. "Hello, is Bill there?"

"Yes, he is," said the voice on the other end.

"May I speak to him, please? It's very important?" I put the "It's very important" part in so she would take the time to go get him. I figured he was out milking the cows or something to do with dairy stuff.

"It'll take a little while he's out scraping the corrals. Shall I have him call you back?" she asked.

"No. If you don't mind getting him now, I'll hang on," I said.

"Alright," she said reluctantly, "But it will take some time."

"Okay, I'll be here," I answered, ignoring her unwillingness to go get him. I waited and waited and waited.

Finally I heard, "Hi, this is Bill."

"Hi Bill, this is Donna. Do you remember me?" I said, kidding and somewhat nervous. "How you doing Bill? Is everything okay with you?"

"Not really," he said. "The dairy's not making it, none

of the family dairies here in Oregon are doing well. We're in the process of shutting down."

"Oh, Bill, that's too bad. I know how much the dairy meant to you," I responded sincerely.

"Yeah, there's too much competition with the bigger outfits," he added.

"Do you miss me?" I asked him.

"Yes, I do," he answered, giving me strength to ask him the next question. "Is there any room for me up there if I decided to come up? I mean permanently." He then said something to me that I liked very much.

"Yes, there's room. I've been waiting for you."

I started to relax. I thought, 'Maybe we can work things out.' "Can you come down here for Christmas and spend some time with me?"

"Sure, there's nothing here that needs to be done that the others can't do."

"Good. It'll be nice having you around again."

"Can you pick me up at the airport?"

"Yeah, okay. Make it in the morning, so I won't miss any work." I told him about the passing of Dr. Boyd.

"I'm sorry, Donna," was all he said. No questions asked, but I knew he meant it. Bill knew how important Dr. Boyd was to me. "Well, I guess I better get back to my chores. I'll be talking to you later," he said.

He was still a man of few words and I was fine with that. I needed the quietness of his persona. Bill had really seemed glad to hear from me. That made me feel good, and knowing I wouldn't be alone this Christmas gave me a feeling of joy. Yes, joy. I actually felt excitement at the prospect of seeing Bill again.

The day before Christmas I picked Bill up. We kissed, nothing passionate, just a peck on the mouth. Neither one of us wanted anything that was even close to passion. A sort of silent commitment to a platonic relationship which both of us wanted made for a comfortable non-threatening relationship for the next ten days. We talked about superficial things: the dairy, my job, my mom, Bill's children. He never asked me about the MPD, and I didn't bring it up in the beginning of our time together. We were just two very good friends who genuinely cared for each other. His extreme lack of emotion was, at this point, in my favor. Too much emotion had already been a big part of my life in the last few months. I told him what happened to Dr. Boyd. I cried a little as I told him and Bill was considerate and comforting. He held me close and told me how sorry he was. We talked about getting back together, kind of a trial run. We both wanted to give it a try, and it pleased him that I was willing to move to Oregon. We spent a quiet Christmas with my mom and family, and our time together was over too soon. On the way to the airport, I told him my past illness was just that, a thing of the past. He said he was glad for me. And there was no further discussion on the matter. No questions asked. Bill went back to Oregon. He would return at the end of January, and we would travel back to Oregon together. I gave my thirty-day notice at work and was more than ready to start afresh.

I spent as much time with my mom as I could. She was so brave, yet I could tell she was sad at my leaving. But, she was happy for me. It was a bittersweet thing for the both of us. I wanted to believe in Bill's and my future, and I was actually happy about being with him again.

During one of my difficult times regarding Dr. Boyd, I cried for awhile. When I had finished, I closed my eyes and felt the presence of God. Spirit was within and without. The tears were coming down as I allowed the One who had created me to fill my whole being. All the tension left my body and I felt radiant with "the peace that passes all understanding." The experience stayed with me for several minutes, then slowly and reluctantly I came back into the present moment knowing I had not as yet traveled through all the stages of grief. But the knowing I would get there gave me hope, hope gave me courage, courage gave me power, and the power would lead me to the finished healing. The still-small voice had whispered in my heart, " I will continue to guide you, as I have always done." I knew I was heading in the right direction.

I had one more thing to do. I went to Dr. Boyd's graveside and sat very still for a very long time before I spoke. "Hi, it's me, Donna. I've got something to tell you. I'm leaving for Oregon. Bill and I are getting back together. It feels like the right thing to do. I hope it works out for us. Boy! The years have gone by so fast. I feel better lately, about you. I'll always miss you. But, you're the one who taught me to stand on my own two feet and that there's only one way to look, and that's straight ahead. I'll remember that forever. You gave me so much more than I could have ever imagined."

I went deep into myself and felt the love I had for him. He was the one that showed me what a father should be. "Thank you, Dr. Boyd." I cried and cried and cried, and then I just stayed there for the longest time, not wanting to go but knowing I had to. "I guess I should say good-bye. I want you to know I'm not going to live like a caterpillar anymore. Nothing is going to stop me from being a whole person. You will be proud of me and what's more important, I will be proud of myself. Good-bye, my friend, my dear, dear friend." I went to my car knowing I was ready to go with Bill. What I didn't know was the unknown was slowly stirring in the hollow of my mind.

The day came. The morning we were ready to leave, the last thing I did was give my precious mother a hug and a kiss good-bye. It was very early in the morning and she was in her bed sleeping. I put my arms around her and realized how frail her little body had become. Mom was ill and her time on Earth was nearing an end.

"Mama, mama," I said softly, trying to wake her. "I want you to know that Bill and I are leaving now. I love you and we'll be back real soon." I kissed her on the forehead.

She reached up to me with tears in her eyes, "I love you too, dear. I'm happy for you. Don't forget me." She gave me a kiss on the cheek.

"I'll never forget you, mama. We really do intend to come back for a visit in about three months. I'll call you once a week until then. Okay?'

"Okay sweetheart." She looked over at Bill and said, "I'm glad she's with you. I want you both to be happy." She spoke with love in her voice.

Bill came over to her, leaned down, and gave her a kiss. "Don't you worry, grandma, everything's going to be okay."

"I trust you, Bill," and again she said, "Please don't forget me."

"How can we forget you? We love you. We're coming back, we really are. You won't even have time to miss her," Bill said gently.

Mom said, "I miss her already." The tears were welled up in my eyes and the sadness within gave me a lump in my throat.

I took a few minutes to get myself together and then, "We're leaving now, mom. Marge is in the front house if you need her for anything."

"I'll be alright, honey. I'll probably go right back to sleep. You go on. I know you want to be on your way." She was so beautiful. My love for her came into full view, and I felt so grateful for having had her for my mom. God had never failed me. Right from the start, He gave me a wonderful mother to live in for nine months. And, the rest of the years with her showed me what unconditional love is all about. Unconditional Love, it's a spiritual thing. Mom and God gave me a most precious gift. Thank you, mom. Thank you, God.

Bill and I left California on the February 2, 1983. I was full of hope and the farther I got away from home, the better I felt. We took our time going back to the dairy, the dairy that was no more. Bill was feeling the failure of losing the dairy. It had been his dream. We were both grieving our losses and being quiet was one of the things we both needed. In this particular situation, silence was indeed golden for the both of us.

We traveled the coast route, and it was beautiful. With no schedule to follow, we went at a slow pace. We thought of it as our vacation. We avoided any attempt at being sexual. In an effort to make things as relaxing as possible, I told him not to feel like he had to try and make love just because he thought he should. "Let's not allow this one major problem ruin our time together. We'll take care of it later." He agreed willingly, and the tension melted down to a wonderful calm. The quietness on the way to Oregon was a blessing. Bill had always been a quiet man, and I wanted to think my own thoughts. It was a journey without emotion, and we were both glad to have it this way. The denial on my part was in not knowing that there was more than one major problem, and it was playing a big part in my wanting to avoid him sexually. I convinced myself it was because of the compassion I felt for Bill regarding his impotence, and my need to avoid anything at all that would arouse me emotionally.

We arrived in Oregon on the sixth day of February. It

had taken us five days to get here. I was totally enthralled with the beauty of the country. Again, I had the feeling I had done the right thing. The dairy was on Hanley Rd. in Medford, and Bill and I stayed in the milkers house, which left something to be desired. I didn't care what it looked like, I only wanted to be free from the pain of the past and live in a peaceful environment. I met a friend the first day we came home to the dairy. Pat was her name. She gave me a big hug and said, "Welcome to Oregon." She, her husband Jerry, and their son David, lived in the front house. That hug and those words meant so much to me. I had never been away from my family and felt I had met a kindred spirit in Pat.

My life would be different without Dr. Boyd, without my personalities and without my mom. My beloved mother died in April of 1983, just several months after my arrival in Oregon. And even though I had been without her presence those several months, we talked often on the phone and she was always sending me cards and letters. I looked forward to my daily short walk to the mailbox, knowing more often than not, there would be something from her for me. I was glad she was no longer ill, but the loss of her took some getting used to.

I fell in love with Oregon. I was especially taken in by the beauty of the country. We lived in an area where we were surrounded by mountains. As spring approached, the absolute loveliness of it all was breathtaking. There were little patches of flowers coming up to remind me of the newness of life that was mine. I felt tranquil at the thought of having lifted myself up from the animal level I had once lived to the human level of the experience I was now living. It was soothing to know I had risen above the ugliness that my father had passed on to me.

The first year I spent taking long walks, sometimes with

Pat, but mostly by myself. I needed a lot of time alone, to reflect and to let the grieving process have its way. Being alone helped me to get to know what kind of person I was, in this new way of life I had chosen. As I walked and observed the flowers coming into bloom, flowers of every color, and trees taking on new life, I was peaceful within myself. I saw life in the birds and butterflies, in the fields of fresh new wheat. Sometimes a gentle breeze would come upon my face, blowing my hair back, and I knew life was good and that I was part of that good. This was the gift my beloved mother had given me from childhood and clear into my adult years. What Dr. Boyd had given me would be the wings that carried me through to the awakening of my oneness with God.

I continued on with my carefree happiness, of the beauty all around me, the wonderful friendship I had found in Pat, and the hope that Bill and I would someday make love. But for now the excitement of my new life and the wonder of it all was enough.

Bill and I remarried approximately one year after our coming to Oregon. We also sought counseling so as to be able to enjoy our marriage, in every sense of the word.

Pat, my friend, taught me how to can. We did it all: fruits, vegetables, jam, turning cucumbers into pickles, and even doing our own picking in the fields. She knew all the right places to go for picking. I could see the signs way before we got there. STRAWBERRIES, CORN, U PICK. It was exciting. It was learning something I didn't know before. It was a different life, indeed, than I had in California and I loved it!

But when the excitement of the newness wore off I grew tired of waiting for the changes to take place in our marriage. The counseling was not working, and Bill stayed deep within himself. His lack of interest in our sex life told me he was okay with the relationship just as it was. That baffled me; it also frustrated me. I wanted to be "normal" which in my mind meant an active, healthy sex life. And because I couldn't "make" it happen, I began to have temper tantrums. I would say mean, hateful things to Bill, and the more aggressive I became, the more passive he became. He would walk out of the house, smoke his pipe and wait for me to cool down.

And so the days turned into weeks and the weeks turned into months, until two years had passed. I felt hemmed in. It seemed the one relief I got was screaming at Bill and telling him how stupid he was for not being a man. I had become my father and the self-hate I suffered after every fit I threw only increased and the cycle would begin all over. I would apologize after every temper episode, which was exactly what my father did. It was unbelievable as to the person I had become. The anger I felt went so much deeper than my anger of not being able to make things work out for us. Underneath the anger was fear, hidden fear. Consciously I didn't feel as if I was afraid, but it was there. I was blocking it all out. To know the truth was too hard to bear. I put the blame squarely on to Bill's impotence. I didn't see myself as mentally and psychologically impotent. Blinded by my own limitations, I could only see that if Bill was a normal man, everything would fall into place.

The instant fear I had felt with the death of Dr. Boyd stayed with me, unresolved, as did the anger. The need to cover up, rather than admit it was there, led me to a plan I was hoping would take care of the extreme stress going on within me. I decided I was going to look for work. I found a couple of jobs that I didn't stay with for very long. I became restless and discontented once again. Frustration and dissatisfaction kept running through my mind, stirring the ones that flourish in the negative condition of my life. They were gaining strength and power. The ingredients of fear and sadness, anger and pain were the very things that gave them the mightiness that would, in time, bring them into my consciousness. I had handled it in the old way of doing things and finally it culminated into a split. My mind broke into three personalities: Edith Rose, Donna Mae, and me. I was once again experiencing the separation. Edith Rose was a child again, Donna Mae was totally committed to the intelligent side of me, and I was the gatekeeper. Donna Mae, once again, waited to be crowned the Queen of us all. The sexual being that I am was completely denied. The sequence of events that would follow brought me to Dr. Sullivan, and then the erotic one would appear. It was all part of the journey.

I grew weary; all efforts to be sexual with Bill vanished. Bill and I gave up trying to have sex. We avoided any physical contact, and in time, we even gave up talking about it. We made the best of what we did have and never mentioned what we didn't have. There seemed to be no fight left in us, more like resigning to that which seemed inevitable. And in all truth, relinquishing our hope of achieving this insurmountable, complicated matter brought about a peace, a surrender to what is. We thought we had given up. It was more like a rescue that brought about a feeling of comfort in our time of helplessness. We had a circumstance too big for any human to resolve. The grace of God had come to us and we didn't recognize it.

The added burden of my unknown world coming into fruition was exhausting, and I craved the much needed isolation that staying home would bring me. I still had my friend Pat when I wanted the company of a real person. Staying home was wonderful… for a while. The stress was off of me, and I could sit for hours looking at the TV. I didn't even know what I was watching. I wasn't watching. I was staring off into space to the world within, the place that was becoming very important to me. Truly, it didn't dawn on me what was really going on.

"I'm bored, Pat. I need to do something but I don't want to be a nurse's aide anymore."

"Why don't you call CSD and see if they need volunteers," Pat suggested.

"What's CSD?" I asked.

"It's Children's Services Division, a State program helping children."

I took her suggestion and was accepted as a volunteer with open arms. Within three months of volunteering, I was hired by Community Home Care, a contract service that hired in "Homemakers." I put my heart and soul into that job. It was a healthy outlet for me. I worked at my profession diligently, with great pride, and within a couple of years I was the contractor for two counties. Bill was the office manager and I had two employees working for me. It was exhilarating to have achieved so much in just a few years. To have climbed so high, especially coming from a place so low, gave me a big boost in the self-esteem department.

There was one hitch... I was becoming aware of missing time. At first it was easy to ignore the signs, but eventually, I could no longer deny the fact that I needed to be in therapy. I was under tremendous stress. Was there anyone here in Oregon who understood my condition? My heart was up in my throat. I didn't want to ask Pat if she knew of someone. I went to the Yellow Pages, closed my eyes, pointed my finger down to the page until I touched it. I opened my eyes and saw the name Richard Sullivan, Psychiatrist. I called and the receptionist said she would take my number to have the doctor call me as soon as he was free. He returned the call. I asked him if he had ever worked with MPD, and he said yes. I gave him a little history of my background and the therapy I had had with this disorder. I made an appointment. The therapy was about to start once again.

My personalities did not come out right away, but there was a definite aliveness that stirred within me in regards to Richard. Edith Rose thought he was Dr. Boyd and came alive with the happiness of seeing him again. Donna Mae was overjoyed at the thought of finally being the only one. I would be the visible one with the perseverance to see it through. A trust had to be built up before I allowed Richard to see us as separate personalities. And from this trust came two more, one of whom was Joyce. Was it the same Joyce that had been with me before? If it was she was much more advanced than she had been before. She was capable and smart enough to be an entrepreneur. She never referred to the past years in California, yet she knew the drill, knew she had to hide because it would contradict what was taught to me as a child: "You're clumsy and stupid." It wasn't that I believed Dad. It was because I had been conditioned to deny all that was truly me. It was a learned behavior. The connection, as to whether it was the same Joyce or not was never determined. I think it was, because there had never been two personalities with the same name. The fifth one lying dormant within was a passionate, high-energy personality.

I find it difficult to describe what happened the first day I met Dr. Sullivan. An arousal in me was something I was not expecting. I had disciplined myself to stifle all sexual desire. I had pushed my libido out of my conscious awareness, using sublimation in its place, that is, until Dr. Sullivan came along. When I left his office that day I would not accept, on a conscious level, the erotic feeling I experienced toward him. But, it happened and awakened in me something I didn't want to deal with. The fifth, unnamed personality had just experienced a wonderful, delightful, seductive feeling.

Dr. Sullivan was definitely different than Dr. Boyd. There were no feelings in me about desiring him in a fatherly way. That had been satisfied with Dr. Boyd. The sexual arousal in me made me nervous and I tried to avoid the feelings going on inside of me. I had gone to Dr. Sullivan only to finish the unfinished. I gave him some of my history, telling him about my past and my years with Dr. Boyd. I talked about his death and how awful it had been without him.

I talked about the insurmountable anger in me that went back to Dr. Boyd's death and up to all the disappointments along the way in Oregon. By bringing up the repressed anger and freely expressing it in therapy, I was able to slowly release these emotions. The fear in me also went back to Dr. Boyd's death. The pleasure/pain principle had returned in full force. I became bitter with all the hard facts of my life. The success of my business was given to Joyce. She was healthy and did not see the pleasure/pain syndrome as any part of her belief system. Her time with Dr. Sullivan was always about my contract with the State, working with the people that needed her and the pride it gave her to be able to be a productive adult. Edith Rose was of the deeper things of life. She loved knowledge, wisdom, understanding, and she was interested in the spiritual realm. Now, the erotic one, not yet named was of course my creative and sexual drive of which is very high. Donna Mae was where the four of us came from. She had found a way once again to live through the personalities, separate from her because of her belief she was not to be seen. Five personalities, this second time around. Five different expressions, in one body. Five different entities, struggling to be.

I told him about my sexless marriage with Bill, and about my strong thoughts of leaving him.

"Is it a good marriage, other than not being able to have sex?"

"I don't feel it is. We went to counseling for awhile, but we don't anymore. Except for me yelling at him, we live without expressing any feelings at all. It's a day-by-day drudge. I know it's wrong to yell at him, but the anger takes over and it's like an overpowering, uncontrollable thing. My main outlet is my profession and I love it." When I talked about my business, I felt Joyce stir within me, as if to say, "Hey! That's my job to tell him about the business."

"A job can be a great diversion from the hard knocks we get in this world. I'd like to recommend group therapy for you, Donna. Would you be interested?"

"I won't know until I give it a try, and I 'm willing to do that."

"The group meets here, upstairs. Talk to the counselor who runs it and find out the schedule. It could help you with some serious decisions you're trying to make."

"He was starting to sound like an okay doctor. He knew it was difficult for me to change from one doctor that I loved dearly, to him, a stranger. I knew I would be going to him for a long time. I wanted to get it all behind me.

* * * * *

I finally started giving him details about the abuse as a child and the rape. He asked me lots of questions, and I repeated to him what I had already told Dr. Boyd, so long ago.

"My mom was in the hospital when it happened," I explained.

"Who was watching your sisters and brothers?'
"They were all in school."
"What about your baby sister. Didn't you tell me she had been born several months earlier?'
"Yes, that's right. I'm not sure. She wasn't there that morning. Maybe Social Services placed her in foster care. Our family had been involved with them before, maybe they helped out." I stopped talking and stared straight ahead. Not down as I used to.
"Hi Richard, it's me Joyce"
He looked surprised, very surprised. "Hello Joyce. It looks like you've come to see me." He appeared puzzled as to what to do next. Joyce knew what to do.
"Yes, I have. All this stuff with her marriage and having personalities again is a bit much for Donna. So I get a chance to come out into this world of yours."
"It's a good world, don't you think," he responded.
"I want to think that it's good, but sometimes with all the troubles Donna's had, it makes me wonder. She does have a good business. She's a contractor for the State of Oregon, you know. I help her a lot with the business."
"It sounds to me like you're a big help to her."
"Yes, I am. Donna likes her work, but she gets a little antsy when she thinks about how much she likes it. That's when she allows me to take over for her." Joyce was gone.
I went on talking where I left off, just as if there had been no interference. "I really don't think I need to talk about my childhood. My childhood has been raked over the coals. It's really not a bother to me anymore."
"Donna, you talk about anything you need to talk about. You seem very informed as to how to handle your situation."
"Okay. We got a deal." He was really making points with me. "I went to that group you suggested to me. One of

the lady's mother in-law wants to rent a room to someone. I'm going to give it a try and see how things work out."

"So you're saying you're leaving Bill?"

"That's exactly what I'm saying."

The trust was coming and so were my personalities. They had awakened and the four of us would carry on conversations with one another. The fifth one was still being denied and was not a part of our conversations. We knew we would all be integrated eventually, and it was not as horrible a thought to see ourselves in one body as it was when I first discovered I had MPD those many years ago.

I rented the room from Aldine. We hit it off right away. She invited me to go to the Unity Church in Ashland with her. And, I was lifted up to another level of thinking that very first time. The feeling that I was home gently filled my spirit. The minister, Colleen Graham, spoke on Christ. She explained that The Christ did not wholly refer to Jesus, but to that Divinity within all people. That Jesus is our way-shower, that He demonstrated to us that real change takes place in the heart and mind of the individual, that to change our outer world we must first change our way of thinking. I knew this to be the truth because of my own experience through the years.

Finding Donna Mae

The therapy was somewhat different this time. My secret world was far better prepared. The previous experience had given us a roadmap to follow. We didn't require someone in just the same way that we did with Dr. Boyd. The quest for wholeness and independence was there; the difference was that we talked among ourselves more than we did in our previous therapy. But still, I needed to expose my personalities in order for Richard to get inside the thought process of my mind. Another difference was in believing that the combination of church and counseling was the way to arrive at my goal of perfect healing. And lastly, we called our therapist by his first name, after several sessions, which is something I never did with Dr. Boyd.

During one of my sessions with Richard, he said to me, "Donna, I want to talk to you about your personalities. I want you to start looking for the positive in each one. Think about it, find the good in them, individually, and let them know that integrating is a good thing. This may help the resistance I see going on in you."

I listened attentively to his advice, and approached this idea with my personalities

"Hi, everyone, it's me, Donna. Can you hear me?"

"Yes, we hear you," said Donna Mae, speaking for the others because she knew every move they made.

I continued, "I talked to Richard, he has asked us to find the positive in each of us, in order to make integration easier. Which as we all know, must happen. Joyce, are you willing to speak first? Tell us what you see as good and positive in yourself. The rest of us will listen without interruption. I was being so precise, with an I-know-exactly-what-needs-to-be-done attitude.

"Well, let's see." Joyce put on her thinking cap. "I do take over the business ninety-nine percent of the time and keep it going at a high level performance. And, oh yeah, Donna, I'm willing to give you a helping hand whenever you need it. You know, sometimes, you wear down to a frazzle." A little arrogance seeped in. "Donna Mae, you have that I'm-the-one-that-should-be-in-charge notion. You try to carry it to the outside world in a way that is not generally accepted. Just ask Bill."

"Maybe you think it's true," Donna Mae said. "I don't have to ask Bill anything."

I interrupted at this point. "We are not here to put someone down to build ourselves up. We are not to throw negative remarks toward each other."

Donna Mae continued speaking, giving no verbal response to what I had just said.

"Joyce, what you said about yourself is true. You are very business like and you do help Donna when she's at the end of her rope. Now, it's my turn to talk about my attributes. I can make decisions and be consistent with follow-through. That's a great plus, especially when all around me are those who pussyfoot around making decisions and then constantly change their minds. And, I must say it gets mighty irritating at times."

"Believe you're talking about me," I said. "I do change my mind a lot but I think if it as being flexible, rather than indecisive. I guess I need to give myself more time to think about what I should do. The good thing about me is I can admit to a mistake and move on to another way of doing things. So, let's move on to another way of doing things." I stopped talking. The silence revealed our negative thoughts, but in our speaking to each other, we could see how well we worked together with the good and the positive in each of us. "Oh my! I forgot Edith Rose, she hasn't said a thing. Come on, Edith Rose, tell us what you bring into this group."

With head hanging down, Edith Rose said, "I feel sad."

"You feel sad?" I said, saying it as a question.

"Yes, I feel sad and disappointed," repeated Edith Rose.

"She's talking about what happened in Richard's office," explained Donna Mae.

"What happened? Can you tell us, Edith Rose?" I asked.

Edith Rose, with her head still hanging, shook her head no.

"You tell us, Donna Mae," I said, knowing that Donna Mae is aware of what goes on with all of us.

"I'll be more than glad to tell you. Is it alright with you, Edith?"

Edith Rose gave her okay with a nod of her head.

Donna Mae proceeded to tell us what happened that day in Richard's office. "It was very upsetting for Edith. It was one of those times that I kept the appointment with Richard. Edith Rose was stirring around in me. She wanted to come out, so I let her. When she looked up at Richard, she became extremely shy and, at first, wouldn't say a word. She thought she was going to see Dr. Boyd, and when she knew it wasn't him, she slipped out of the chair she was sitting in onto the floor and scooted behind that rocker that Richard has in his office.

"I thought you were Dr. Boyd," Edith Rose said, all curled up behind the rocker. "I'm very shy with strangers, when I'm all alone, without the others."

"It's okay to sit behind the rocking chair if that's where you're comfortable," Richard said to her.

"I remember now. Dr. Boyd is dead. I think I'll go back to my chair." At this point Edith Rose scooted herself back into the chair and pulled herself up into it. She looked away from Richard and, pointing to that stuffed polar bear in Richard's office, said, "I want to hold that bear."

Richard said to her, "I'll let you hold it if you promise to return to Donna Mae, when I ask you to."

"I will, I promise." Richard handed her the stuffed animal and, holding onto the bear, she said, "I was really surprised to see you here, I mean, to see someone I didn't know." Edith Rose hid her face behind the polar bear.

"I understand. I'm shy, too," Richard told her.

"You are, really?" Edith Rose said, with a delightful look on her face.

"I am. I wouldn't lie to you," Richard said to her. "Would you like to go back now? You don't have to stay here if you don't want to."

"I want to go back." She gave him the polar bear and left.

"And that was about all of it," Donna Mae said.

"Do you want to say anything, Edith Rose?" I asked.

"I feel sad that I can't see Dr. Boyd anymore. I felt disappointed that day when it wasn't him."

"We feel sad, too. But Richard is a fine doctor, and you'll like him if you give him a chance," explained Donna Mae.

"I think I've come up with something pretty special with the four of us." I said, getting on with what this meeting was all about. "Let me share and then tell me what you all think. First there's Edith Rose. She's the sensitive one. She's better able to get deeper into our spirit, more so than the rest of us. And Joyce, she's the capable one, the intelligent one. Donna Mae, you're the one that sees that things get done, the one who oversees the rest of us, and that's a good thing. Me? I don't spend much time in guilt, and I don't beat myself up when I make a mistake. I just set out to right the wrong as best I can and move on. So, what do you think? Does that pretty much summarize us all, in a positive way?"

"I think so. I like what you said," responded Donna Mae.

"So do I," added Edith Rose.

"It sounds good to me," added Joyce.

"Can you see then? We'll be better off integrated than the way we are right now?" I said, hoping they all had the same vision of being together as I did.

"Yes, we see that. We will be better off and happier, too," said Donna Mae. It wasn't long after that that Donna Mae and I integrated. That left Edith Rose, Joyce and the fifth personality, who I had learned was named Ashley. The fullness of her was nothing short of dynamite. She was uninhibited and directed all of herself onto Richard. Very little work toward the rest of the integration was accomplished when Ashley counseled with Richard. Her focus was phenomenal, always concentrating on the hot sexual attraction toward him. She was totally seductive, telling him what she could and would do for him. The sexual tension while in the same room with Richard mixed with the chemistry flowing both ways was boiling hot.

Meanwhile, Joyce kept Richard informed of what was important in the business she ran, most of the time. Giving it to her kept me from dealing with the pleasure/pain conditioning that still plagued me.

I was able to return to the house on Flanagan's Ranch where Bill and I had lived.

Renting a room was not enough for me. I missed the little country house that I had fixed up. So when Bill moved in with his dad to care for him, I returned to the place I loved. Bill's stepmother had passed on several years earlier.

I continued going to the church Aldine had introduced me to. I was inspired with the teachings. The church is not about being born a sinner or about God's punishment upon us for being "bad people." It isn't about God punishing us at all. It is about the natural consequences of our God-given freewill. Through transforming our minds, we can become what God had intended us to be from the beginning. This sure was what I was looking for, and found.

The battle of Ashley with her obsessive/compulsive behavior, and my desire for wholeness would be a strong one. In my efforts to bring us all together for the purpose of wellness, I opened the gate for Ashley to present herself to Richard. I was always aware when Ashley visited Richard. It wasn't a loss of memory situation. It was more like being in the background, watching her every move and her every word. I thought keeping my eye on her would tone down her sometimes aggressive ways. But, I soon learned that Ashley did what Ashley wanted to do when she was in control of my consciousness. Exposing her didn't seem to diminish her one iota.

"Hi, Richard, it's me, Ashley. Will you play a knock-knock game with me?"

"I guess so," he said.

"Knock-knock," Ashley said.

"Who's there?" he responded.

"Boo."

"Boo who?" Richard said, with a smile on his face.

"Peek-a-boo," Ashley said, while at the same time lifting up her blouse. She was not wearing a brassiere. Richard was taken back for the moment but gained his composure rather quickly.

"You want to play the knock-knock game again?' Ashley asked.

He shook his head no. Ashley was gone.

Most of the time away from therapy, I was buried in my work, and even though Joyce helped me a lot, I, too, worked very hard in my business that I was very proud of. Eventually I was awarded a third County. This gave me the entire Southern Oregon Region as the family resource services contractor. It used up almost every bit of my energy. What was left was used in therapy and church. I had boxed up all my strength into these three channels, in order to divert my sex drive. It worked very well and would have continued to do so except for one thing. Ashley's driven', irrational thoughts of Richard.

"I love you, Richard," Ashley would tell him. I think about you all the time. And I have great fantasies about us."

Richard would ask her to talk about the fantasies. Should he have? I don't know.

"It's like all the other fantasies I have about you. We're naked and I come to you, wanting you, and you satisfy me in every way. We're in love. It's so wonderful, Richard. I want us to be together.

Richard would say, "It's only a fantasy. It's not real."

"I know, but it seems so real. We can make it real. Can't we Richard?"

Richard never answered this question, seeming very uncomfortable.

It was a known fact that Richard's wife was terminally ill with cancer, and Ashley's fantasy was about waiting for Richard until he was through his grieving time. Then he would see for himself that it was Ashley he wanted to be with. It was an illusion that Ashley would not give up, not easily anyway.

I had reached a point where I just wanted to be left alone. I could lose myself in my business, in the church, and in my yard. My yard was something beautiful. The neighbors would stop and tell me how much they enjoyed it as they passed. Except for wanting my personalities to integrate, I was content to live almost in isolation. The integration took time to achieve, but eventually, while I was gardening, Joyce came into my being. In among the beautiful flowers and greenery, we melted into each other.

Edith Rose and Ashley were a different story. Ashley wanted to remain separate, until her and Richard were together. She explained that if she took the risk of integrating with the others, they might be stronger than her and would make her give up waiting for Richard. This was Ashley's reasoning. Breaking through this illusion was another painful task to be resolved. As for Edith Rose, she wanted a little more time for me to get to know her. Edith Rose had been ignored. And through my becoming closer to her I would be able to better understand myself.

The search for my true identify had been a much longer, deeper and more intense journey than I could ever have imagined. I was lonely and lived an empty existence, and Ashley gave me no peace of mind. I could not figure out how to get her to integrate. There was a conflict going on between the two of us. The conflict was in my willingness to accept the fact that Richard and Ashley would never be together and Ashley's immense belief that we were going to be with him, in time, someday. Try as I may, I could not convince her it was only a fantasy, an illusion that had gripped her mind and would not let either of us go until we were integrated.

"Ashley, this waiting has got to stop. It's unbearable. I see Richard every time I have a session with him, and he shows no sign that he wants us to be together." Of course, in Ashley's eyes this meant he wanted to be with her. The ambivalence between illusion and reality personified within the two of us caused a great disturbance in me, and I was ready to face the truth. But, the strength of Ashley was equal to my strength. I prayed to God to end the struggle. I learned something about God during my pleading, or I should say, I realized what my thoughts were in regards to God, thoughts that had to change from my perception of God to the Truth that would set me free. I had made God in the image and likeness of my humanness, and basically said to him, "Let my will be done." I learned that God will not wave a magic wand and make all unwanted things or events go away. The Spirit of God has, however, given me, given the world, the way to overcome through innate gifts that come from our Divine Nature. Some of these gifts are faith, strength, love, power, understanding, and life, just to name a few. These are the elements that give us the ability to live the human experience abundantly. Changing my perspective helped me to see the light at the end of the tunnel. There was no instant healing, no instant miracle. The miracle was a day-by-day trust and confidence, evolving from within, letting me know that the conflict would someday be over.

Facing up to the truth, I realized I was letting Ashley believe in the illusion. In reality I wanted to be with Richard as much as she did. I needed Ashley to feel the pleasure to avoid the still prominent conditioning of avoiding the pain that followed. As I began the work of coming through Ashley's illusion to avoid the unavoidable, a quiet desperation of doom would spread all through my body, and a voice would whisper, "You and Richard will never be together." As these words reached my consciousness, I would instantly shake the dread from my awareness and quietly return to the false belief that contradicted the words that I had just heard, and Ashley would continue to remain within my inner world. My need to allow her to keep the illusion would also continue. The fear of what I had to face in giving up the illusion, through Ashley, gave her the power to deny the facts. We resisted integrating with each other. I was afraid of her sexuality coming into my being. I felt threatened because of her uninhibited nature.

To keep from facing a truth that I was not ready to face, I turned my attention to Edith Rose.

I was surprised to discover how insightful she was. Edith Rose was sensitive, gentle, and non resistive, whereas Ashley was a more dominant personality, strongly resistant. I had always thought of Edith Rose as a child, but now I could see she had become a woman, a woman with much wisdom. It pleased her to have me give her some attention. She had been waiting for just the right time to tell me something.

"Donna, I need to tell you something. I don't mean to be harsh, but it's for your own good. Do you know that to constantly think you are separated from yourself is really sick."

"That's what I'm trying to do, Edith. I'm working on coming together."

"That's what I mean. You're trying to 'get' to Donna Mae."

"Isn't she the one I need to get to?"

"You are Donna Mae. Your believing you're separate is the problem."

"Oh," I said. "What can I do to not think, ha, believe this way anymore?"

"You just did it," Edith Rose said in a most loving way. "Seeing the need to change is a step in the right direction. Being willing to let the change take place is a giant step," Edith Rose said without judging.

"I know nothing seems to be working in the direction of integration. I want to face the truth, no matter where that might take me."

"Good," Edith Rose said. "Instead of 'trying to get,' think about it as 'giving life to them' and graciously receive all that the Universe is willing to give you."

"Wow, Edith Rose, that is profound. I don't know what to say except you're beautiful."

"What you see is the beauty within yourself. You see in me the reflection of your own unique self," Edith Rose said with a knowing in her voice.

I was struck with her understanding of life, but I wasn't able to see her beauty in me, not just yet. "Do you know how difficult change is for me, that I have bitterness in me. And, what about all the years taken from me?" My anger surfaced. "What about it, Edith Rose? Do you have something profound to say now?" I said angrily.

This is the advice I received: "Detach yourself from all the drama, get in touch with your child within, your child of the past, and bring her with you to the child of the future. Then you will know you have been valued from the beginning of time. Give your attention to the feelings of the past, and then let them go. Let go of any and all things that are now keeping you from your oneness with God. Take in the air of freedom, use your will to survive, walk through the mental obstructions to the Spirit within you, and you will see, Donna Mae. You will see."

"What will I see?" I said, noticing she called me Donna Mae.

"You will see that you are only one. That there is only *one*."

Edith Rose had just knocked my socks off. There was a knowing in her voice, and I decided to take the advice, to regard the child within.

I looked beyond Carol, my first little personality, and saw myself. Sweet Donna Mae, not quite three. I reached out my hand to her and said, "Come with me, my darling. Don't be afraid. I am with you and together we'll walk through the years of the past. I'll bring you with me to this present moment. Nothing traumatic will happen to you. Trust me, please trust me! I have gone through great pain to clear the way."

And in my creative imaginings, little Donna Mae took my hand and we slowly walked through the years for a second time. This time, we walked with all the emotional security that this child within needed. From the taking of the bottle to the here and now, with patient persistence, she came with me into a new emotional home. She found her peace and I found mine.

Was the turmoil over? Indeed no. There was still Ashley to deal with, and she was furious. From the journey of the child within, Ashley saw the reality of never being with Richard, and from this awareness, the thought of killing Richard entered my mind. The emotion was highly volatile! The aggressiveness of this plot showed me something that was next to impossible to believe. I looked around for Ashley, she was gone. Just like that, she disappeared. I didn't know where she was and it worried me. Again, I turned to Edith Rose.

"Edith, Ashley is gone. I don't know where she is. I'm frightened. It's never been like this before. I've always known when an integration has taken place. If Ashley had come into my being I would have known it. I'm having terrible thoughts about killing Richard. It's not like me to think this way. It sounds more like Ashley." In desperation, I asked, "Do you know where she is?" I was highly excited and anxious.

"Calm down, I know where she is. Calm down. She's integrated into me. There's only you and me now." Edith Rose was very compassionate towards me as she spoke.

"What! She integrated into you? What about these feelings I have about killing Richard? It's scaring me. Ashley's always been the antagonistic one, always ready to fight for her belief in being with Richard someday."

Edith Rose spoke with total calm. "You've forgotten again, Ashley's feelings are your feelings. Your feelings have always been Ashley's feelings. You need to become open to this truth I am telling you."

"I know what you're telling me is true. But the personalities have always been so real to me. And, Ashley seemed so real. How could they not be real?" I said, calming down a bit. "And what do you mean Ashley integrated into you? How could I have both Ashley's feelings and my own feelings in me if she's in you? Can you explain that?" I was completely out of my comfort zone. I had been thrown a curve and it was mind boggling.

"All this has come from your thoughts. It is your thinking process that needs to be reckoned with. It's you and me that's left to integrate, and the last of believing in the separation. Ashley needed to come to me so you can come to terms with your feelings of separation. You believe this can happen and so it does. Believing this way is not reality."

"But it seems so real," I said.

"I know it does. But remember, in your thoughts, you can make the unreal seem real. Acting out your illusions is very dangerous."

It was not Ashley that wanted to kill Richard, it was me. My ego had gotten the best of me. In my anger, in my fear, in my rage, a thought came... then an idea... then the decision... and the plan to kill Richard was born. There was no one to blame. I had to take responsibility. I had turned to Edith Rose to help me. I didn't understand all that she was telling me, but I knew that Edith Rose was telling me the truth as she saw it. In an effort to help me understand, Edith Rose said, "For right now, Donna, think of it this way: now that Ashley is in me, she knows what I know and someday you will. too."

"Why don't I know what you and Ashley know, now?" I asked, still puzzled and confused as to what was going on.

Edith Rose answered. "When you no longer deny my existence or think you can make me go away when we integrate with each other, then you will know what I know. That there is only one of us."

This last bit of information was clear to me. Edith Rose was the autistic one and the one dad always called for when he was in one of his psychotic episodes. I had denied this part of me because I believed that I had been born a freak, that I was a mistake, a misfit in the eyes of my family and especially my father. I also believed, at times, that my mother felt sorry for me because of this mistake that had come out of her body. I suffered almost as much from this false belief as I did from what my father had done to me. In essence, what Edith Rose was telling me was that it's okay to be autistic, that it's okay to be, whatever that entails.

The subconscious conversations between Edith Rose and myself helped me in my conscious world. I advanced in my thinking to a more positive way and my ability to reason became much more evolved than it had ever been. This gave me less tolerance for the illness that had plagued me most of my life.

I worked diligently through my violent plan to kill Richard. I went to Richard's partner, Dr. Steve. Each week that I counseled with Dr. Steve, the rage in me lessened. It took seven once-a-week sessions before I was out of the danger zone. Exposing the terrible plot through the emotional release of talking it through was eventually eliminated in my struggle to be free. And although I had the support of Dr. Steve, the encouragement of my church, and Edith Rose, there was still a speck of fantasy about Richard and me that lingered. It was hanging by a thread and the fantasy balloon was about to burst. It was in a session with Dr. Steve. He was about to tell me something that would shake me from my head to my toes. He was trying to be diplomatic about it. "Donna, did you know that Richard is going to move to Canada?"

Appearing calm, I said, "No. I didn't. What made him decide to do that?"

"Richard has become quite serious about someone. She lives in Canada and they've been commuting back and forth. They want to be closer to each other."

"Oh," I said. There was a world within about to explode. How I hated Dr. Steve at that moment. He had just given me the worst news I could ever hear. It was quiet for a couple of minutes, and then I started screaming. My arms and legs floundered about. I knocked over the lamp next to me. Letting out all the raw emotion brought me fully into the reality of my truth, and it took what seemed like forever to settle down. Dr. Steve hadn't said a word the whole time. I was the first to speak. "I didn't know I was going to behave like that. I never thought I'd let anyone see me so out of control."

"It's okay, it's okay," he said. I don't remember the rest of the conversation that day. I remember that we hugged when the session was over. Whatever was left in me that still believed Richard and I were going to be together, that day, took it all away. With much prayer, meditation and sessions with Dr. Steve, I began to replace all my illusions with the positive thoughts of Truth. My ego was bruised for a very long time.

I turned to the fact that Edith Rose and I had not integrated as of yet. I learned that Edith Rose, on that awful morning, had found the door to Higher Consciousness. She not only found the door, she went in and discovered the place of perfect bliss, where Love dwells, and received the Grace of God that is offered to everyone. Edith Rose asked and was given guidance to the steps that would bring "us" to the Truth. She was able to go in and out whenever she wanted without my knowledge. But when she would come back into the place of forgetting, she, too, would forget and the consciousness of Earth-Life would take over.

One day, as I rested on my sofa in a somewhat meditative state, the vision of so long ago came clearly into view. This time I knew it wasn't the milkman. This time I saw a beautiful lady in a white lace dress surrounded in white light. It took awhile for me to understand that it was the reflection of that spark of Divinity in me. Such a wonderful thing to behold! It left me knowing that the awakening from the deep sleep of the false belief of separateness had ended, that Edith Rose was home. We had integrated. There was only me. Donna Mae had been found.

The healing finally came in the removing of layers of false thinking over the many long years. Nothing gave me more awareness than my personalities. This "condition" got me into myself, and I never dreamed where it would take me. As I removed the armor concealed what needed to be stripped away, I discovered the light within me through Edith Rose. I now know her wisdom was coming from the depths of me. And I also know that it's okay to be autistic. The awakening that I am a spiritual being having a human experience was far from my goal. I just wanted to be healed from MPD. That the Presence of God is always with me is a knowing I greatly cherish. The only "devil" I have ever run into is my own personal ego, and the "devil" can disappear through the transformation of my mind. Letting God out of the box of limitations and setting Him free gave me the freedom to be. No longer creating God in my likeness gave me a power to see the reality of my long awaited self. As I became more willing to let go of all false beliefs, I was better able to make choices that eliminated the negative. In my vision to see life situations and events in a more positive way, I became more grateful of the gifts that the Universe so freely gives. Not only grateful, also aware that I was in the beginning stages of seeing my world from a whole different perspective.

It would seem a natural thing to live a normal life, but for me, it was strange and difficult, not spontaneous at all. In my quest to know the "I am" of me, I turned to thoughts of my autism. Could this have been some of what was blocking the way to my healing? I remembered the day I read, "Autistic Characteristics" on the insurance form that had mistakenly been sent to me. I wanted to know what this meant and if it handicapped me in someway toward the integration process. My search brought me to what is now recognized as The Borderlands of Autism. One subtype of autism referred to as "pervasive development disorder" could apply to me in so many ways and is referred to as pervasive developmental disorder not otherwise specified (PDDNOS), which occurs in less severe and prototypical form. The closest of all subtypes that gave the definition of the possibility of my characteristic's pertaining to autism is known as Asperger's Syndrome. The description includes pedantic and stereotyped speech, clumsiness, obsessional interests, and deficient social behavior.

Asperger's Syndrome is a synonym for autism of a less severe kind (Scopler, 1985). This pretty much described me. In my early years, I did express a precisionist-like language, quite preachy. I came to realize this was not the way other people spoke. The words I spoke would have been in a monotone fashion; I had not observed in others that this was not the way it was done. The insightfulness I utilized in knowing I was not like others taught me to be like "them" in my speech, as well as in other ways. The clumsiness could have been there all along as an autistic person, augmented by the demeaning remarks my father made toward me, emphasizing my awkwardness. I was definitely obsessive. Eye gazing is another symptom of autism of which I had. It was staring off into space with a trance-like appearance, noticing nothing or no one but what was going on inside.

Both my autistic world and my outer world were confusing and threatening to me. Being autistic caused an isolation within me that made it difficult to reach out. I had an inability to relate to others and situations outside of myself in a normal, natural way. I was unable to comprehend, at times, the things that were said to me. Processing what I understood sometimes took a very long time. As a child I was labeled dumb, clumsy, and stubborn, mostly by my father. His tone of voice let me know that the names he called me were not good things. I felt ashamed of myself. I attached myself to inanimate objects, such as my bottle. I clung to my mom and to others in a dysfunctional way through the years. I needed the sameness of structure. This gave me a sense of security that would waver in the strangeness of change, such as when the bottle was taken away.

As I grew and progressed in the developmental stages my sensory function improved and some of these behaviors were eliminated. I didn't seem to have any learning disabilities, and I walked at fifteen months, as did my other siblings. As a child, the sounds in my environment seemed very loud to me. This is known as being hyper-auditory. If I heard several different sounds at once, the noise would appear distorted because of the loudness. Hearing a dog barking outside while at the same time hearing a car go by made my head fuzzy, and then the fear and the confusion would come. This, too, improved as I got older, yet I continued to be bewildered as to the interpretation of what was being said to me, way into my older years and sometimes to this very day. I also use to use my peripheral vision. I have, in my later years, taught myself to make eye contact, but still feel more comfortable looking just left of the face. I learned how to read before I went to school. My mother sat me on her lap and read me stories. I easily learned the words she was reading. I learned to compensate my deficiencies by watching what others were doing and would concentrate until the learned behavior began to internalize. In time, I felt the "realness" of it. I would let go of that which was comfortable for me in order to bring myself into the thing learned. To my knowledge no one ever noticed the autistic characteristics in me. If they did, they never confronted me on the subject, not even Dr. Boyd. He never said a word to me, maybe he would have someday.

Donna Mae Rose

While I was adjusting to my single-mindedness, I felt a gnawing in my soul, a sort of Divine restlessness. A spiritual discomfort as it were, that remained a constant. I was sure I had made peace with the past, yet there seemed to be a next step to take. I didn't have one iota of an idea as how to move into that newness that was so uncomfortable for me. I needed guidance. The answer came. The gifts of the Spirit that is my Divine inheritance needed to be cultivated. There was something for me to do. Like playing an instrument, the gift is there but needs to be developed in order to manifest. Like anything else, it was going to be practice, practice, practice. For instance, when fear sets in, think of it as an opportunity to give faith a chance to intercede. It's not God testing us, rather receiving from Spirit that which is needed in any given moment to meet the challenge. It was a hard lesson to learn. In essence I was being told that I would need to let go of the old belief system and negative thoughts that lay dormant in my mind for so many years. In other words, I let the spiritual gifts of overcoming become a part of my being through the practice of my every day life experiences. With this awareness came the reality that the lessons would go on. And I would continue to evolve. A way has been provided for each and every one of us to change in our own individual way, at our own pace, and in our own time.

It actually took courage to see myself as God sees me, courage to know that this is not blasphemy but a knowing that I could unite my consciousness with the Christ Consciousness and remember who I am. I can return to my beginnings and see the Truth, never again to be a puppet on a string. I was free to make the choice to live life abundantly. And, I embraced that choice with the greatest of love for all of those who had lived within.

The Way Back Is Forward

I believed in my oneness and looked forward to the fullness of life. I stopped going to Dr. Steve. To better understand the spiritual aspect of myself I read books by Gary Zukav, Wayne Dyer, and Deepak Chopra, great spiritual writers in my opinion. I prayed, meditated, and continued going to church.

When I realized the obsessive behavior was gone, I was elated. This revelation of knowing the addictive behavior was over and done with was a wonderful gift. Another revelation that came to me was just as exciting. I had been feeling a pull in two directions. On the one hand I wanted to know more about my Divine origin, while on the other hand I feared the god that I had believed to be a punishing god, a god that sent people to the Hell of burning fire. A god that said, "I give you free choice, but if you don't see it my way, off to the eternal fire you go." What kind of free choice is that? Sounds more like a threat, a manipulation. But, searching for the Truth and finding it revealed to me that this way of thinking is a lie. Finding the Truth dissolved the darkness that had blinded me from the Light. Returning to my beginning was the way I was able to engulf myself in the Peace of God, the peace that had been with me all along. Renewing my mind brought about the withdrawal of my faith in these "devilish thoughts" and to trust once again in the Truth.

Am I giving you the impression that this changing of the mind is an easy thing? I hope not. Am I leading you to believe that I could and did do this all on my own? Again, I hope not. I believe that the Presence of God is with us at all times, and Divine Grace is the unconditional Love that will in time bring us to our Knowing. I believe in the Divine Patience of the God that created each and every one of us that loves us with an everlasting love. I believe that for us to know our oneness with the Source of all good is God's greatest joy.

In the realm of the Sacred Place, where human thought is not allowed, Spirit does its good work cleansing the memories of the past thoughts and experiences and reminding me of who I am. This remembering reaches the consciousness of Earth-Life, and the Real Self takes form.

I tried to be normal in my youth, to avoid the fear of being ostracized or ridiculed. Now I know being the Real me, right here, in this moment, wherever I am in my learning, is exactly the place to be. That it is okay to be human and to allow others to be human. I am a willing participant with Spirit. That which needs to be changed in my life will be manifested.

While searching my soul for answers, I took a drive to the Oregon Coast. It was something I had done on several occasions when I needed to be by myself, to reflect. I sat on a rock, looked out over the beautiful blue ocean, a calm ocean on this day, little waves that would break into nothing, showing the beauty of the minute white foam as it reached to the sand. The years past came back for me to ponder. It had been a strange life, but in a sense, an extremely rewarding one. The challenges I had dealt with gave me an awareness of myself that helped me discover far more than I had ever anticipated. It had been revelation after revelation. And after a very long journey, as the façade of concealment lay bare before me and the fear had lessened, I could see the Real Me, my spiritual self. The travel had been worth every step I took.

I kept watching the water and staring into myself until I could see all of "them," playing on the sand, close to the water. Some of "them" were getting their feet wet, swirling around in a frolicking, playful way. I looked at each one and remembered how, in my mind, they were able to separate themselves by their outer appearance. Carol wore pink when she was dominant; she was the innocent, trusting one. Susie always wore her hair down; she was so full of life, carefree. Susie definitely never had a problem expressing her feelings. Her love of life gave her a determination to survive, right up to the end. And, Joyce (the first time around) always wore her hair up in a bun. Her enthusiasm for learning and sharing her intelligence was the way she showed her love for me. Joyce really cared what happened to me. Wanda wore black and would dye her hair black when in control of our body. Her creative ability was the love she showed for dad, distorted and twisted but nonetheless a genuine love for him. Dear Beth, I saw her as the exquisitely beautiful one, her beauty an inner elegance. She was courageous and had no qualms protecting me. The love we both had for my brother Bill was the bond that brought us together.

Some of the others were more of a energy rather than a show of outer appearance. Laura, the protector of the cocoon, and Mildred, protected me while I was coming out of the cocoon. Both had the protective spirit of my mother. They, too, cared what happened to me. And Mary, what about Mary? She, like Wanda saw things from a distorted point of view. Mary wanted to avoid pain of any kind, at any cost. She didn't want to deal with the problems that overwhelmed me. She couldn't see the good that would come from struggling through to the resolution. Mary was blind to the Spirit that led us to victory. Then there was Edgar and John, the masculine aspects of myself. Edgar had that masculine protective nature. I felt so good being around him. I loved the bible verses he read to me. The one I hang on to is, "Lo, I am with you always." John was the companion to Edgar. I guess I didn't want John to be the only male, in an otherwise all-female personalities. I had been my brother's companion in an all girl family. My older brother, Ray, had already moved out of the house during the time Billy and I spent time together. I knew how good it felt to be my brother's friend.

The second family of personalities was the second Joyce, probably the same as the first Joyce, but this one had risen above her previous intelligence. She was now capable of running a business and was superbly effective, exceptionally accomplished, and willing to do what had to be done in order to be successful. Her energy and enthusiasm were extraordinary. She brought me to a level of high self-esteem. I was living up to my highest human potential as far as being an entrepreneur was concerned. The second time around, she didn't wear her hair up; she had a blunt cut, just below her ears, very kinky curly with long bangs down to her eyebrows, even the bangs were curly. And her hair was bleached blond. She always wore her glasses and dressed right up to the style of the time.

Now comes Ashley. Wow! What does one say about Ashley? The passion that was in her was determined by her adamant nature. She was resistant to seeing things in any other way but her own. Her power to fantasize stopped her from listening to any other persuasion. Her enthusiasm was insurmountable! And try to tell her that to live in fantasy land was living in "Heartbreak Hotel" didn't cut any ice. She just blocked out the "noise" that got in her way. She could not stand the fear of losing something, even something that was never going to be. Ashley wore red most of the time because Richard had complimented her one day while wearing the color. But she was not opposed to wear any color that suited her fancy. She never wore glasses and put the blunt cut behind her ears. Through the human events of my experience, Ashley finally wore down and truth prevailed. I eventually became the strong one in this struggle between fact and make- believe.

Edith Rose had many attributes. She was courageous, fearless, compassionate, and able to set herself aside for the sake of another. She was receptive to my inner world. Edith was the door to my wholeness. And now I come to Donna Mae, she was with me from day one and was the product of environmental conditioning, which was difficult to break down. Not impossible, thank God, but part of my struggle because of the brainwashing she had endured. And me? I am the total of all the others and am proud of all their gifts that they brought into our working through to our victory.

As I watched my people, so joyous and content, I knew

311

why they were all so happy and playful, digging their toes in the sand then running into the water to wash them off. They were aware they lived fully through me. I was their source, and the energy, spirit, feelings, emotions, and desires within were the subtotal of all that we are together. Bringing us to wholeness, the desired goal had been achieved.

Upon coming home from the drive back, I lay down to rest a bit and thought of the many years that it had taken me to get this far. I was sixty-eight. It had been a sometimes steep mountain-climbing adventure. It had eventually transcended the human awareness, taking me beyond the five senses. The revelation came gradually and the way took me from the belief in the separation into the knowing of oneness. I awakened to the truth of who I am. I began to relax from the rest I was having and went into a meditation. I experienced the sensation of spiraling down into a "black hole." It wasn't the feeling of falling, more like floating downward. The black was all around me. There was no fear in this experience, only the wondering who was going to catch me at the bottom. After what seemed a very long time, I saw a dim light getting brighter and brighter. Finally, I reached the bottom with ease. I sat down and, there before me, was the vision that had come to me the morning I crawled into bed with my mother after her return from the hospital, after the horrible, devastating ordeal with my dad. I stared at the vision until I could see that the bright, glowing image was a projection from my mind of the Christ Nature that lived within my being and had been covered up by my forgetting. I felt just like I did the first time the vision came to me on that beautiful morning when lying close to my mom, feeling safe and secure.

As I floated through the blackness to the moment of again seeing the vision, I knew, with a knowing that excluded all doubt, that everything is okay. The message was in more detail. It told of a Love that knows no beginning, no end. That to bring us into the remembrance of this Divine Life, which is our birthright is Spirit's most precious desire, wanting more for us than we could ever want for ourselves. I knew in this most wonderful moment that of all the gifts that are ours, God's Love is the greatest gift of all. That the human journey that is mine to walk was, and is, for the purpose of awakening to my Real Self. The human facts and events of the happenings in my personal life brought me to the place where I didn't even know I wanted to be, deep within my Oneness and knowing the Father. The meditation had been a marvelous, amazing participation with the One Power, God.

In my own personal human understanding, as I was growing up, I would disappear into my personalities to escape my father's dreadful ways. When I started therapy as a young adult for the purpose of "finding myself," God used this as an opportunity to eventually awaken in me the gift of being fully alive. Feelings of being unworthy, not good enough to take up space in this world, kept me a lesser person. As I began to open up, I found the Sacred Door within. It was in the silence that I was led right to my Spiritual Being. The release from the bondage of disbelief, freed me, and as I turned inward to the deepest part of me I was able to leave the illusion of not having the right to exist.

Having been abused as a child, my growing up came with a twisted thought process. That twisted thinking followed me into my adult years and in my middle twenties, I realized there was something wrong. I sought psychiatric help with the belief that within a year's time, I would have my "head on straight." Wow! Was I wrong. Having repressed all terror and abuse from my memory, I was diagnosed schizophrenic for years by many different doctors. Dr. Boyd was the one that saw through the façade and recognized the illness as MPD. I was approximately forty-five at the time I met Dr. Boyd. Remembering the past was horrendous. The immense anger suffocated me, making it extremely difficult to breathe. And the overpowering, all-engulfing fear was unbearable at times. The struggle to set myself free caused conflict and confusion to the point of exhaustion. Finally, I triumphed. I thank God those years are over.

The legacy my father left me was atrocious from all outer appearances, but from the truth lying dormant within me, the journey that was mine to walk brought me to my Steady Companion. "Have courage, my daughter; your faith has healed you; go in peace." Luke 8: 48. My journey still continues, but I approach life differently. The Divine Love within gives me the joy of living for something bigger than myself.

This whole evolving thing is not about belonging to a specific religion. It's not about religion at all, and it's not about getting into therapy. This was just the chain of events that occurred in my life. It's about self-discovery beyond the human spirit. It's about a personal walk that only you can travel.

God meets us where we are each and every day. He guides us, directs us, and brings us to our desired goal. The Presence of the Divine was not always consciously with me. But, I do know I was given strength to continue when I didn't have an ounce of willingness to go on. Somewhere in all this, I was offered the energy to move ahead and somehow I accepted the gift. Thank you, God. In my experiences, a Self not yet known was rising from deep within, attempting to clear the obstacles that kept me from my True Nature. The hard shell of the chrysalis would stop me from remembering from whence I came. I lived the life of the caterpillar. I had forgotten my oneness with God. But God had not forgotten, and that alone was my salvation, grace came in when nothing else would work.

The freedom from fear was not received in an instant. It would be a step-by-step evolving. God had always been willing to reveal the Truth to me, yet Spirit knew just how much my darkened mind could accept, and I was given only that which I was able to take in, according to my limitations and ability to receive. God is not limited. Man limits himself according to what is believed in the mind. The thoughts themselves are the blocks to what really is. And then there's Grace. The Universe guided me along the way. Cosmic correction would come to me again and again, not punishment. The worth of my soul was slowly brought to my conscious attention. God had been good to me all along, going only at the pace in which I was able to cope. My desire to live with dignity would come to pass, did come to pass. In the midst of my confusion and the seemingly limited appearance, the Light of Truth was making its way into my heart. My heart would open and I would know. It didn't matter how slow it took. What mattered was that my mind was awakening from the sleep, and the sense of separation was disappearing.

I learned that body, mind and spirit need to come together. These three elements come into harmony when I do not deny that each is a member of a set, requiring equal care. If one of the three is denied, there will be an imbalance in my character and personality.

I realize the path that is mine to walk is no less important than the destination. Each step I take brings me closer to the essence of my Being. Each experience was and is necessary. I live here on Earth, the Learning Place, and I will continue to learn.

The radiance of my future blinds me to the specific details of where the road will take me. Should I stumble, I'll get up, brush myself off, and continue to evolve. God in His wisdom gives us freewill and allows us to learn our own lessons, even seemingly failing at times. When we've learned from this so-called failure, we'll know it is no failure at all, just another lesson learned and a clearer insight into our Real Self.

Even unaware, deep in the soul's memory,
We know we are one with God.
Therein lies the seeking.

DONNA MAE ROSE

The Epilogue

Wile lying on my bed one evening at dusk, I went into a deep meditation. As I began to leave this earthly place, the doubt, the uncertainty, the fear, and the appearance of all things unlovely began to fade away. Then the darkness came. It felt as if I was floating. I waited in silence, patiently, unafraid, knowing something was about to happen. Time ceased to be; the Light appeared and dissolved the darkness. I was in the Presence of the Divine. The veil that had been hiding my true self was removed. I rejoiced in what I saw. I felt tranquil, clarity had come. I had returned to the place of remembering. I had looked beyond the appearance to the vision I was experiencing, and I was delighted in the wonder of it all. The Divine Presence that is in everyone had led me into Eternity back to where I was when it was time. Yes the time had come again to return to Earth-Life. I knew because the one perfectly equipped to be my personal observer was giving me the guidance and direction as to the family I would choose to be born into. The Presence of the All-Knowing, All-Wise One was with me, giving me the Truth of Our Oneness. I would forget many, many times during my stay on Earth. For now there was no forgetting only the joy and the comfort that comes from being with the Source of All Life.

I was a spiritual being about to embark on a human experience. In the beauty of the Universe I dwelled in perfect bliss. Why, then, would I choose to return to Earth-Life? The answer is easy, now that I understand it. Oblivion! That's why! I was in perfect bliss, yet I was unaware of my perfect state of being.

Earth-Life is a gift, in that, it gives us the experience we need to distinguish Light from darkness, pleasure from pain, sadness from happiness, freedom from imprisonment. Earth-Life gives us the duality. Spirit gives us the gift of enlightenment, the joy of knowing perfect bliss, of know what God has done and continues to do for each and every one of us.

As I slowly started to come back from this state of completeness I was reluctant to return to the present time and place. I eventually did, vaguely at first then I felt my five senses come into my consciousness. I continued to lie on the bed until I came fully into the awareness of the here and now. Was this all a dream, an illusion? Perhaps my imagination was playing tricks on me.

No! It happened. The vision had taken me to the Truth that goes far beyond believing into absolute knowing. It's all part of the journey. My life here on Earth was, is, and will continue to be the way back to the perfect healing of my soul.

There is an unanswered question here that needs an explanation. Why in the world would anyone choose such tragedy if they could choose a warm, kind and loving parent instead? Why would I consciously choose an abusive father in this lifetime? This is an important question, and an equally important answer is needed. I could say, "The purpose of the human experience is for the total healing of the soul." And even though I believe this to be the truth of our earthly existence, it's just too simple an answer. The clarity of the purpose needs to be explained.

First of all, my personality did not make the choice. It was not in the world of time, space, and matter that I elected to live my experiences. My soul selected the path I would take because of the joy I would awaken to. The physical world is the learning place that would reveal the Light that would remove the darkness in me and bring me into wholeness. The Truth within my heart would show me the way of overcoming, the way of victory. It was the lessons I would learn through my particular experiences that were the intention behind this undertaking.

It was not the pain, the fear, the vulnerability, or the struggles that came my way that were the motivating factor. They would only serve as the doorway to my turning deep within to my conscious awareness, an awakening as it were, to the truth of my spiritual nature, and the need for my soul's healing. When my soul voluntarily decided to take on the task of these experiences its sole purpose was for my spiritual evolution, in order to heal. It's the journey back, through choice, to my highest good. The situations in my life awaken within me the birthright that was mine from the beginning that went beyond the five senses. Yet the results of the healing of my soul would extend to my body and mind. For it is God's desire and pleasure to see us a happy, healthy, peaceful, and harmonious people.

Donna Mae Rose

In my own personal experience, discouragement would come in great sweeps. I would grow impatient with the waiting, and it all seemed more than I could bear. It was in these times of enormous frustration that what appeared to be the absence of Light would dim my vision, and my progress towards wellness was brought down to a slow pace, almost to a standstill. My thoughts could only see the condition of the difficulties of the present moment, and the prison I was in would not let me get away. When I could not face it any longer, I would turn inward and enter into the realm of the invisible, the nonphysical, and there I found peace with the comfort of being nurtured. The Presence of the Divine gave me the Truth that my damaged soul could be healed. As I came out of this beautiful place, I could feel the courage flowing through me once again with the knowing that God does not put us through our trials, rather God brings us through our trials to the place of releasing the past and to continue on towards our desired goals. I am not there yet but am willing to go the rest of the way, because I know there is something more than Earth-Life. And, I want to see the complete healing of my soul.

I believe each and every one of us have a spiritual nature, difficult to detect some times, but nevertheless it's there and can be seen when we observe it through a compassionate heart. Bringing us back will not be accomplished in "the twinkling of an eye," nor will it be a "quick fix." Realizing our own spiritual nature will take time, time to evolve, time to learn our own special lessons of seeming failures, crisis, and the appearance of the "bad" that is happening to us, giving us the feeling of powerlessness until we learn how important it is for God to patiently wait for us to open up our hearts and fully receive our good.

Yes, we are kindred spirits, all of us connected to one

another. Our fear and anger, weaknesses and vulnerabilities are all parts of our humanness. The way to freedom is a strong drive in us all, and we are a powerful force when it comes to wanting our good. If our desire is strong enough, we can go beyond our human limits and transcend to the infinite potential of our life. Something within our consciousness will awaken to the Truth of our Being, and the shackles will be removed.

So when you attempt to face a difficult situation but cannot, don't despair. Feel compassionate toward yourself. Not pity, Compassion. Attempts at overcoming is a noble, arduous but possible endeavor. Just let your spiritual nature enhance your humanness and you will know you are worth every bit of what it takes to achieve your goal.

We are all like the flowers of this Earth,
Coming into full bloom.

With Light from the Son and the nourishment
From the Source of all good,

We, too, will come into our perfect loveliness.

DONNA MAE ROSE

Printed in the United States
201445BV00002B/172-207/A